C000055540

EAST SUS
COUNTRY CHURCHES

A Strictly Personal View

JAMES ANTONY SYMS

S.B. Publications

By the same author:
Kent Country Churches (1984)
Kent Country Churches Continued (1986)
Kent Country Churches Concluded (1989)

First published in 1994 by James Antony Syms
in association with S.B. Publications
c/o 19 Grove Road, Seaford, East Sussex BN25 1TP

ISBN 1 85770 056 2

Typeset and Printed by Island Press Ltd, 0323 490222, UK

CONTENTS

CHURCHES ILLUSTRATED

Front cover: St John the Baptist, Ripe

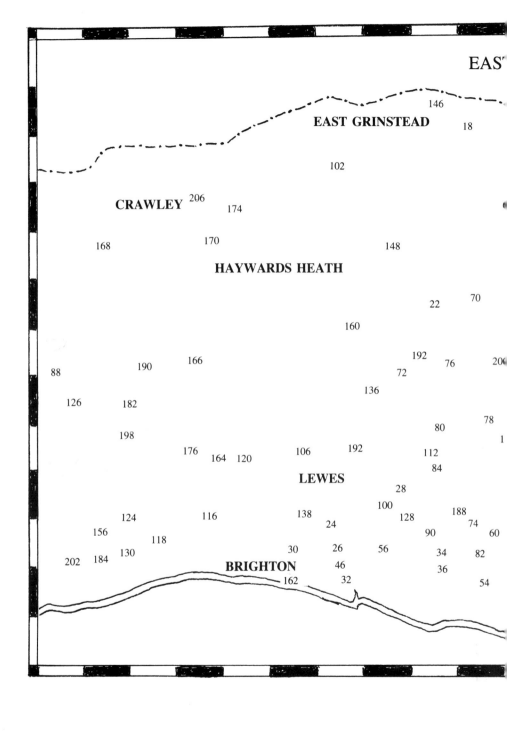

EAS'

EAST GRINSTEAD

146

18

102

CRAWLEY 206

174

168 170 148

HAYWARDS HEATH

22 70

160

192
166 76 200
190 72
88
136
126 182
78
198 80
176 192 112 1
164 120 106 84

LEWES

28

100
124 116 138 128 188
24 74
156 90 60
118
202 184 130 30 26 56 34 82
BRIGHTON 46 36
162 32 54

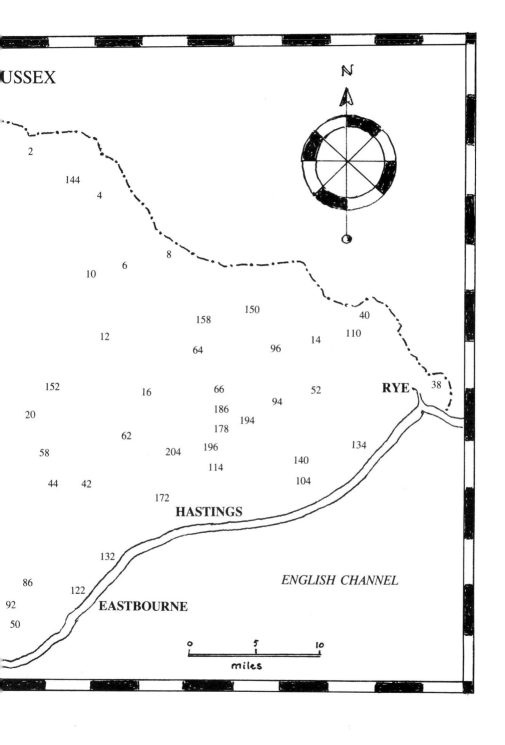

INTRODUCTION

Does anyone read introductions? I don't know but possibly not many. For those who do read this one, I hope their time won't be wasted. I have enjoyed writing it even if most of the churches which follow need little introduction from me. There is no great significance in the order in which they are shown; it is simply the chronological sequence in which I visited them as may occasionally be inferred from the text. The only exception is that of Worth which comes last; after Worth anything is in danger of anti-climax.

It is the churches of eastern Sussex that fill the pages of this book for the good geographical reason that they are the most accessible to someone living in Kent. The many old churches of western Sussex may loom invitingly over the horizon but that, I fear, is where most must stay so far as my explorations are concerned. If I have strayed across the border from east to west Sussex in a few cases, who would blame me who know these churches. After all, when they were built there was no administrative division dividing the county. Distance, rather, has been the limiting factor for me. As it always was in parochial terms. That is why medieval churches are so thick on the ground. They needed to be; salvation afar was salvation denied. Before venturing into Sussex I had occupied the first decade of the carefree leisure that retirement brings in getting to know the country churches of Kent. Ten rewarding years exhausted (revealed would be a better word) this treasure trove but not my enthusiasm for churches, churchyards, their atmosphere and history — Sussex has proved a worthy successor and I am now at a loss to say which has most claim on my affections. Affection and admiration undoubtedly they all inspire as one contemplates them across a deserted churchyard. Nostalgia and a sense of identity with the past can be given free rein.

Genuine Victorian churches, of which there are several in the county, have not been included in my peregrinations, worthy certainly as many are and deserving, of course, as their parishioners undoubtedly are. The unavoidable fact is Victorian churches have not had time to gather the moss or accumulate the history which provides the mental stimulus to the occasional visitor. After a couple of centuries of weathering and if there is a softening in the attitudes of the authorities to the sterilization of the interiors, Victorian churches will surely join their medieval predecessors as treasure houses of the past and adornments of the countryside. Such is my excuse for their omission from this book and hope for their future.

So all country churches in time become quite magical and the effect they can have on one is profound, if not necessarily religious although better so. They are the unrepeatable feature of our countryside and it is, to my mind, self-deprivation for anyone to ignore them or merely give them a cursory glance. They deserve far more than that and we are blessed in having them whether we deserve it or not. To overlook them brands one a philistine who may have small claim hereafter on heavenly bliss — if such exists. Who would want to take the risk of such opprobrium or mortgage his or her future so casually? But I suspect the only people likely to read this book (if any) are already church enthusiasts and I therefore do them an injustice with the imputation of philistinism. Apologies are offered.

Our country churches can, and do, speak eloquently enough for themselves do we but listen. But where, for some reason or other, the opportunity is lacking, this little book, like many others, attempts to supply the want in its own way; it is also, one must admit, very satisfying and addictive (and therefore self-indulgent) to write about them and assert one's view about this or that. What follows, then, in these pages are the strictly personal impressions of one lay individual as he enjoyed the hospitality of Sussex.

Let me confess, at the outset, that I can make no pretence to any qualifications in architectural or ecclesiological matters; those who seek expert guidance should look elsewhere but at least I can honestly claim a degree of familiarity with country churches because I have sketched so many from the outside and admired them from the inside. To buttress personal inexperience, untutored opinion and ill-informed prejudice there is a wealth of qualified commentary about churches which may be called in aid. My sources may be of interest and a help to newcomers to the enchanting world of country churches and their churchyards. In any case, it is only right that I record my debts.

First, and one might almost say an indispensable vade-mecum, is Pevsner's 'Buildings of England'. This monumental undertaking, by a German incidentally as the originator but helped by the native English, lists and evaluates briefly all the buildings of consequence in England, county by county, town by town and village by village. Pevsner and his collaborators rarely if ever sleep or stumble. Needless to say, it is the local church that takes pride of place; only the great houses, far fewer in number, can compete. Armed with the appropriate volume of Pevsner, one will never leave a church without a clear idea of how long it has been standing, its development and what one should have noticed. I never move without the master which is why I am able to describe the architectural fetures of a church with such an air of authority, even if it is invariably second-hand authority.

On a par with Pevsner in terms of authority and coverage but highly condensed is a pocket-sized book by Frederick Harrison. His 'Notes on Sussex Churches' is a dear little book, first published in the early 1900s and now, I am sure, out of print and only obtainable from second-hand bookshops of local interest. Whenever in my text I refer to 'my Notes', it is to Mr Harrison's invaluable book that I pay homage.

Next, of a more gossipy less architectural nature but also county by county and village by village, is Arthur Mee and his 'The Kings' England' series. One can be confident that, if someone of historic renown or notoriety was associated with a church or village, Arthur Mee will have caught and preserved him or her. Fairly comprehensive, too, but distinctly more opinionated at a discriminating Betjemanesque level are the 'Collins Guide to English Parish Churches'. Whereas one knows that Pevsner or Mee may not themselves have visited every church in their great survey, how could they, one feels that John Betjeman did visit and assess in his own idiosyncratic way all the churches he listed as worth a visit. In the case of Sussex he found 91; in Kent, I can proudly note, 169 receive his approval. However, if a church did not receive the Betjeman accolade, that is no reason to ignore it; he was not infallible. As a Catholic, I feel at liberty to be more catholic.

Not so comprehensive but much more scholarly and often over my head, are the occasional papers about churches by antiquaries, frequently of a clerical caste, which are issued annually by the Sussex Archaeological Society. Their 'Collections', as the annuals are called, can be found in a good public library. The reports therein are an absolute mine of informed knowledge, mostly written by Victorians and sobering to our self-conceit to read in this ill-educated and secular age.

At an individual level are the church guides which one finds, if one is lucky, just inside the church door. Church guides vary, naturally, but all are proud of their church and eager to convey information. Where there is no guide, there is sometimes a portable information board — full of description and small type and often rather difficult to make out in the half light of a church. And, where there is no guide or board, one feels disappointment and one's mite to the church restoration fund can suffer although it shouldn't. To offset the apparent neglect, it should more properly be increased.

Late in my explorations, well into the eleventh hour, I came across H. R. Mosse's 'The Monumental Effigies of Sussex'. This is an excellent little book of the 1930s — compact, detailed and comprehensive. With this to consult (if one is available) enigmatic memorials are clarified, latin is translated, figures are brought to life and the shadows of unlit chapels dispelled. I suspect that only public libraries have it now, in the reference section from which it cannot be withdrawn, regretfully.

There is, of course, a host of books about country churches and church architecture, more general geographically and technically, which usually list the author's recommended selection, county by county. I might just mention in particular that authority on building in stone, the late-lamented Alec Clifton-Taylor and his 'English Parish Churches as Works of Art'. Also, if one wants to find out where the best towers are, for instance, or the best bench ends, or the best wall-paintings, or the best fonts, or the best almost anything else, Lawrence Jones' 'The Beauty of English Churches' will provide the answer. One could go on endlessly; colour photography has given a great fillip to the recording of country churches and there are now pictorially seductive books to be found in most bookshops (or on coffee tables). As an amateur in black and white, I find them altogether too attractive for my peace of mind.

One last specific compliment must be paid to a source of knowledge on which I have much relied. At the head of each piece of text in this book about an individual church is given the Saxon derivation of its village place name. Anglo-Saxon derivations suggest that the place was inhabited before the Conquest, a supposition worth a mention, I think. To avoid any presumption that I am fluent in Anglo-Saxon or Old English, it is only fair to Judith Glover to acknowledge that the derivations have all been culled from her erudite little books 'The Place Names of . . . .', in this case Sussex. She is the Pevsner of place names, I maintain.

I must admit that the religious element is almost totally lacking in this book. As my age advances this is probably a grave mistake and the question 'is there life beyond the grave?' becomes more pressing. Pascal provided his solution to the dilemma —

'Let us weigh the gain and loss in wagering that God is. Consider these alternatives: if you win, you win all, if you lose, you lose nothing. Do not hesitate then to wager that He is!'

But unfortunately I am not a betting man. Nor can belief be summoned at will. It comes from the grace of God, so it is said. Thus my fascination with country churches is purely secular and more disposed here to the past than to the hereafter. Our country churches are irreplaceable as stores of our past, even when shut and locked. They speak of our unlettered forebears when, in some extraordinary way, they created in profusion all over the land buildings of beauty, purpose and permanence that we seem unable to equal today. Their work (although work is hardly the word to use) speaks of our history, national as well as local, and one may often surprise a hero of one's schooldays recumbent in the shadows of an empty chancel. It is a remarkable, possibly unique, heritage that we now enjoy and, I must admit, do look after rather better than before, pace the brief interval of the Victorian rescuers to whom we should also genuflect. Without their well-intentioned restorations we should be a great deal the poorer and the countryside deprived of many of its most potent landmarks. If there is a church tower in prospect, that is what locks the eye.

Which brings me to the architecture of our churches. For those of us whose memories are not as reliable as we would like them to be, a few facts for reference may not come amiss. First, the architectural periods, taken from Lawrence Jones' 'The Beauty of English Churches'; then how we may identify them, taken from a variety of sources in an amateurish way but more or less accurately, I hope. What follows, therefore, are the rash pontifications of the amateur overruling the timidity of the tyro. After all, if one let a craven fear of error stifle all comment or opinion, one would forever be silent and that would never do for a would-be author.

ARCHITECTURAL PERIODS

PERIOD	DESIGNATIONS	DATES	REIGNS
Romanesque	Saxon	Pre-Conquest	The As, Aeths, and Eds of Wessex
	Norman	1066-1190	Will I, II, Henry I, Ste, Henry II
Gothic	Early English	1190-1280	Rich I, John, Henry III
	Decorated	1280-1380	Edward I, II, III
	Perpendicular	1380-1550	Rich II, Hen IV, V, VI, Rich III, Henry VII, VIII
Renaissance	Tudor	1550-1600	Edward IV, Mary, Elizabeth
	Stuart	1600-1690	James I, Charles I, II
Classical	Georgian	1690-1840	James II, Will & Mary, Geo I, II, III, IV, Will IV
Neo-Gothic	Victorian	1840-1900	Victoria
Nondescript ?	Modern	1900-	Ed VII, Geo V, Ed VIII, Geo VI, Eliz II

The dates on the previous page are, I caution, approximate; styles can lag especially in country places. They also intermingle in churches that have been developed structurally over the years, as almost all have.

I find it stimulating to one's appreciation of a church to relate its architecture to great contemporary historical events. For instance, the Saxon period with the Danish incursions; Norman with the Conquest, of course; Early English with the Crusades and Magna Carta; Decorated with the Hundred Years War; Perpendicular with the Plague and the Wars of the Roses; Tudor with the Reformation; Stuart with the Civil War; Georgian with the birth of the modern world; Victorian with industrialisation and the Tractarians; Modern with the great killing wars and war memorials of the 20th century. Others will have quite different points of reference but it is almost impossible to contemplate a church and not wonder what things were like when it was built and the circumstances associated with many of the memorials.

RECOGNITION

I hope that my earlier caveat about lack of architectural qualifications will have warned the reader to take my attributions about particular churches with a pinch of salt. However, for newcomers to the subject, who may not have an authority like Pevsner or the church guide to hand, here is how I try to identify what I am looking at. It is the great man's Penguin 'Dictionary of Architecture', spiced with unintended misinterpretation, that provides the essentials of what follows.

Saxon

When complete, Saxon buildings were tall and narrow in their walling but what mostly remains of their work in medieval churches is low to the ground and frequently mutilated. I identify Saxon work by small, roughly dressed double-splay windows; by long and short quoin stones (see Worth church); by pilasters (embryo buttresses) and by V-shaped arches. There is not much of it about — Worth is a complete Saxon church, at ground level anyway, and Bishopstone has a celebrated example of long and short quoin work.

Norman

Mostly distinguished by solidity and round arches with recessed ornamental motifs (orders) in the case of doorways; and by small, simple, slit-like windows, widely splayed within. There is a gratifying amount of Norman work still extant. Although my sympathies make me regard the Normans as invaders, deprivers and despoilers, it is nevertheless always a pleasure to recognise their almost millenial petrified finger prints.

Early English

The only feature that says Early English to me are narrow lancet windows with pointed arches. If one is knowledgeable, the capitals of columns can signify this period but not, alas, to me. It was, I think, a fairly unsophisticated time but it did mark the change from round to pointed arches, always held to be a turning point in architectural terms.

Decorated

Windows are the great give-away here. Windows of the Decorated style display a sumptuous arrangement of flowing, cusped stone tracery — flame-like, hence the Continental description of flamboyant. These windows were probably very difficult to make but rewarding in terms of prestige; they are certainly not easy to draw. Most medieval churches are resplendent with Decorated windows; they fill one with admiration and respect for those who made them. It must have been a prosperous time. Wool?

Perpendicular

As the name implies, Perpendicular architecture is essentially vertical, most obviously demonstrated by the stone mullions of windows continuing to the apex. Less extravagant than Decorated, its dignified austerity seems to me to be exactly right for ancient, unassuming country churches. It is my favourite style aesthetically although said, I believe, to result from the general impoverishment after the Black Death.

Tudor and Stuart

I don't think I can characterise this Renaissance period better than by observing the substitution of small rosy brickwork for stonework. There are also Tudor arches of a sort of flattened four-centred arch. This was the age of Inigo Jones, Wren and Hawksmoor. Twineham, early Tudor and endearingly simple, is an example of a complete brick church; I can only remember one other in this book but there is inevitably the occasional Tudor chapel attached to a medieval structure as, for instance, at Herstmonceux.

Georgian

Georgian churches are fairly distinctive, if rare. If they did not have a tower or bell-cote for bells one would hardly recognise them as churches in the traditional sense. They are descended, I think, from the classical basilica; Glynde, built by Bishop Trevor in 1763, is an excellent example of a complete classical, Palladian church, in immaculate flint work.

Victorian

Victorian and Victoriana is everywhere and no church escapes their well-intentioned restoration or 'improvement'. I would describe Victorian work as a manifestation of unrestrained garish Gothicism using the latest materials and I will be probably be criticised for so doing. Only rarely would most of us go especially to see a Victorian church and that must be a criticism.

Modern

There is only one completely modern-built church in this book — Worth Abbey and that is only as an afterthought — splendid though it is. Despite all our technology, we still seem unable, exceptions apart, to build as handsomely as they managed in the primitive days of, say, the Plantagenets. It is not only that we suffer from the absence of the benevolent effects of wind and weather, it must also have something to do with building for the glory of God which may be lacking to-day or, less spiritually, with neglect of local building materials and the necessity to be less labour intensive. Nondescript does seem an appropriate title for our times but perhaps I am guilty of the prejudices of old age.

As a nervous author's comment on his beginner's guide to architectural styles and how their more prominent features may be recognised, heaven forfend that the knowledgeable should trouble with the inevitable faux-pas above. It is not meant for him or her, only for such as myself.

Architectural styles and periods are one thing. Another relates to the purpose of the design — why is it as it is? There must be some good reason governing the design of any building; all churches in this country exhibit the same general layout and I have often wondered why they have come to adopt the shape they have, that is a chancel and nave in more or less separate compartments. That may do as a generalisation but there are, of course, the odd exceptions to emphasize my point. A delightful little book 'The Church Explorers Guide' by Frank Bottomley provides an explanation that I find eminently satisfactory. He says 'the chancel is seen as heaven, the chancel arch symbolises death and judgement and the transition from time to eternity and the nave, representing the world, is devoted to the laity! Exactly right; from those few words one can appreciate what a church is all about in terms of our hunger for some sort of alleviation from the trials of this world and longing for immortality in the next. One might say, if carried away, that a church is a philosophic expression in stone. One could hardly say the same about the banks, those temples to mammon, which play such a conspicuous part in the economy of our lives. One should be cherished, the other used. As indeed both are.

No visitor, to my way of thinking, should content himself with just the church. The churchyard, with its tumbled and worn and mostly inscrutable monuments and headstones is a haven in which to observe and ruminate. It is open to all of us; one cannot be a trespasser even though one may walk upon the graves of those long since buried there. They do not mind. I am sure of that. Just as we seem unable to build structures to-day to compare with our medieval churches, so we seem to have lost the art, or will, to create funerary memorials to match those of the 18th century with their charming cupids, warning skulls and lapidary testimonials. Victorian and modern headstones will never look as elegant and elegiac as their predecessors. Green marble chips, polished granite, curbed stones and various other vulgarities should be forbidden by a pastoral measure from Lambeth or something equally draconian. Unfortunately the vandals who demolished the protective railings in churchyards in the name of wartime necessity are probably now beyond the reach of earthly retribution; maybe their desserts will be administered above. Churchyards are precious and should be spared all that mistaken care which converts hallowed ground into what Betjeman describes as a 'garden of some suburban villa'. They are better as sepulchral oases of non-cultivation, open to all nature.

My comments and the sketches herein, full of error, inaccuracy and opinion as they may be, do represent enchanting hours spent in largely solitary contemplation of the countryside churches in the eastern half of Sussex. They are a vanishing species, albeit at a glacial pace, one hopes; weather and indifference have taken and will take their toll but it is surprising how many have survived all those turbulent centuries from the Middle Ages to our present secular state. We are incredibly fortunate to have such riches as common property, looked after and cherished by the devoted few. So may I, a stranger, offer my benedictions to those unsung, village volunteers who look after so well what beyond any doubt whatsoever is the jewel in their village crown. If heaven there is, they will assuredly end up there. I would love to come back (from where?) in two hundred years time and repeat this voyage of discovery. But as a confirmed pessimist, I fear Andrew Marvell may have it right with his ominous verse —

'But at my back I always hear
Time's wingèd chariot hurrying near.
And yonder all before us lie
Deserts of vast eternity'.

Let us therefore enjoy what we may while we may.

Hadlow
1993

As the first in my exploration of Sussex country churches, St Alban's in Frant, and indeed Frant village itself, make a good start. Both church and village seem to bear the hallmark of Abergavenny which is hardly surprising observing that the Eridge estate marches beside the village green. Both look to be in excellent condition with no sign of neglect or dilapidation, rather the reverse with gleaming fresh paint and trim gardens the rule.

The present church, a Regency successor to a medieval predecessor, was completed in 1821 and was thus spared some of the excesses of later Victorian exuberation. What chiefly distinguishes this dark sandstone church in appearance from a conventional medieval church are the aisle windows which each exhibit similar white-painted (iron, I gather) mullions and transoms. To me they seem more appropriate to the windows of some Gothic country mansion — Rochester's house in Jane Eyre, for instance. However the conventional west tower soon dispels that fanciful illusion.

Inside, all is very much spick and span if a trifle clinical. Here again much use is made of white paint — on the walls and on the slim cast-iron columns that support the roof. The ceilings, though, escape this austerity and those of both nave and chancel glow with colour. Consequently the whole effect is bright and airy with a lot of attention to the detail of the furnishings as might be expected in a church with the wealthy, landed parisioners that Frant enjoyed and enjoys. Examples of this care and affluence may be seen in the matching multi-coloured alabaster pulpit and reader's desk, neither of which would disgrace a cathedral, the delicately carved choir stalls and reredos, the loving work of a Frant postmaster. Similar quality is present in the tall, fretted front cover that puts one in mind immediately of that other font cover in the Abergavenny church at Birling in Kent. Both are impressive examples of the cabinet makers' art. I was surprised, therefore, when reading an old magazine shortly after visiting Frant, to see that a comparable font cover was sold at auction in 1988 for £300. For such an important and decorative item of church furniture, £300 seems an absurdly low price, but then I suppose secular demand for font covers must be limited, not to say eccentric.

The church stands in an extensive churchyard that commands sweeping views to the north towards Tunbridge Wells and across the Weald to the west. On arrival one is greeted by a contemporary lych gate designed like a graceful open rotunda. It is out of the common run and distinguished enough to measure up to the gabled estate houses that face the church — they get a mention from Pevsner, too. Several headstones from the time of the medieval church survive in the churchyard; small, chunky eroded stones of the head and shoulders shape still silently hint at long-gone worthies who have rested for centuries in the shade of Frant church, old and new. One I managed to date as 1745 but the church pamphlet notes one bearing the extremely early and rare date of 1570 — the year incidentally when Pope Pius V excommunicated Elizabeth I. How that edict would have affected a country church like Frant I can't say but possibly the vicar never learnt of the anathema. Horizons at Frant must inevitably have been localised and parochial in those far-off days.

Not so in the 19th century for Frant can now claim a link that crosses the Atlantic. Memorialised within the church and buried in the churchyard is Colonel By,* Royal Engineers, who one learns founded Bytown in 1830 on the banks of the Ottawa river in Canada. One may also need to learn (I did) that Bytown is now known as Ottawa, the capital of Canada. To-day, Frant must be a place of pilgrimage for Canadians on that account. We are not disgraced by church or village and perhaps the link is one reason why both look so seemly and well-preserved.

---

* Apart from Colonel By and Romulus and Remus, how many other individuals have founded a capital city ab initio?

On a cold January week-day, temperature 0°C, it was a welcome surprise to find this church not only open but being warmed by its central heating. Nonetheless no-one except me went in or out during the one and a half hours that I was there; I was the sole beneficiary on that raw morning — an extravagant expenditure for which at least one visitor was grateful.

This is a large Decorated cum Perpendicular church, standing in a large open churchyard bordered on all sides by the houses, old and new, of its village. A handsome oil painting in the nave depicts the church in an almost treeless churchyard; for instance those two Irish yews, evidently youthful, that guard the porch in my sketch are noticeably absent in the painting. It always astonishes me to see old reproductions of treeless churchyards but that is often so. Churchyards need vegetation, preferably yews, as well as their due complement of mellow headstones. It seems we are improving, in that respect at any rate.

The most attractive feature of the church, for me at least, must be the 14th century north porch. It is storeyed and buttressed and vaulted, bearing on its central boss the criss-cross, fretted, arms of Echyngham, the family which rebuilt this church and also that at nearby Etchingham. Its inner door, perhaps made from the same local timber on the Courthope estate at Whiligh as that which went to make up the roof of Westminster Hall, is a massive, double-skinned obstruction guaranteed to keep out interlopers. But not draughts apparently for it is backed up internally by a small draught-excluding lobby. In a church too large to be warmed by the press of bodies one should not complain about central heating or double doorways however anachronistic they may be.

In the clerestoried nave concern for comfort, or possibly a thriving WI, has led to the provision of a dazzling array of pew-length kneelers. They are quite exceptional; scenes of the village, clearly recognisable, the story of Noah and his ark and other religious themes, and a kaleidoscope of birds, flowers and fruit native to the district. They looked far too good to be knelt upon — a sort of rustic Bayeux tapestry.

Now one must remark on the memorials. These are concentrated in the north, the Courthope chapel, and in the south, Pashley chapel. The north contains memorials to the Courthope family, in battalion strength it seems, but there are no Pashleys now in the Pashley chapel (though there is still a Pashley manor not far away). However, to make up, there is a large eroded iron slab bearing the May coat of arms almost hidden under the clutter of the chapel. Even so, pride of place and appearance must go, I think, to three enormous black slate armorial ledger stones on the chancel floor commemorating members of the Roberts family. Although unprotected from the tread of unwary feet, the slate remains perfectly preserved and the engraving as crisp as the day it was cut. In contrast the iron slabs in the south chapel seem far gone in rusty decay. But as ever, ledger stones and paving slabs are much to be preferred to encaustic tiles and carpeted wooden flooring; the pity is the latter is so prevalent. Austerity and religion and the hereafter go together — comfort and pleasure are the imperatives of this world but they are not, fundamentally, what one goes to church for. To be honest, though, I must admit that exploring churches like Ticehurst does give me great pleasure of a secular nature — even in the most austere of weather.

Neither my sketch, nor my inadequate commentary, do justice to a church listed in 1961 by the Ministry of Housing and Local Government as of 'special architectural and historical interest'. How many village churches can still boast a rood screen with cross above as does Ticehurst? How can a sketch of this church virtually ignore its prominent sandstone tower? How can one omit the 16th century font cover or the stained-glass Doom in the chancel — Betjeman doesn't. Almost more so, how can one draw Ticehurst church without including the characteristic village houses that surround the unfenced churchyard? Blame that embattled, escutcheoned, storeyed porch.

The Assumption and St Nicholas

I wonder what Sir William de Echyngham would say if he could see his tall, proud church to-day for it is still almost exactly as he had it built in the 1360s, towering high above the Rother and Dudwell rivers and with his banner blowing in the wind atop the central tower. He would be mightily impressed that his church has successfully withstood the changes of architectural fashion and the ravages of time. His manor house beside the churchyard has not been so fortunate — it no longer exists having been replaced by a Tudor-style railway station. Why little Etchingham needs a railway station at all and why it should have to be next to its medieval church is something that only the Victorian railway promoters could possibly justify. To-day it looks like a contrived vandalism to place the two in such close juxtaposition but at least the commuters should get off to a good start in the morning.

The church is magnificent, more imperious than parochial. Severely constructed of dressed blocks of sandstone, it looks good for another six hundred years in the Sussex countryside. But external appearances can be deceptive as a glance at the hymn boards which hang on the central tower supports in the nave will reveal. The boards hang freely and are vertical. Under the weight of the ponderous tower the massive piers strain to remain vertical but, as the boards demonstrate, without complete success. In a church one should perhaps contemplate the hereafter and those leaning piers with the tower above do tend to concentrate the mind in that direction. Apparently there was a vault under the crossing which was filled in at an earlier attempt to underpin the sinking pillars. The worry now must be that any further attempts to regain the vertical might well displace insecure bonding and result in a general collapse. Which would be a tragedy.

Because there is more to this church than its commanding shell. As much as its unchanged 14th century structure, it must be the Echyngham brasses on the chancel floor on which much of the fame of this church rests. Here, their only protection is a low rail; nothing hides their medieval pride and they are, I think, an example to those churches which hide their treasures under protective carpeting. It is true that the founder has suffered the indignity of losing his head and I expect, if he could, he would have something to say about that although I doubt if he would wish to be covered up.

As well as the brasses, the chancel is blessed with a contemporary set of choir stalls, each with its carved misericord, decorative or moralistic. Medieval misericords are held to be evidence of a monastic connection, here said to be with the Cistercians at Robertsbridge. If the Cistercians have gone from Robertsbridge, at least their misericords survive triumphantly at Etchingham.

There is much ancient, faded heraldic glass in the upper lights of the windows — even I could identify Echyngham. From the Collections of the Sussex Archaeological Society I learnt that others were those of Edward III, his son the Black Prince, another son, Edmund of Langley, his son-in-law the Duke of Brittany, William de Montacute King of Man, and the earls of Arundel, Devon and March. They read like the cast of a Shakespeare play, or more correctly, like a lesson in our history. Arthur Mee records sadly that a boy with a catapult broke four of the six hundred-year-old windows. Equally sadly I can record that another window was damaged two days before I arrived when thieves broke in and stole the Jacobean communion table that served as an altar in the south aisle. This church has had more than its fair share of theft — William de Echyngham's head, a 17th century funerary helmet and now the communion table — no wonder it is kept locked; the wonder is the key is so accessible.

Two puzzles occupied my mind as I carried my investigations to the pub across the road — why should a substantial tower house but one bell and why should there be a mass dial by the north door where the sun can never cast a shadow?

BODIAM
St Giles

Very much second fiddle in repute to Bodiam castle is this withdrawn little Early English church. It is only too easy for the stranger to miss and, compared to the famous castle, few people can come to admire, I would imagine. Skirted by the sunken approach road and screened by the high bank and a thicket of trees, one eventually finds it, with difficulty in my case, isolated from the passing traffic and hidden from nearby houses. It seems to keep itself to itself. When I was there the rooks cawed in the surrounding tree-tops, pigeons cooed mellifluously in the distance and squirrels foraged industriously amongst the fallen leaves; and I was able to sketch undisturbed which is more than could be said if I had tried to draw the eminently more sketchable castle in its moat half a mile away overlooking the Rother.

The path from the lych gate leads around the base of the west tower to a neat Victorian porch on the north side of the nave. Inscribed on the stone arch above the chained and padlocked doorway are the words:-

'This is none other but the house of God
But this is the gate of heaven'

One does hope that the gates of heaven are not so forbiddingly barred or, if they are, there is some advice as to how they may be opened. One can understand and sympathise, in this irreverent age, why churches are kept locked and Bodiam church is certainly very vulnerable to an unoverlooked break-in, although I doubt if there is much inside of a readily marketable nature. What the thief would incur for sure would be dishonour and, one hopes, due retribution at those heavenly gates.**

So the casual visitor must content himself or herself with the exterior for the accessible windows are every bit as impenetrable from the outside as is the padlocked porch. This is a church in which the 13th century origins are very much overlaid by Victorian restoration and it is easy, as one looks at the unweathered sandstone, to forget that it antedates the much more weathered and tumbled castle down by the river. It would, I am sure, be a surprise to Sir Edward Dalnygrydge, the builder of the embattled, towered castle with its machicolated gateways,* and protected by its broad and tranquil moat, to find that the unpretentious church has outlived his grandiose creation.

The church's Early English ancestry is manifested by the irregularity of a few uncoursed rubblestones at the base of the tower and by the lancet window at the west end of the south aisle and, so Pevsner says, by the unattainable chancel arch. The rest is restoration work by a Victorian architect; how much Mr Carpenter changed or renewed needs expert knowledge to establish but surely the catslide roof on either side must be the product of an earlier age. Clearly, though, he did a good job and it is evident that the 13th century church is in a better state of furbishment, if that's the right word, than its grander neighbour. One is a romantic ruin, the other a modest but usable country church that serves its purpose as well in the 20th century as it did in the 13th, possibly even better since I dare say there are pews in the nave now and bells in the tower.

So the question provoked by an extrinsic view of both church and castle in one not exactly religious observer is why a modest, other-worldly structure like the church should so signally manage to outlast, both in use and in preservation, a fortified stone edifice, massively designed to withstand the onslaughts of man. One might think it had something to do with the staying powers of Christianity as opposed to the tendency to obsolescence in technology, or perhaps to both. The castle now seems rather like the dinosaurs of the distant past whereas the church still looks to the future — or should one say to the hereafter? We can, of course, be grateful for both.

* Machicolation, the medieval equivalent of modern bomb doors.

** I read subsequently that there are two brasses in this church. One, dated 1360, is that of a headless, legless knight in armour, said to be the 'earliest military man' in Sussex. Others, no doubt, may be lucky enough to admire this human. Failing the key, volume 76 of the Sussex Archaeological Collections will supply the deficiency.

A gracious street like that at Burwash needs something striking as a finial and St Bartholomew's meets that responsibility with distinction, placed as it is 'looking down on the site of the old park and palace of the Burghershs'. So much the Sussex Archaeological Society Collections tell me. The Burghershs were the lords of the manor here when this church was built and, although not commemorated in stone, a bit early for that, they are remembered by the dedication which was a family name. One might add that this church should not properly be described as a finial to a much more recent street — it is the street that depends from the church. As it should be in a Christian country.

Little of the original church survives from the Burghershs' day; only, I gather, the tower, the aisle pillars and the chancel arch. The rest is restoration or rebuilding but not disconcertingly so. Two things I found engagingly odd. First the arcade pillars — all octagonal except one round. Why the singularity? Even more odd, although I didn't realise it at the time, they are asymmetrically disposed if the ground plan of the church in the excellent guide is accurate, as I've no doubt it is. The north arcade was apparently built fifty years after the south and possibly they were a bit cavalier with their measuring rods in 1250. After all, times were unsettled then, they invariably were in the Middle Ages, and the wonder is they managed to build as well and lastingly as they did.

An equally stimulating question, for me, surrounds the bell apertures in the Norman tower. From a precarious position in the churchyard above the sunken road to the valley below they looked authentically Saxon — small, double-headed and divided by a tiny recessed column. How can you have Saxon windows high in a purely Norman tower? I can't believe that Victorian restorers would insert neo-Saxon windows; no, my belief is they were inserted by a stubborn local mason of Saxon extraction who had not yet accepted the new-fangled Romanesque style of architecture. Arthur Mee supports me and says these openings 'look like Saxon'. Hurrah for Mee.

For a church that stands in what was the centre of the medieval wealden iron smelting industry, it is entirely appropriate that St Bartholomew's should contain, in the north east corner of the south chapel, the 'oldest existing example of a Sussex cast-iron grave slab'. Safely and unobtrusively secured vertically to the wall, it is now exposed only to atmospheric damage; so far it has lasted 650 years even if its inscription has become almost totally indecipherable with the passage of time. The church guide, however, does record the inscription; it is always sad when inscriptions become obliterated or lost — they were put there painstakingly for a purpose. To revert to this inscription — to a female says the guide, to a male assert Pevsner and Mee (it seems to turn on the disputed gender of 'Jhone'), to a member anyway of the family of a local ironmaster. They lived, incidentally, where Rudyard Kipling came to settle. His house in the valley below the village, the present Bateman's, is a successor to that of the ironmasters. Otherwise, perhaps it would be known to-day as 'Collins'. Either way, its real fame rests on Kipling.

The church guide ends with a reproduction of the 18th century drawing by the Sussex artist, Grimm. Apart from showing the since-removed dormer windows in the aisle roof, his sketch is interesting for the almost total absence of trees in the churchyard. Many of the trees now there look more than two hundred years old and there must have been yews in the churchyard in 1784. Presumably they were sacrificed by Grimm to reveal the church without obstruction. No doubt he reasoned that you can see trees anywhere, especially in the Weald, but there is only one St Bartholomew's, Burwash. A highly developed regard for the priorities, one might say.

A gorgeous, unspoilt church on its hilltop in its walled churchyard beside Brightling Park aka Rose Hill. My view, the one inevitably chosen by the similarly impressionable*, includes the monumental pyramid that no-one can ignore and few reproductions disregard. It is wholly out of scale with the other monuments in this pleasant churchyard but, one reads, apparently appropriate to the larger than life 'Mad Jack' Fuller whose mausoleum it is. 'Mad Jack', aka 'Honest Jack' one should record, was sufficiently sane and public-spirited to save Bodiam castle from demolition. Brightling and Sussex have every reason to be grateful for his eccentricities; and the rest of us too.

The little church is a delight, mostly 13th and 14th century but with a rare, embattled Georgian south porch, proudly dated 1749, which I was very relieved to find unlocked. Inside, one first encounters two cast-iron headstones propped against the wall — rather dark and forbidding, they look like firebacks as iron headstones invariably do. To reach the diminutive nave one enters through a Norman (sic), arched doorway that looked to me tall enough and narrow enough to be Saxon despite being cut in a wall shown in the guide as post-Norman 13th century — an intriguing contradiction over which to ruminate as one contemplates the solid sandstone walling. Through the doorway, the overwhelming impression is one of a cosy intimacy accompanied by that familiar incense of a country church — the odour of damp which is so appropriate to their age. Here the modest internal space seems largely to be occupied by two substantial octagonal pillars dividing the nave from the north aisle and by one low, chunky pillar dividing the chancel from the north chapel. As is sometimes the case, for our benefit now I need hardly say, when there has been a prominent local family anxious to assert their ancestral pride, the chancel although lit by a very handsome Decorated east window, is upstaged by the small family chapel to its side.

It is the memorials to the Collins family that lift the chapel into the limelight here with a profusion of elaborately scrolled, armorial cartouches confidently proclaiming the history and virtues of this numerous family of ironfounders. The most famous memorial to this family, though, is firmly clamped to a wall in Burwash church which is not altogether surprising since the Collins lived roughly midway between the two parishes. In Burwash church the memorial is dated 1343 whereas Brightling declares the date to be mid 16th century — how is one to adjudicate between the rival claims? I incline to the latter date.

At the west end of the nave there is a small, raised gallery on fluted columns which imagination says might have been specially designed to accommodate the Tranter and his rustic quire from 'Under The Greenwood Tree'. There is also a commodious squire's pew in the aisle (Jack Fuller, a bachelor, must have rattled about a bit here), several pieces of salvaged brasses and traces of wall paintings. Altogether there is an old-fashioned, tranquil atmosphere to this church as if its parishioners have never been unduly troubled by the great world and with every reason to be satisfied with their rural situation. They have certainly well populated their churchyard which is noticeably full of those tiny headstones, so ancient they have barely kept their heads above ground.

As I reluctantly left, the clock in the tower chimed one o'clock melodiously. I don't know whether it was the ringing of the bell or my presence but I found myself subject to an aerial display by a solitary fluttering bat circling erratically between the western buttresses of the tower and then being led away towards the churchyard gate by a solitary, ambling cock pheasant. It was almost as if the souls of those buried there were politely thanking me for coming to admire their resting place and were then asking to be left in peace.

*   For instance, by Derry Brabbs in his book of delightful colour photographs of English country churches.

PEASMARSH
St Peter and St Paul

Pea marsh

This little church stands well away from its village in park-like surroundings across an open field from the august Peasmarsh Place. Built in 1839 as a rectory, the Place must have been a very grand rectory and quite disproportionate to the modest church whose rector it was designed to house.

But the church was here long before the Place and indeed before the village which I was told had migrated to its present position a mile away astride the road to Rye. I must say I found the notion hard to credit; although high up, the ground underfoot in the churchyard was distinctly marshy and unconsolidated. That may explain the substantial buttresses propping the Norman tower and would surely have discouraged domestic settlement. If so, why a church without a parish? Unless built by the lord of the manor as a more or less private chapel attached to the great house, churches and their parishioners generally go together; parishioners may move but churches never*. Peasmarch church, being Norman in origin, owes nothing to the Place so possibly I was not misinformed, merely opinionated, and the Black Death has something to answer for here as it frequently does when one finds an isolated church.

This is still basically a Norman church in which the nave walls were breached to make Early English north and south aisles. It is constructed of a rubbly sandstone and presents a grey, weathered appearance. The arcade pillars which are all that remains of the original nave walls are ample and rectangular and possess, in some cases, nook shafts at the corners in an attempt at rough and ready embellishment of plain and primitive piers. Such sturdy supports speak eloquently of antiquity; less eloquent are the deal chairs, which have replaced the pews in the nave, or the unsightly litter in the north aisle. There was a complete restoration here in 1926 and that, I imagine, was when the pews were swept away. It must be pure prejudice on my part but chairs never seem to convey the same pious message that pews, particularly those with carved bench ends, manage to evoke.

However, apart apparently from gravity, nothing has disturbed the original chancel arch which is, or was, the conventional Norman semi-circle. Said by that respected antiquarian, Canon Livett of Wateringbury in Kent who missed nothing and analysed everything here, to have subsided under the weight of the wall above, this arch has now perforce developed a slight horseshoe shape. It is remarkable as well for shadowy representations of leopards, vaguely heraldic and animalistic, which long ago were carved in relief below the spring of the arch on either side. I wondered what their significance might be — Canon Livett would have divined it, I daresay, — but St Peter's emblem is 'keys' and St Paul's a sword, so the leopards can have nothing to do with the dedication of the church. Could they have been carved there to intimidate those who presume to trespass in the chancel. They are not large but they are mysterious and they do add an intriguing feature to an already arresting arch.**

When I left after completing my sketch I chatted to three workmen by the churchyard gate who had been working there. They were clearly interested and well-disposed towards the church — it was they who had volunteered the information that the original, pre-plague village of Peasmarsh had been centred around the church — but they had not ventured inside. Despite my urging to inspect the carved animals on the chancel arch, they would not be persuaded. "Next week" they said but I doubt it. There seemed no good reason why they should be so unwilling to spare five minutes of a working day and I could only conclude that the church was somehow looked upon as private property inaccessible to the public except when a service was being held.

---

* I stand corrected; Ebony church in Kent was taken down from Chapel Bank and re-erected at Reading Street.

** Can't have been leopards; leopards apparently symbolise evil and sin, cruelty and antichrist. Hardly the thing to defend a chancel and sanctuary. Lions, which are a symbol of Christ and His resurrection, would be more appropriate and perhaps that is what these arresting carvings represent.

It is always a bit disconcerting when one's favourite mentors contradict one another. A case in point is the dispute over the date and identity of the iron grave slab at Burwash. Here at Penhurst, Betjeman roundly declares 'dedication unknown'; not so — see above. St Michael has presumably been the patron saint since the first recorded vicar, Robert de Tring, was inducted in 1288. More subjectively, Arthur Mee described this church as 'forgotten and neglected'; not so again or not so on one first Sunday after Easter when the church was open and bright with flowers even to the extent of a font cover bedecked with primroses like an Easter bonnet.

No-one who comes here is likely to forget Penhurst. The church stands in a churchyard alive with daffodils in the spring but of a village there is not the slightest sign. Instead, immediately to the south, with its kempt lawns merging comfortably with the long grass of the churchyard, stands the manor house. This is an Elizabethan jewel in greyish sandstone — tall and symmetrical, five bays wide with balancing pairs of chimney stacks climbing up the gable ends and reaching high into the sky. It is a perfect relic of an elegant past and one cannot help feeling envious of whoever has the good fortune to live there although when the post arrives I can't imagine and the daily papers must be fetched from afar. The compact group of church, manor house, barns and old oak trees makes an enchanting scene although my view, from the south east, cannot include the manor house. Anyway I wouldn't want the church to be upstaged and it was the church I came for. The manor house was an unexpected bonus to be savoured in memory only.

So, belatedly, to this modest church which offers no more space to its scattered parish than a narrow nave and small north chapel — but adequate no doubt. Externally, the feature that will attract attention is the truncated, Perpendicular west tower with a stair turret that nudges the squat, pyramidal roof. 'Cut short — finished with a bit of tile hanging' says Pevsner. That curtailment would explain why the stair turret bites into the tiles and why there are no belfry openings.

Being so close to, virtually part of, the Ashburnham estate, the woodwork is of particular interest at Penhurst. The first sample to greet the newcomer are the emaciated timbers of the south porch — deeply eroded, they must have sheltered the church doorway for many a winter, for as long as the pitted, coralliform 14th century chancel screen has divided the interior. Later, but from the same source no doubt, are the low box pews of the nave and the wall panels of the north chapel which give the latter the air of a snug parlour or closet, magicked in some way across from the manor house. It is all very intimate but, for some reason I don't understand, observing the manor house and the Ashburnham connection, the walls and floors are surprisingly bare of memorials — medieval simplicity consorting happily with Elizabethan elegance and both preserved by our 20th century fascination with the past.

Nevertheless, it has not been neglected of late. The church guide tells us that it was extremely dilapidated in the 19th century with the whole of the north slope of the roof falling into the churchyard.* You would never guess that now but you might have expected attack from the death-watch beetle, as was the case, calling for remedial spraying. Now, if my daily paper is correct male beetles can be attracted away from their boring habits by a synthetic female scent and ensnared on sticky traps. Poor beetles but good news for us and for all that hidden framework that supports the church bells in safe operating order in their towers. Still, as well as safety, bells do need apertures to release their message. Have there always been too few here to be summoned?

* Arthur Mee would have been very cross.

16

WITHYHAM
St Michael

Were it not for the Sackvilles I doubt if Withyham would be a place on the map or indeed if there would be a church at all to-day on the hillside above the winding road to East Grinstead. The original church, probably a Sackville endowment, was struck by lightning and burnt in 1663 necessitating a rebuilding in 1670. While they were about it, the Sackvilles, or more fomally the dukes of Dorset as heads of this family, took care that their memorial chapel should adequately represent their status; which it does, being larger and loftier than the chancel. We are lucky that they were as concerned to see to their laurels as to the repairs to the damaged church.

The present church consists of a west tower, nave, north aisle, chancel and the celebrated Sackville chapel. Pevsner says that parts of the 14th century building were used in the 17th century rebuilding. Certainly the south doorway looks ancient, even Norman — a low semi-circular arch, much stained with iron streaks as if the sandstone blocks had once been subject to intense heat. The whole building is of golden brown standstone with no attempt to clothe the walls inside with plaster or paint except above the chancel arch where an Earl de la Warr (a Sackville rector) painted the Last Judgement in the 1850s; it must have been a precarious undertaking. There are also occasional painted crosses on the arcade pillars; modern they looked and with what significance I have no idea. Otherwise the stone walls look untouched and glow with their natural colours.

So one comes to the north, Sackville chapel, which seems so obviously the raison d'etre for this replica medieval church. The dominant feature of the chapel is a central, free-standing tomb chest for a Sackville youth thus described:-

> "Here lies the thirteenth child and seventh son
> Who in his thirteenth year His race was run."

The life-size effigies of his parents kneel sorrowfully beside their departed son, the duke in armour as was the convention. There are other sons, dukes a-plenty, duchesses too, commemorated by memorials large and small, plain and armorial, legible and illegible but none so grand as the tableau to young Thomas Sackville, deceased 1677. Why was he so signally honoured, one wonders. One of the legible tablets is that to the recently deceased Vita Sackville-West who created her own living memorial in Kent with the gardens of Sissinghurst Castle. Faded banners hang down from the shadows of the distant painted ceiling, hatchments decorate the walls and what I take to be the essential Sackville symbol, a pattern of the diagonal 'bend' of alternating mini-shields, is repeated in diapers across the tiled floor. But for others not commemorated in stone, the great neo-Perpendicular east window provides a family tree of coats of arms. Twenty eight there are and the window is full and blazes with colour. Inevitably there will be future bereavements; perhaps the large blocked north window may have to be unblocked to provide space for successive achievements as they fall due. Or have we given up heraldry and the display of family pride? I hope not but fear so; ostentatious display is now held to be non-u and is avoided.

After so much Sackville pomp, one can hardly overlook the only pub, the Dorset Arms, which I didn't and where I learnt that the locality was also the birthplace of William Penn, the Quaker founder of Pennsylvania. Lately I have found country pubs infested by the ubiquitous old-age pensioner, like myself (not so in churches, I may say), but here to my relief I was greeted by ''Ah ha, a customer at last'' from the landlord. Withyham, if not the Dorset Arms, is fortunate to be so unobserved and I hope that my remarks above do not disturb this peace. It seems unlikely.

WARBLETON
St Mary the Virgin

Waerburh's farmstead

A nice, gentle red-brick path winds up the churchyard of this golden old church resting on its knoll above a farm and a row of one-time workhouses. The latter are now desirable country cottages as mellow as the church although younger by four hundred years. On arrival, instead of my customary preliminary survey of the prospect from a sketching point of view, I found myself helping a young man negotiate the lych-gate steps with his headstone-laden barrow — presumably for further inscription; headstones are surprisingly heavy.

The basic structure of St Mary's is 13th and 14th century to which had been added a 15th century tower, slightly out of line. There is a nave, north aisle, chancel and north chapel, all lit by an assortment of lancet, Decorated and Perpendicular windows — nothing new. The brick path leads one past the chancel to the south porch and the first surprise here is to encounter an external recess in the chancel wall, 'Probably a canopied tomb, perhaps an Easter sepulchre' says the Young Persons' Guide. Here might have rested, suggests Arthur Mee, Warbleton's most celebrated parishioner, the 16th century martyr, Richard Woodman. He sounds an obstinate, if principled, man who more or less provoked a martyrdom that might well have been evaded. To-day it is difficult to understand anyone behaving like Richard Woodman however strong the conviction. They must have been made of sterner stuff, persecutors as well as the persecuted, in those far-off, burning days of Queen Mary.

Leaving aside the gargoyle water spouts that intersect the string course of the tower, unusual in their prominence in this part of the country, the other surprises here are inside the church. The first to attract attention must be the squire's pew, set high on stilts above the lesser pews of the north aisle. From this commodious crow's nest one can examine at close range the arches of the arcade pillars even if denied a view of the altar. I suppose though, that in the days of the squires' pews the altar was of less importance than the pulpit and the squire might certainly have wished to glower directly down on the parson if the latter persisted too long with his sermon.

Presumably Sir John Lade, who died in 1740, was one of those landed squires fortunate enough to enjoy this upraised private pew. His marble monument, which now graces virtually the whole north wall of the chapel, is very grand indeed; 'of the highest order ... Sussex has little like it' says Pevsner. It is by Rysbraek and obviously was meant to be admired as well as to commemorate else why go to the expense of employing so famous a sculptor. The surprise, therefore, is to find the organ in front of this work or art so that the latter is invisible unless one penetrates the dusty recesses behind the organ. The arrangement is almost as much a desecration as covering medieval wall paintings with whitewash. The church is not large but surely the organ could have been fitted in elsewhere or swapped for something smaller. As it is, it essentially deprives the church of its second-best possession.

The most precious possession is also hidden, this time necessarily, under a long strip of carpet leading up the centre of the chancel to the sanctuary. Here is immortalised in brass, seven feet long, William Prestwyck, who was rector here from 1414 to 1436 — those fateful years when Joan of Arc was captured, tried and burned at Rouen. Prestwyck has that sorrowful face that makes him one with all other priests so delineated and his hands are clasped in the conventional medieval attitude of prayer. He is worth the trouble of rolling back the carpet; in fact it is no trouble at all to be so well rewarded.

Notwithstanding my strictures regarding the treatment of the Rysbraek, I was very taken with Warbleton church, attended by its orderly rows of weathering headstones and by its elevated position. It is somewhere that one would be happy to await the last trump oneself but just so long as one wasn't behind that offending organ.

20

Confidently proclaimed within the porch by John Betjeman as 'one of the most charming medieval churches in Sussex', it is something of a surprise to find he then omits Fletching from his selection of Sussex churches in Collins Pocket Guide. So do Laurence Jones and Alec Clifton-Taylor; they are both very economical in their favours and those they do list must be very special to outrank Fletching. It is closely surrounded by the houses of its small village which frustrates a stand-off view and maybe that is the reason for its exclusion by the pundits. Not fair considering the quality of the village.

The tower is Norman, early Norman to judge by the belfry windows, each divided by a central baluster echoing Saxon practice. One learns that the tower is not an exact geometrical rectangle which must have presented problems when they came to fit the broaches of the spire. Nevertheless they managed so well that now the spire reaches like a stiletto, 64 feet, high into the sky.

One is admitted to the nave through a marvellous old door in the porch. Embellished with Perpendicular mouldings like window tracery and equipped with an enormous locking apparatus, it is dark with age and clearly was never meant to be passed with a casual indifference. Once inside, there is a slight problem with the nave, or I found it so. Based on Norman foundations, it is said to rise gradually from west to east. But the short, round arcade pillars also increase in height from west to east; one would have expected the reverse to compensate for the rise in floor level. However, unless one had been fore-warned, one wouldn't actually notice this architectural conundrum. It is in character with the iregularity of the Norman tower.

So to the elongated chancel through a Perpendicular canopied rood screen that still retains its rood. Pevsner says the present chancel dates from a restoration of 1880 but at all events the style is mainly Early English with three pairs of lancets to light each side plus a Decorated east window, tall and complicated that is a challenge to the would-be sketcher. It would be convenient to hide one's deficiencies under the accommodating branches of a yew but none grow near enough to shade the church.

It is the two transepts, or rather their contents, that most distinguish Fletching church. The south is the more copiously furnished. It contains, for a start, an enormous bible dated 1701 (don't touch). Then in ascending order of importance (my ranking) a coffin slab rescued from under a buttress, a memorial to a local glove maker in the form of a brass depicting a pair of medieval gloves, an alabaster tomb with the life-size recumbent effigies of Richard Leche and his wife Charitye (commissioned incidentally by the lady in her lifetime) and, last and most majestic, the massive architectural table tomb and elaborate brass of Sir Walter Dalyngrygge and his wife. Their over-arching stone canopy has gone but a stone unicorn's head and shield with engrailed cross remain to proclaim their association with Bodiam castle. They have been here since 1380.

By comparison the north transept seems at first glance bare and uninteresting until one opens the unlocked door in the north wall that gives on to a narrow compartment that is the mausoleum of the Holroyd family. They are (were?) the earls of Sheffield seated at the adjacent Sheffield Park. Although it is their mausoleum, the Holroyds have gracefully given pride of place to their family friend, the immortal Edward Gibbon whose memorial tablet immediately confronts one and is the mausoleum's proudest possession, I would say. Possibly the church's too.

It is recorded that Simon de Montfort heard mass here with his followers on the night before the battle of Lewes in 1264. Thus refreshed spiritually, next day he rode, others marched on foot no doubt, the ten miles or so to the battle field and was successful in defeating and capturing his brother-in-law, the king, Henry III. History credits the outcome of this battle with the foundation of parliament democracy in this country., Can it really be fair to blame poor Simon for the Tory party or the Labour party especially as the earl was decapitated the following year after losing the battle of Evesham. Kinder perhaps to remember him at prayer in his battle armour that fateful night in June in Fletching church.

IFORD
St Nicholas

Iford, the first downland church in Sussex that I attempted to capture on paper. Here along the brief stretch of road between Lewes and Newhaven there are five such churches that look east across the open levels to the river Ouse and west up the bare slopes of the descending downs. That this delightful tract of countryside has not yet been spoilt by its proximity to Newhaven is surprising and the continuation of this happy state must be an argument in favour of the Channel Tunnel (which, as a Kentish man, I naturally oppose). Newhaven presumably will decline in importance and its trade no longer threaten this five mile ribbon of sleeping country churches. Good.

Iford is no more than a hamlet, if that; just a prosperous farming community with a Norman church to knit the whole together and lend distinction to its focus. While I was there more farm tractors passed by the churchyard than did cars.

The church looks comparatively new — flint work in good repair, pointing perhaps a bit overdone and the stone window dressings seemingly unweathered. This pristine condition externally is all down, the church guide informs one, to a major restoration in 1868 and two subsequent campaigns after 1945. There may not be many people living at Iford but they do seem to be able to look after their little church successfully. Which is as it should be for a church that dates from just after the Conquest.

The central feature of the church is the tower which separates nave from chancel. There are no aisles although blocked arches suggest where one once stood. Lack of population in Iford would have made any aisle superfluous, I should imagine. However, to revert to the tower, splayed outside near ground level and supported by four tall moulded Norman arches inside, it was apparently the original chancel here. It must have been a minute chancel and can't have been one for long for those three level east windows in the present chancel are also plainly Norman. Above them, the small window is, I understand, technically known as an 'oculus', a term I have not encountered before.* The theory that the tower and nave antedated the chancel is open to doubt, however, when one reads in the guide that 'the alignment of the chancel and nave are different and the whole tower skews as it rises'. If the tower was adjusted to accommodate the differing alignments , they must have preceded the tower, I would have thought. Irrespective of which came first, those internal tower arches are sufficiently imposing to dominate a restricted interior and must have induced a suitably impressionable frame of mind in the medieval congregation and invested in mystery the priest at the distant altar — that is if they could see him for the clouds of incense and the bell ringers in between. Too much mental daylight in religion can encourage doubt and disbelief rather as the electric light has exorcised ghosts; I am sure they were adept at impressing their congregations in the Middle Ages and this little church would have provided an effective setting to that end, it seems to me. However immaculate the window dressings are to-day, St Nicholas at Iford is definitely a relic from the past and one in which one's imagination can easily be stimulated. It is better inside than out and that, of course, is what the canons of the Church would properly prescribe for the faithful.

'Next is Iford with straw blowing free and cows in the meadows' — thus E V Lucas in his 'Highways and Byways in Sussex', written in 1904 and containing 76 exquisite drawings by F L Griggs ARA. Mr Griggs was a master and his illustrations are mainly why I have a copy of 'Highways and Byways'. The scenes are invariably heavily wooded in marked contrast to the arboreal austerity of Grimm, his 18th century predecessor. There was no straw blowing when I went to Iford, it was early May, but there were cows over the churchyard wall and there was also the first call of the cuckoo from across the river levels. Perfect.

* My wife, no architect, or foreigner for that matter, says it is also called an 'oeil-de-boeuf'.

One of the most primitive and early churches that I have yet explored. Its origins are Saxon, being sufficiently established in 966 to be granted to Hyde Abbey by 'I, Eadger, Emperor of All Britain'. For an abbey at Winchester to exercise its authority over a small church in east Sussex suggests unexpectedly good communications obtaining a century before the Conquest. Even to-day the association might seem tenuous.

How much of the Saxon building remains is open to question, perhaps only the foundations. The circular tower, nave and chancel are Norman supported by later, rough and ready, non-uniform buttresses. The tower, of course, has no buttresses — being circular it almost amounts to a flint buttress itself, all the way up to the Phrygian cap on top. Lack of available quoin stones is said to be the raison d'etre for round towers but there are a few reliable quoins made of stone and brick at Southease and plenty to be seen in the neighbouring churches with their rectangular towers. Still a round tower is a sufficient rarity (although not along the valley of the Sussex Ouse) to be a memorable sight and this one houses the third oldest bell in Sussex. The parish, I have little doubt, would not be without their bell for all the world.

As a general rule one finds that country churches tend to grow by accretion; a tower may be added, walls are breached and aisles created, transepts thrown out and chapels optimistically commissioned as the price of admission to heaven. (Well worth the money too observing the difficulty for the rich in passing through the eye of a needle.) Obviously there must be exceptions to organic growth and Southease is one such. Here the chancel and the aisles have all gone leaving behind above ground no more than a few voussoir stones from the blocked arches and a fragment of an aisle piscina. Why? The Black Death or the excessive burden of ecclesiastical exactions by Hyde? Who knows.

A church can manage without an aisle, many do, but all need chancels — must have one to function as a church. So at Southease in the 15th century they solved the problem economically by allocating roughly one third of the still-extant nave to the priest for his chancel. It was all done in the simplest possible manner; first by inserting a rood screen, which apparently soon followed the original chancel into oblivion (death-watch beetle or Cromwell's Triers? — both unwelcome), and then by what looks to be a make-shift wooden chancel arch supporting plaster and studding post above. It looks very unsophisticated and flimsy and, together with the unceiled nave roof, gives the interior a strongly rustic atmosphere. The effect is quite enchanting. Like the tower, the screen between nave and chancel may reflect the difficulty of obtaining good workable stone in these parts.

Of memorials, there are four coffin slabs to 18th century divines set amongst the faded plum-coloured quarry tiles of the floor but otherwise there is nothing in the interior to commemorate local dignitaries. Not that there were none, as the churchyard attests, but for the very good reason that the walls are almost entirely covered by medieval paintings, so faint as to be barely discernible. Nevertheless, there they are, another irreplacable distinction to an already distinctive little church. Local commemorative pride has properly deferred to prior medieval art.

It is a mistake, of which I am guilty now, to draw attention to an unspoilt church like Southease if one hopes that it will remain unspoilt; better let it sleep on unremarked and undisturbed. But then I am not alone in a tendency to nostalgia. For instance, in the unpretentious little 16th century porch there was a curling notice promoting the 1990 Sponsored Bike Ride in aid of the Sussex Historic Churches Trust. Like its Kent counterpart, the Friends of Kent Churches, this admirable body raises annually considerable sums of money from the unlikely exertions of bicyclists pedalling round from church to church. The riders benefit from the exercise, and probably spiritually too, and the churches benefit astonishingly in material terms. I have no doubt that Southease, amongst others, owes a small debt of gratitude to these muscular pilgrimages each September.

Glynde church is not to be confused with, or overshadowed by, its neighbour a mile away, the Glyndebourne of operatic fame; both buildings enhance the Sussex countryside and both, in their different ways merit a visit, one of which will be expensive, the other fortunately free. It is the latter, of course with which we are concerned here.

The church, under the lee of the enormous flint range of Glynde Place, is virtually the creation in 1763 of Richard Trevor, Lord Bishop of Durham, whose family seat was Glynde Place. If the bishop didn't actually design the church, he must have had a great say in what he wanted and he did pay for it all. What he got in place of its medieval predecessor was a stone and flint temple in the Palladian style, modest in size but finished in excellence down to the last squared flint. It seemed to me to be the architectural equivalent of a Fabergé jewel. For instance, precisely matching flints above an ashlar base suggest the most exacting standards of external construction while internally the severity of stone is softened by a sheath of patterned cloth. The moulded ceiling is picked out in grey and white, the pews are boxed and there is a west gallery for the choir. Complete and perfect in itself, nave and chancel a single unit, the whole design of this church conforms to the architectural precision that a prince of the Church and a great landowner could no doubt command and did.

The west door was unlocked. "It always is" said the lady topping up the flowers but there was no guide to tell the stranger what was what and why in this family chapel. Fortunately Volume XX, dated 1868, of the Sussex Archaeological Collections makes good the defect. Here one reads that the original church at Glynde was pulled down in 1763, that work on the bishop's replacement started in August that year, and that it was completed on 30th June, 1765 and that it cost all of £2,300 which even in the currency of the 18th century cannot have been an exorbitant sum for a building of such elegance and quality. The coat of arms, which prominently adorns the western pediment above the porch cost the bishop £26, well worth it for so permanent a profession of status.

The history of the parish of Glynde in the Collections of 1868 provides a contemporary report of the bishop's new church. I cannot resist quoting it as an example of how tastes have changed. Here is what is said in Volume XX:-

> "Every part of the interior corresponds in simple elegance with the outward appearance of the edifice. An air of neatness pervades the whole, and where ornament is needed, it is under the direction of the chastest judgement. The greatest contrast prevails between this elegant structure and most of the Sussex churches, not only in its external appearance, but also in its internal accommodation. Generally speaking the churches are a disgrace to the county. They are mean in appearance, whilst the interior too often presents an aspect of the most chilling neglect. In many instances neatness seems to be purposely banished from them, as if it were necessary to lacerate the feelings, in order to excite the spirit of devotion. At Glynde, however, elegance and comfort are happily combined. The feelings of the worshipper may borrow their tone from the cheerfulness of the temple, and the sacrifice of the heart may be of gratitude and love and not of fear and trembling."

Certainly not fair to the medieval churches of Sussex if no more than just to Glynde. Evidently the author looked on the contemporary with approval and to the past with disdain. I think alarm at the recent and nostalgia for the past is more conventional to-day. Who can say which attitude is correct, if ever there can be a right or wrong in matters of taste. In this world, things seem to move in cycles with the passage of time; By the time my brand-new grandchildren reach my advanced age, the cycle will have circled and the present may dominate again at the expense of the past. I hope not entirely as by then I shall be part of the past too.

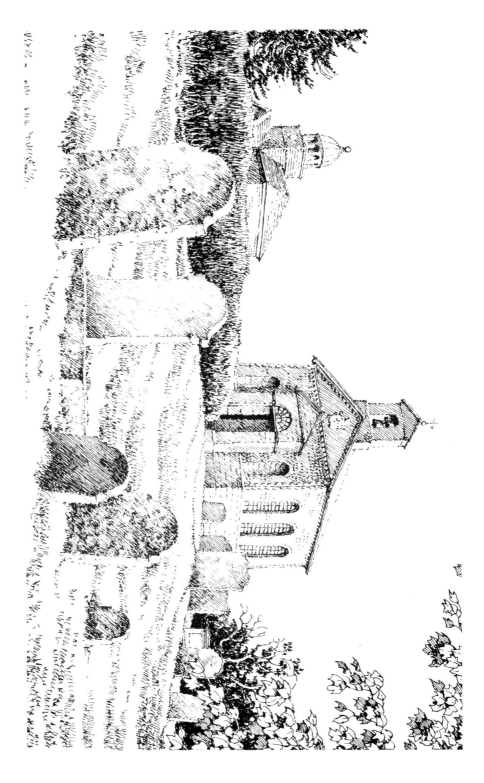

Unless one had been there, one would hardly believe that a place like Telscombe could still exist. But exist it does, two miles into the Downs up a 'no-through' road above Southease. Secure in its combe, Telscombe is protected by the Downs which swell, magical and bare, in all directions as they whisper of far older works of man than the little grey church which shelters in their lee. And yet those modern works of man at Peacehaven on the cliffs facing the Channel are no more than two miles away again — happily invisible and part of a quite different world.

Telscombe is apparently one of only three hamlets in Sussex lying above the 200 foot level which makes one wonder why it is where it is. What in fact is it? No more than a farm or two, a comfortable house or two and a few cottages with all the land on which the village stands now in the care in perpetuity of six trustees on behalf of the Corporation of Brighton. And, of course, the church, in the care of the Bishop of Chichester, while all around are the precious empty spaces — pasture for sheep, habitat for larks and lapwings, walks for hikers with everywhere reminders of our half-sensed prehistoric predecessors. They have all chosen well. But still, one would like to know why the church is here in this tiny, remote hamlet. For that one must get inside and, with luck, find a church guide to enlighten the ignorant. Without luck, though, as I was, for the lady with the only key was away shopping, there is a problem. Windows occasionally come to the rescue but, although at eye level here, all were complete with stained glass and impenetrable. So one is forced back on what the exterior reveals to the amateur and what the invaluable Pevsner proclaims.

Let us begin with the exterior and see what may be deduced. The west tower is plain, unbuttressed and standing on a modest plinth, and topped with a red-tiled pyramid cap. The tower windows are long and narrow, no more than slits really. The body of the church, nave, chancel, north aisle and chapel, is simple and, like the tower, is constructed of a mixture of stone and flint, arranged here and there in herring-bone courses, the whole covered with vestiges of soft-grey mildewed cement rendering. Its sits snugly on, or rather is embedded in, the slope of the hill opposite the principal farm in the hamlet.

It would be difficult to date the church from the external appearance. The unpretentious tower looks old but some of the chancel windows look newish or, more likely, renewed. I can't remember a buttress anywhere which I would think means very old or very new. It certainly isn't new. Let us see what Pevsner says. Based on the jamb of a north window in the chancel, a somewhat exiguous clue I would have thought, he pronounces the nave and chancel to be Norman. The aisle and chapel are held to be 12th century additions, based on 'a multi-scalloped capital' to one of the chapel piers. The tower is undated by Pevsner but, if its lancet windows are round-arched inside as he says, then they and the tower would be Norman too, I suppose. Arthur Mee agrees.

There are no memorials to excite comment although Mee finds the 13th century font 'a veritable treasure'.

Considering the limited number of houses that make up the present-day Telscombe, the churchyard is amply stocked with headstones — few really old, most with a Victorian or later look to them. They suggest a more populous village than exists to-day but they can give no hint of the population here when the church was first consecrated. The village is on the road to nowhere — lucky Telscombe — not where one would normally expect a settlement to be since there are no particular geographical features or lingering traditions associated with some sacred, pre-Christian place to concentrate worship here in this encircled valley. So why the enduring grey church? We may be lucky to find it hidden away so unobtrusively in the brooding immensity of these empty downs but nevertheless reason there must be, even if unfathomable to the passing stranger.

If one listens carefully one can almost hear Stravinsky's Rite of Spring echoing faintly in the wind.

PIDDINGHOE
St John

Spur of land belonging to Pyddi's people

Before the sluggish river Ouse can reach the sea at Newhaven it must first wind round below the tower of Piddinghoe church. This was a fishing village once, known for its herrings. Now it is a backwater, by-passed by the main road and all the better for that. It is the sort of village where, in 1988, they put up a framed notice illustrating all the houses in the village and listing all the names of those who lived therein. One learns that the church is a listed building, grade 1, and that the emaciated, but unprotected, set of stocks in the churchyard is also listed, grade 2.

The church, which is 12th and 13th century, but looks much more recent as a result of a major restoration in 1882, was the scene of considerable activity when I arrived to sketch and explore one hot morning in summer. I found that I had coincided with the members of an art club from Hove who had the same idea. They seemed to be everywhere in the churchyard but in no way put out at my intrusion. That is the great virtue of churches and churchyards — no-one is ever a trespasser or unwelcome.

The church itself was also under attack — attack, I think, is the right word. Here bettle was the enemy and two men were busy stripping the boarding that enclosed the ancient roof rafters so that the enemy could be engaged at close quarters. The operations high in the roof and the supporting scaffolding in the nave had put the church completely out of commission; everything that could be taken down had been taken down and dust sheets used to cover immovables like the altar and the font. It seemed that only the odd little head that peers down on the pews from the north arcade had been left to take its chances.

In their lunch break, the two workmen proved to be very forthcoming and ready to discuss the problems of the church. For instance, without their guidance I should never have noticed that the voussoir stones of the north arcade were of that unreliable building material, chalk. The arches of the north arcade are round headed, the south pointed, and both cut from the original walls of the nave but at different times, no doubt. Only the north are dressed with chalk, though, I seem to remember. Another idiosyncracy of this church, of which I was informed, was the sunken level of its interior floor — well below the level of the churchyard outside. It is almost as if the church has been bedded down for stability leaving barely sufficient room for the windows of the aisles.

Inevitably the most striking feature of Piddinghoe church is the round west tower, entirely constructed of flint and heavily repointed, at the Victorian restoration, no doubt, as was the rest of the exterior which accounts for the generally unweathered appearance. The tower, I was told, is nevertheless cracked right through towards the top and the arrival of the architect to pronounce on preservation was anxiously awaited. Round towers are so scarce it must be preserved even if the bells are condemned to permanent immobility. I was encouraged to climb the ladders to inspect the aged roof timbers but cravenly declined. I was discouraged from climbing the tower ladder; quite right too. I would not like to have to attempt a single vertical baulk of timber with nothing more than horizontal slats for rungs. The architect will not be allowed to duck that ladder though. Perhaps he is younger.

To-day (July 1991) this church looks sadly devastated as would any building when under major repair. It is difficult to picture it restored to health — the scaffolding taken down and dust sheets stowed away, the sun shining through the stained glass on the polished pews and flowers on the altar. Lots of money is needed to pay for the work with only a small village to call on but I am sure that it will all be successfully carried through in the end and services resumed and sketching parties again attracted. If anything will do the trick, that round tower with its golden fish for a weather vane will do the trick. It is now like a ship in dockyard hands — sad to contemplate but certain to emerge resplendent and good for another century or two.

32

LULLINGTON
Possibly dedicated to St Sithe (an unrecorded saint)

Lulla's farmstead

To-day, this withdrawn little building may seem more a curiosity than a church. Invisible from the road, it is reached up a narrow, brick-lined path on the slope of the downs that face Alfriston across the Cuckmere river. What one finds when one gains the clearing that does, or did do, duty for a churchyard is the chancel, topped by a white-painted belfry, which is all that survives from an earlier complete church. The remaining interior is simplicity itself — roughly 23 by 18 feet — containing an altar, a font and a few chairs plus a single bell in the belfry above. Services are still held here, evensong every third Sunday in the month. In summer at any rate.

In 1965 the missing parts of the church were excavated by the pupils of the Ratton Secondary Modern School of Eastbourne under the direction of Mr A Barr-Hamilton whose detailed account of the proceedings and of his findings were published in the Sussex Archaeological Collections of 1970. It appears from this scholarly report that there have been three versions of Lullington church here, the second and third being reimposed on the footings of the original. The first in line, consisting of a west tower, nave and chancel, is dated as 1180, at the transition from Norman to Early English; the second version, nave, chancel and south porch but no tower, is dated as C1350, that is towards the end of the Decorated period while the third and final version, also nave, chancel and south porch, is considered to be 16th century. Later, fire in the time of Cromwell is thought to have been responsible for the elimination of the nave and porch leaving us no more than the small chancel that we see to-day. In 1780, the remains of the church were painted by James Lambert; there was then no belfry evidently. Such, very briefly, is the history of this tiny relic as revealed by painstaking archaeology assisted by the enthusiasm and muscle-power of schoolgirls and boys.

Notwithstanding the chronology outlined above, the slim lancet windows of the chancel are perplexing and would seem to contradict a 16th century ancestry. Pevsner and the official leaflet put the windows as 14th century but my 'bible' (one of them) allocates the Decorated style to the 14th century. These lancets are not Decorated or I am a Dutchman. All of which says to me that the chancel, chapel should we call it, is a survivor from the original construction. These idle and amateur speculations may seem pointless and pretentious but they do add spice to the solitary exploration of an apparently straightforward and abbreviated building of some rarity.

Not everyone is so stimulated. While I was there a group of three adults inspected the church for all of three minutes before proceeding on their way — probably to 'take in' the Long Man of Wilmington as part of their day's holiday programme. On the other hand, the visitors' book that rests optimistically on the font bore an address, from the day before, of a visitor from Gettysburg, Pa, USA. That is an address to stir the imagination.

Not surprisingly, there are remarkably few memorials; an external wall tablet to an 18th century vicar and a modern headstone to a father and son who gave their name to the Foundation for the Preservation of Lullington Church. Nevertheless, despite a lack of above-ground evidence, the archaeological dig reported identifying nineteen graves in, or rather under, and around the nave. There must be many more lying under the rough grass that now constitutes the hidden clearing in which this little fragment of a country church still survives. It is worth more than three minutes!

LITLINGTON
St Michael the Archangel

Lytela's farmstead

After the fragment that is all that remains of Lullington church, Litlington, a little further along the road that winds down the Cuckmere valley, seems a model of completeness and convention. It is, or was, Norman in origin but was 'restored' (in inverted commas to emulate the parish guide) in 1863 — a blessing or a misfortune, depending on one's point of view, that Lullington obviously failed to experience.

It is extraordinary how many medieval churches were 'restored' in the 19th century. Where would we be without the efforts of the well-intentioned Victorians with their ample purses. Some ancient relics, like the carved oak screen which once separated tiny chancel from diminutive nave at Litlington would still be here for us to admire (possibly) but how many churches would have succumbed to decay and collapse and how bereft the countryside would look without them. Old etchings too often demonstrate the octopus-hold that ivy had on the towers and roofs — now one never sees a church in danger in that way. So while regretting the occasional Victorian or Puritan iconoclasm, if that is not too harsh a word, one should commend the former for their conscientious preservations. The churches were, for once, ahead of the lay community.

This little flint church shows no sign of disintegration after at least eight hundred years of wear and tear. Essentially it consists of a Norman nave and chancel with more recent additions of a south porch, vestry and white-painted western bell turret. The Norman evidence consists of miniature north windows, beautifully enriched with stained glass in the chancel but blocked in the nave. There are Decorated windows to let in the light from the south and Perpendicular windows east and west replacing lancets, traces of which remain to intrigue one. There is an Easter sepulchre and sedilia in the chancel and a dark pillared, octagonal 16th century font covered elegantly by a polished, concave wooden cap. Also of interest is the roof; externally of slate, which is uncommon in this part of the country, and internally supported by king posts, the whole resting on an embattled wooden plate running around the top of the nave wall. One can't help but be impressed by the latter's detailed workmanship — an example of painstaking ornamentation in something that hardly attracts the eye. It must be a symptom of the pious philosophy that said that everything connected with a church is to the greater glory of God and therefore that no pains should be spared. It is not an attitude much practised nowadays, rightly or wrongly. And that about sums up the interior — old and rustic but without a memorial to excite historical associations.

Except for the floor, which apart from weather-proofing, is where the Victorians really left their mark in the shape of their ubiquitous coloured tiles. Floors are important and can make or mar an interior. I wonder what happened to the stone slabs that they must have had here once. Did they, perchance, migrate to the rectory, which earns admiration in the parish guide, or to Church Farm which looms over the churchyard on the northern side. I wouldn't have minded a few myself, especially if they bore armorial engravings, as I expect they did. But would they bring their ghosts with them?

Forewarned by my wife, I kept a sharp eye out for the Litlington Tea Gardens to which she had been taken as a schoolgirl from Eastbourne. There they are, still going strong, if overcrowded as was the village pub, whereas of course the church was an oasis of peace (maybe there is something to be said after all for a secular society). That is the problem for the villages that lie along the east bank of the Cuckmere. They are too attractive and well known for their 20th century comfort when everyone has too much leisure and transport, myself included.

EAST GULDEFORD
St Mary

After Sir Richard Guldeford

I have always thought that this church more properly belongs to Kent along with all the other churches of Romney Marsh. It stands on that western level which was reclaimed, 'inned' one should say, by Sir Richard Guldeford in 1500. From a Kentish point of view it is on the wrong, Sussex, side of the Kent Ditch — if it is Sussex's gain, it is certainly Kent's loss.

Before departing on a terminal crusade to the Holy Land, ending in his death at Jerusalem, this supporter of Henry Tudor before Bosworth and one-time Sheriff of Kent had this little church built at his own expense. By 1505 it was complete. East Guldeford church is so untypical of its time that one wonders to what extent Sir Richard, who was sufficiently conventional to go off on a crusade, had a say in its design.

Quite unlike any other church on Romney Marsh, high and cliff-like, it is almost square and made exclusively of those dear little Tudor bricks, 9 inches by 2 inches, which enhance any building lucky enough to be made of them. They are laid in successive courses of headers and stretchers, in the bond known as Old English, and they are overlaid, only patchily now, by mellow, discoloured rendering. Being as broad as it is long, one roof cannot easily span the width of the building — hence the twin hipped gables with a central valley in which the tile-hung bell turret sits so snugly. Despite a recent campaign of repair, I noticed three very alarming cracks in the brickwork running vertically from ground to eave through the windows of the north wall. I trust the Marsh will remain quiescent.*

The church is as uncomplicated inside as it is straightforward outside. Bare, white-washed walls look down on plain, deal box-pews separated by a wide brick gangway. Nave and chancel are virtually all one with only the altar rails to imply the division. The decorations are recent — an elegant painted frieze of angels above the east window, some corbels acting as brackets for flower arrangements, two inconspicuous memorials and a representation of the arms of Guldeford. There is also, I must mention, a small ship's bell attached to the west wall which was salvaged from the two-masted, square-rigger Alliston, wrecked on the Camber sands in 1879**.

Attractive and inconspicuous in the reclaimed fields as this church now is, it might not be so remarkable, I think, were it not for the date of its construction. I have consulted the history books — Henry VIII had not yet ascended the throne and Martin Luther's declaration had yet to see the light of day. Rome still dominated Western Christianity and the conventions of the Holy See were still generally accepted — in the shape of its churches as well as in everything else. Essentially the churches were divided into two — a secluded, privileged holy space for the priest to conduct his mysteries with a larger, open space for the duly-impressed laity. Thus basically are all medieval churches. Chancel for the priest and nave for the parishioners. But not so here; the distinction is eliminated and the priest brought to the level of the people as the Lollards had wanted a century earlier and the Puritans were to preach a century later.

I daresay I might be wrong in all this and that my theory is the outcome of an over-excited imagination brought on by the austerities of East Guldeford church. It is odd, though. When this church was built the Papal fiat still ran in this country and churches were no doubt built to accommodate the Roman rite. Exceptionally, in one small backwater on the edge of the marsh someone, possibly not Sir Richard, decided to do his own thing and leave a signpost for the future. As such, this herald of the Reformation is well worth a second glance and a second thought. Now it looks entirely rustic and innocent.

* Two years later the bricks are crumbling and the pointing of the brickwork of the north and east walls seems to have deteriorated to an alarming degree — not far short of terminal, I would say, unless something is done.

** The Alliston was registered at Whitby where one of the owners was a coal shipper which makes one suspect that she was much the same as the ex-collier, Endeavour, also from Whitby, in which Cook explored the wide Pacific. By coincidence, my wife's name is Alison and her father hailed from Whitby. I feel a personal involvement with that bell.

All Saints, Iden, does not figure prominently or indeed at all in the lists of the favoured churches of Sussex so I was surprised to find, hidden away down a side lane, a handsome building that would do credit to any village, or town even. Apart from a relatively recently discovered Norman window in the tower, it is almost all Perpendicular in appearance. Its conventional tower, with its south east stair turret, has a grand transomed west window and dates from the late 12th century; the wide, uncluttered nave is early 12th century, the equally wide and uncluttered chancel is 13th century and the north aisle and chapel are 15th century. There has also been a south aisle, the traces of which are more obvious from the outside where two sets of coloured voussoirs remain as evidence of past capacity. Such, briefly, is the sandstone church at Iden, in plan roughly two inexact squares joined together at the junction of nave and chancel.

Nowadays I try never to be upset when I find a church locked and, if I was responsible for its care, I would lock up with the best of them. Imagine, therefore, my relief when the elderly husband of the lady churchwarden arrived to open up in anticipation of a party of bicycling bellringers from Yorkshire who were 'doing' Sussex and Kent. Right on cue the brightly clad throng turned up and were followed gratefully into the church by me. I would say their bell-ringing was somewhat perfunctory — 'Little Bob minor' it was, they said — they seemed impatient to find the nearest pub for lunch before pressing on to Peasmarsh. Still without them I would not have been able to wander round the interior; exteriors are fine, all important from a sketcher's point of view, but it is all so much better when one can learn about the inside as well. In mathematical terms it might be described as synergy or two plus two makes five.

After the departure of the thirsty bellringers the church was very properly promptly locked again. Properly locked in Iden's case because there are some eminently collectable and portable antique statues which would not last long if made too accessible.

The overall impression that one gains of the interior is of open space; the good looking pews are relatively few in number and the choir stalls have been swept away. I suppose that some of the mystery that a church needs has been swept away too — the modern altar is distinctly clinical — but the general atmosphere is calm and unshadowed. Of the distant past, apart from the imported statues, there is now, clamped vertically to a chancel wall, a 28″ brass of a rector who died in 1427. It seems to be in excellent condition but, so placed against the light, it is difficult to make out. Better in its original position on the floor would be my verdict. I am always in favour of retention in situ even if preservation is handicapped thereby but then I am only an observer and can't be held accountable. There are also some crude scratchings on one of the arcade pillars, supposed by the church leaflet to have been scored by returned crusaders. They reminded me of the equally faint scratchings on a pillar in the magnificent church of St Margaret-at-Cliffe near Dover.

Iden church may not, so far as I know, have felt the brush of fame; it looks altogether too peaceful. Nevertheless the name, Iden, does have its niche in history for it was immortalised in the second of Shakespeare's Henry IV plays. In 1450, the fugitive Jack Cade was surprised by Alexander Iden, squire, in his garden and mortally wounded followed by judicial quartering, post mortem!

"Is't Cade that I have slain, that monstrous traitor?" Thus Iden, or rather Shakespeare. In actual fact, Sir Alexander Iden lived near Heathfield. Iden must be content with the realities and lesser excitements of a descent of bellringers and the purely nominal association with a medieval hero of Sussex. Fame, however tenuous, need not be discounted, all the same.

A subsequent visit, later, to redraw Iden church confirmed the injustice of expert opinion; it is a very fine church with a noble tower that well deserves its immense transomed window.

This is a heavenly church in a heavenly spot with the nearest house, Court Lodge, barely visible a quarter of a mile away across the fields. One finds the church at the end of a narrow lane, surrounded in summer by pasturing cows and cylinders of rolled-up hay awaiting collection. The leafy lane is only wide enough for a single car and must be the medieval road that led to the medieval village which, I am sure, crowded about the church before the onset of the Plague — or so the deserted situation would seem to suggest. To impute a heavenly outcome to the after-effects of the Plague may seem perverse but time has certainly worked its healing magic at Hooe.

My history books tell me that the Black Death reached this country in 1348 with sporadic outbreaks continuing until the 17th century. Therefore, the village here might have been evacuated to its present site a mile or two away any time up to, say, 1600. Departure from the church confines after only a relatively few generations of villagers had enjoyed its protection seems a poor reward after so much effort on the part of their building predecessors. On the other hand, the outcome from a sketcher's point of view could hardly be better. Wind and weather and fire are the enemies of structures; it is only the members of the congregation that suffer from the Plague and people are eminently renewable, preferably at a safe distance which is where they now are.

The plague-proof church, built of dressed sandstone blocks, greyish in colour, consists of a resuscitated 12th/13th century north chapel (now the locked vestry) and a 15th century chancel, nave, south porch and west tower. It is all of a piece with Perpendicular windows everywhere except for two lancets in the one-time chapel. There may have been a different-period window at the east end of this chapel — now it is bricked up to provide a chimney for the vestry — a very Victorian 'improvement', I feel. All the hood moulding of the south-facing windows terminates in little heads, mostly forlorn and vacant in expression except for one malicious imp which surely sprang from the pages of M R James's ghost stories (or vice versa).

To enter the church one steps across a tomb slab minus its brass but still bearing a faint impression of its indent. It came from the nave; a pity it was moved because there are singularly few memorials inside. I missed the famous dug-out chest, Saxon says Mee (perhaps it is locked in the vestry, very sensibly), but one cannot miss the disproportionate inlaid sounding board above the pulpit. I suspect this overbearing aid to accoustics was liberated from some large town church. Anyway it looks very imposing here and the sermons from it must carry extra weight.

With a tower of such obvious substance, a well-found ring of bells is to be expected and with the absence of nearby households to object to noise, it is understandable that bell ringing should feature prominently in the church activities as framed notices in the ringing chamber make clear. Apparently, in the early 1980s the Sussex County Association of Change Ringers rang (if that is the right term) 4 peals of 5040 Doubles lasting two hours and forty odd minutes on each occasion. Such marathons would test the patience of anyone living next door to the church, as I do at Hadlow. I did once complain when my Sunday afternoon nap was disturbed but very soon was made to realise that I had committed a tremendous faux-pas. Never again.

As I sketched, I was made to listen with half an ear to an eccentric who explained that the church had induced in him a powerful urge to poetic composition. Not being a poet, I could only grunt without understanding at his disquisition on iambic pentameters and such-like mysteries. Possibly I had encountered another Gray; I would like to think so and he would too, I gathered. For my part, I would aspire respectfully to be another Samuel Hieronymous Grimm.

WARTLING
St Mary Magdalene

Not quite at the end of the road but from here, at the boundary of Wartling churchyard, the fields begin their uninterrupted sweep down to the sea at Pevensey. Its a bit like the rim at Romney Marsh. Four minor roads meet to form the nucleus of a picture-book village of church, pub and a few houses. So close together it puts one in mind of Defoe's quatrain.

> "Whenever God erects a house of prayer,
> The Devil always builds a chapel there;
> And 'twill be found, upon examination,
> The latter has the largest congregation."

Thus it was as I found it at noon, on a Friday admittedly — an empty elegiac church and a crowded little inn, more full of flowers and women than men! Are we being shown the future by rural Wartling?

This is an attractive little church consisting of a 13th century chancel with a mostly 14th century nave and abbreviated north and south aisles. There is no tower as such; the nave continues westward to form the base for a wooden bell turret and broach spire. There is only one bell rope so presumably only one bell in the turret. The walls of the church are a harmonious medley of honey-coloured dressed sandstone blocks patched here and there by rubblestones and brickwork. It all looks solid and substantial, as it should having lasted six hundred years — an impression of enduring stability which is somewhat belied, however, by the alarming outward belling in a length of 13th century walling in the nave that is clearly visible from the inside. Perhaps it has always been so since there are two 14th century buttresses outside to contain it.

The windows are all Perpendicular with much clear glass except the east window above the altar which is Decorated and stained, if my memory serves. There are two later porches, north and south, and that about sums up the geography of what is essentially an unpretentious church appropriate to a remote hamlet. It is exactly how one expects and hopes to find a country church.

The straightforward exterior is mirrored inside by the simple interior where dark box pews still survive in the nave. A sudden exception, unfortunate in my opinion, is a yellow memorial lectern in the shape of a heron with outspread wings. The excuse given in the church guide is that there have been heronries near the church since the 1600s. Quite so, but not yellow birds; the weather vane would have been a more appropriate position for this emblem. Of memorials, the Curteis family and their connections predominate and more or less clothe the chancel with their wall tablets, some of sufficient quality to earn the favourable comment of Pevsner.

Outside there are other memorials with one that cannot escape mention although it is inconspicuous enough to escape notice. It is the Pelham Buckle in stone relief outside the south aisle. Arthur Mee infers that the buckle insignia was awarded to a member of this illustrious Sussex family after his capture of the French king, John, at the battle of Poitiers in 1356. Although many Pelhams appear in the Dictionary of National Biography, not our Sir John. Nevertheless the valiant French king was captured by the archers of the Black Prince and then ransomed by Edward III (I learn) for £500,000 plus La Rochelle. When the French proved unable or unwilling to find all the ransom money, John voluntarily re-surrendered to end his days in London in 1364. I am sure all the French school children are very familiar with their king's noble behaviour; we are less well-informed. My visit to Wartling church has supplied a deficiency in my education.

RODMELL
St Peter

All the churches of that unspoilt tract between Lewes and Newhaven seem to be Norman or have Norman origins still visible and this one particularly so if its chancel arch is anything to go by. Semi-circular as it should be, the arch consists of an elaboration of at least three orders of deeply-cut mouldings — zigzag, chevron and billet. Very impressive it looks and it was only after I had noticed the squat, polished marble columns that support its imposts that a doubt of its authenticity crept in. It turns out that the arch is in fact a modern replacement of a 12th century (ie Norman) predecessor. I thought the reproduction arch looked fine — unlike most imitations — and quite in keeping with the rest of the church which is rather a mishmash but genuinely old for the most part.

The nave, chancel and south chapel are Norman while the south aisle, west tower and the small adjoining compartment, known as the baptistry, are just post Norman, that is Early English. Only the porch and vestry are modern, Victorian I imagine and purely utilitarian. Seen from the outside, the general impression is one of glittering, black, irregular flint stones separated by generous ribbons of pointing except at the east end where crumbled rendering and the outline of earlier lancet windows soften the effect of hard, unyielding walls. Two things strike one at a first inspection; one, an odd little trio of windows at the gable end of the nave looking along the ridge of the chancel roof and the second, the silvery oak shingles on the tower which strongly resemble fish scales. Oak shingles are conventional, of course, for church spires but I feel sure that openings in the gable end, two circular bracketing one dark lancet, are unusual and it is difficult to see why they are where they are. I could not resist them and, despite the pull of the fish scales, managed to include them in my sketch plus the 'new' Perpendicular window in the place of the chancel lancets that once lit the interior.

Although attractive enough externally to merit a drawing by the admirable F L Griggs (when he could still depict the church enclosed by 'immemorial elms' — alas, no longer), it is the interior that arouses most interest by its inconsistency. For instance, the circular pillar which divides nave from aisle is topped by a carved and ornamented capital, square in section, while the plain, chamfered arches, cut from the earlier wall, are round as they should be but spring from differing responds. Still inconsistent, the arches which separate Norman chancel and chapel are pointed and Transitional — how can that be, one wonders. Then, when one turns to the Norman baptistry arch in the west, one finds its responds vary again. Altogether this intriguing interior is, as I say, a bit of a mishmash which suggests more than one begetter or masons with ideas of their own.

Three movables attracted by attention. First, windfall apples for sale by the door (harvest festival on the horizon); second, what looked like a native spear in the south chapel and, most evocative of the past, a great square columned 12th century font — reputed to be Saxon says Mee.

One reaches the churchyard through the playground of the Rodmell primary school. Fortunate children to receive at an impressionable age such unavoidable contact with a medieval country church.* On the other side of the churchyard lie the gardens of Monk's House where Leonard and Virginia Woolf settled. I think I could end my days very happily at Rodmell too. It is a most beguiling oasis with its Sussex vernacular houses and cottages lining the side lane to the ancient church and with the track up the Downs to Breaky Bottom and its vineyard close at hand.

* Very likely it was the children who collected the windfalls.

46

WEST DEAN
All Saints

One can very easily become confused by the 'Deans' of Sussex. There are at least four Dean churches; a West and East west of Eastbourne and a West and East north of Chichester. Pevsner spells this church with one word, Westdean, perhaps to distinguish it from the Chichester West Dean but the church guide unequivocably opts for two words. It is so gorgeous here in this secluded valley on the seaward edge of the downs, where the Cuckmere river hesitantly approaches the sea, that All Saints presumably feels no need to compromise with its identity.

One can readily understand why a procession of people should come to admire this old flint church. Once, Alfred the Great had an estate here. Now, many centuries later, the village still maintains an exclusive air, undisturbed by the pressures of the 20th century. The cluster of houses and church are inevitably a magnet (they attracted me) and it is a wonder that all is so unspoilt. Alfred lived from 849 to 899. He must, I imagine, have had a chapel here at his royal residence so maybe the tiny Saxon window in the north wall of the nave may be a surviving fragment of the royal chapel. As one's eyes rest on the small aperture it is romantic to reflect that the eyes of the shadowy king of Wessex may also have rested on these same stones a millenium ago. He had the Danes to contend with; the churches to-day have scepticisim and apathy as their enemy and it is doubtful if they will have a comparable success. The issue does seem to be in the balance.

All Saints is basically a simple structure if one excludes for the moment the curiously capped tower. The nave and chancel are virtually one, separated only by a low step up to the chancel, and defined of course by the pulpit at the head of the nave. There was a rood screen but this was removed in the 1840s. Nevertheless, despite its simplicity, the interior is full of interest. The most striking architectural feature is the Norman arch at the base of the tower. Like the reproduction arch at Rodmell, the moulding of All Saints' arch also rests upon diminutive columns; having been deceived at Rodmell, I viewed this similar springing with suspicion only to be deceived again. All Saints' arch is genuine.

The monuments are impressive — two 14th century canopied tombs lining the north side of the chancel face a grandiose 17th century sculture of two kneeling figures under a columned entablature. Compared to the restraint of the former, the latter is both magnificent and ostentatious. As one contemplates such gradiloquence cloaked in piety one cannot help wondering how much of the deceased's estate was diverted towards its cost. A lord of the manor doubtless could afford it but it is not often that one sees generation after generation repeating the display or expenditure. Nonetheless, we should all be the poorer without the Thomases of this world, or rather the next. Less elaborate are two small modern busts — one to a sad-looking painter, Sir Oswald Birley, the other to a Tory politician, Viscount Waverley, by Epstein. Epstein gave the noble lord a wing collar and tie but cropped his shoulders. The effect, as might befit a wartime chancellor of the exchequer, seemed pinched to me.

Apart from the reputed Alfredian connection, the Saxon window, and the extraordinary half-hipped spire to the tower, All Saints has also the distinction that it is approached across a grass verge which gives on to what is now the Old Parsonage — a 14th century house (built by and for the Benedictine monks of Wilmington Priory), still complete with solar, newel staircase and other medieval featues, Pevsner tells us. It is a private house to-day but the key of the church is kept there and is readily obtainable, as I found. How nice to live in this unspoilt, hidden valley in a medieval house (with modern plumbing, I am sure), beside the ancient flint church with only the importunities of church visitors to disturb the peace. And with no maurauding Danes on the horizon, either.

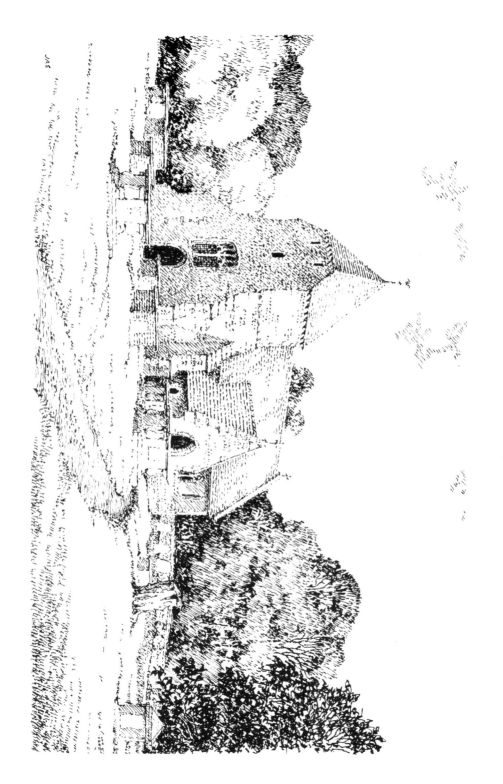

The first time, I think, that I have encountered St Jude, a name that sounds, etymologically speaking, rather too close to Judas for comfort. In fact, I find that our St Jude (otherwise known as Judas not Iscariot as opposed to Judas of Iscariot) was one of the apostles and was martyred with Simon the Less in Persia. St Jude, apparently, is often invoked in 'circumstances of special difficulty'. It is difficult to see what problems thay can have had in such a cosy cleft in the downs as Eastdean but possibly the Danes had found the Birling Gap an easy point of entry and the memory of past assault lingered on.

One approaches this church through what is known as a 'Tapsell' gate; that is a churchyard gate which pivots centrally to offer a temporary resting place for coffins. Once past this local invention, everything in the churchyard is quite immaculate (or was when I was there) with grass that would do credit to Lords cricket ground. To be honest, I felt the effect was slightly clinical but that is an opinion which is certainly unjust to whoever takes such meticulous care of Eastdean churchyard. It puts my gardening efforts in the shade.

The church is small and very old and very new. Old is the solid, stepped north tower which is 10th century. Its walls, three feet thick, are constructed of flint consolidated with rendering and with little in the way of apertures to admit the light or an intruder. Clearly it was not meant to be easily overthrown — Perhaps the Danes had not been long gone when they built it. The nave is partly 11th century and partly modern with traces of pointed arches against the base of the tower at the older, eastern end. There is also the outline at ground level of a tiny apse abutting the eastern face of the tower which suggests that the base of the tower may have served originally as a miniature nave. Later a 13th century chancel was added. This offered an opportunity to correct the orientation of the church and to-day there is a very obvious deflection between the alignment of nave and chancel.

Against the blocked archway in the nave rests a coffin slab bearing the arms of Bardolf. The Bardolfs lived nearby at Birling Manor from 1240 to 1423. They also figure in Shakespeare's Henry IV and Henry V. There are two Shakespearean Bardolfs in fact; one, the rebel lord Bardolf, the other, the braggart and crony of Falstaff. Whichever it was he took from life, if indeed it was either, Shapespeare perpetuated the family name in print while Eastdean has preserved it in stone. No family can complain of such a double.

Reverting to the church, the medieval structure gives way to Victorian architecture midway down the nave where the organ holds sway high on its platform overhead. Organs are bulky things and invariably trespass in churches which were never designed to accommodate them. Overhead is a novel and successful way of getting round the problem. Beyond the organ gantry, the Victorian nave terminates in a 1962 apse which houses, and was presumably designed for, the font. This receptacle (if that is the right word for a font) looks to be a modern version in the Celtic style. I read, actually, that it embodies ancient stonework, the pedestal once having done duty as a mounting block at a local inn. To-day it looks very safe and secure in its own special chamber.

It was a somewhat chilly weekday in October when I explored Eastdean. In the church, though, the central heating was on and it was pleasantly warm; extravagant maybe but one way to attract people into a church and keep them there in winter.

In my pantheon of country churches, the church at Udimore will hold an honourable place — old enough and secluded enough to be interesting and romantic and unspoilt by modernisation. It stands well back from that microcosm on the road to Rye that passes for Udimore village and it is surrounded protectively by the haphazard collection of farm buildings of Court Lodge Farm. It is claimed that Edward I (1272-1307) and Edward III (1327-1377) each stayed at Court Lodge; in 1912, however, the Tudor replacement Court Lodge, a long studded house, apparently in an advanced stage of decay, was uprooted and rebuilt at Groombridge in Kent. It is difficult to see what justification there could be for such a move. The historical association with the Plantagenets remains at Udimore and all that is shifted, after considerable expense and effort, is an accumulation of antique, dismantled timber. What's gained by that, I wonder.

The church, or part of it, was undoubtedly here when the two Edwards stayed and no doubt they attended. That there was a Norman nave is attested by a small window, high up, and two doorways, all now blocked, in the north wall. A south aisle of three bays was added, only to be taken down later, leaving behind the outlines of pointed arches as evidence of its existence. It was, therefore, a surprise, after stepping through the door of the relatively new porch, to find myself in the space that once constituted the central bay of the departed aisle. Two cylindrical pillars and a pointed arch face one to prove the point. I felt rather like Dr Who on entering the Tardis. There is no church door proper; only the modern outer porch door with its utilitarian yale lock. My sketch, accurate I hope, shows a porch with a roof line reaching to the eaves; in a drawing, c1920, by F L Griggs, the porch is small and mean and climbs nowhere near the eaves, confirming that all three bays of the aisle had at one time been blocked out. Udimore is lucky to have regained its central bay and a return to its past.

The chancel, 13th century and handsomely floored with black and white marble, is lit by nine tall, clear-glass lancets. There are as well lancets now in the north wall of the nave which suggests that efforts have been made to revert to a more consistent whole than prevailed in the middle centuries when the church was allowed to fall into disrepair and dilapidation. 'No communion service for three years, walls damp, timbers rotten, tower unsafe, floor uneven and mean, ceiling full of holes, bells cracked and windows broken' to quote a litany of censure reiterated in the church guide. Nothing like that now. 'Tower unsafe' might account for the two buttresses on which this church relies — one visible in my sketch, the other, elephantine, props the west front of a tower that scarcely overtops the ridge of the nave roof. Otherwise, like a good Early English church, Udimore makes do without buttresses.

I liked the carved oak pulpit. Jacobean says Mee and it certainly looks it. Not so, says the guide with the benefit of local knowledge. It was carved by a parishioner, when a girl of eighteen, in the early 1920s. She did a first class job; I do hope she left her signature carved somewhere on that darkened woodwork. I would have in the unlikely event that I could make anything remotely as successful as did young Kate Papillon.

On the other hand, I was saddened by the memorial in the porch to two sons of one family; the elder killed in the cruiser Southampton off Crete in 1941, the other in France in 1944. One must lament the unfairness of life which inflicts a double tragedy on one family. Their mother is beautifully remembered by an elegant engraving on the glass of one of the chancel lancets. Now, one might hope that the spirits of the three members of this family can finally rest at peace together in the shelter of this comely old church. Who could cavil at such a fate.

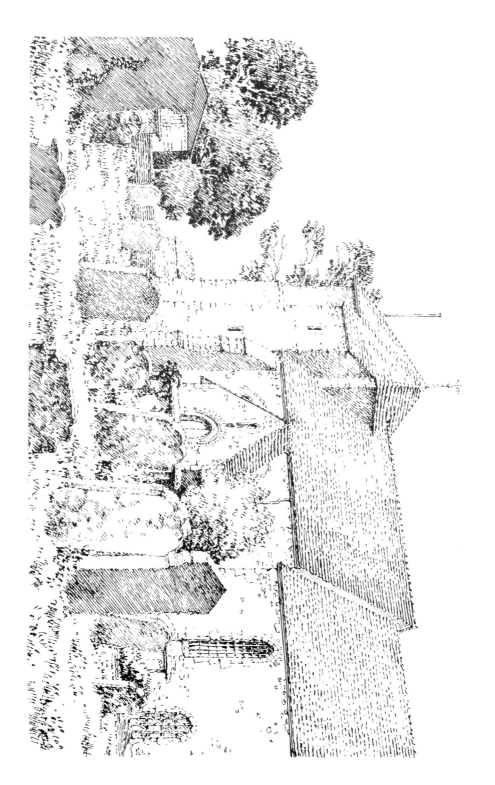

BISHOPSTONE
St Andrew

Bishop's farmstead

When one first encounters Bishopstone church, however much its fame may have gone before, it is difficult to accept that this tall, flint building has stood here on the seaward edge of the Sussex downs for well over a thousand years. The ordered flints, almost submerged under a coat of rendering, look hardly weathered by the weather and yet the church guide puts the foundation of this church as 'probably before 950 AD', Pevsner as 'early c8' and the Sussex Historic Churches Trust claims 'it may be the earliest church in Sussex'. Despite the well-maintained appearance, the evidence to support these opinions is most obviously provided by the quoins of the south porch, porticus more accurately, says Pevsner. Here still survives that archetype of Saxon practice, long and short stones acting as quoins. The long vertical slabs must be about five feet in length — the western one very pitted and original, brand new the eastern quoin — the twentieth century replica of the Anglo-Saxon predecessor. I might mention in passing that it seems to me almost sacriligeous to pin modern drain pipes to these historic stones, as has been done here. Above the added Norman entrance is a Saxon sundial, inscribed with the name 'Eadric' (he sounds indigenous, all right), and marked, so they say, with four divisions indicating the 'tides of the day'. As well as the south porticus, the remaining walls of the nave are Saxon, although how one would know if it wasn't for the quoin stones, I don't know. The rest of the church is Norman, apart from the tiny Early English sanctuary which enables the Sussex Archaeological Collections to state there is nothing post 13th century, except the roof and, of course, the modern 'Saxon' quoin replacement on the porticus which probably doesn't count.

I was lucky to have chosen a Sunday for Bishopstone. There was a service just ending and, after that, the church remained open for a further hour before firmly closing for the day. Once inside, the extreme antiquity of the church strikes one most forcibly. Although the windows, pillars, arches and mouldings appear to be Norman rather than Saxon, they can only be a sort of veneer overlaying the basic native structure. Whichever it is, one cannot help but be rivetted by this architecture contrived at the edge of our history. However hard one tries, it is impossible to envisage the characteristics and circumstances of those Saxons and Normans who chiselled and placed the stones that stand here. One can only admire them after an enormous lapse of time.

The compartmented interior suggests to me that the original intention might have been to erect a tower over the central space that separates nave from minute sanctuary. However, in the event, the Normans added their impressive, four-stage tower at the western end which necessitated converting the south porticus into a porch. I have always thought that a central tower is far more logical if it can be managed without too much interference between nave and chancel. I suspect that piecemeal construction, possibly extending over a great many years, is the explanation for western towers. Wherever it is, the tower is what beckons from afar and enhances the view.

In its own little niche in the downs, Bishopstone lies happily apart from the modern world and gives at least one casual observer every sign of liking it that way. So it was perhaps not surprising to read on the churchyard notice board that 'in this parish is upheld the faith of the Holy Catholic and Apostolic Church received by the Church of England as by Law Established and enshrined in her formularies and in the Book of Common Prayer'. No concession here to the Alternative Service Book and an evident determination to continue what Cranmer began, one feels. The present flux in the Church may be too much for Bishopstone to-day; how much more of a challenge must it have been when the Church in England broke with Rome four hundred years ago. Beliefs may fail and the liturgy may be changed but the stones of this church have proved far more durable — as they have in most country churches. What are we likely to build to-day that will last a thousand years? Not much. As an amateur author, perhaps I may be permitted to observe that words can last even longer than stone.

TARRING NEVILLE
St Mary

Teorra's people
(Where the Neville family had an estate)

Not surprisingly, none of the authorities whom I consult for enlightenment, Pevsner, Mee, Harrison and the Sussex Archaeological Collections, have much to say about Tarring Neville. It is, manifestly, not an important church; it is demure and unassuming and admirable for its situation. There cannot be much doubt about that. So I must do my best, helped by the excellent church guide, to make good the ostracism by the experts.

The church stands, bracketed by Court Farm and Manor Farm, about a hundred yards back from the busy road that follows the Ouse on the east bank down to Newhaven. Westwards, the level fields stretch across to the river and are the haunts of cattle and wild birds; beyond the river, below the line of the downs, can be seen the circular tower of Piddinghoe church. Eastwards, the downs swell in solitude, broken only by tumuli, perhaps those of the Teorras, until one reaches the next river to pierce the downs, the Cuckmere. Away from the immediate vicinity of the coast, it is all pretty magical down here. At the time of the Domesday survey there were 23 people at Tarring; by the 1800s the population had quadrupled but to-day it has fallen back again to the Domesday count. I daresay one could constuct some sort of sociological/agricultural thesis on the basis of those figures but I expect the vicar's comments would more likely be 'Where's my congregation?'.

Although it was the Saturday before Armistice Day, I was still surprised to find this out-of-the-way church open with flowers on display. The congregation may be minimal but the church is obviously cherished even if it enjoys little acknowledgement from the critics. The building itself is neat and compact with an overall blanket of rendering on the underlying walls of flint except in the case of the east end of the chancel where the basic flints are revealed. The rendering does give the church a somewhat anodyne appearance as there are no buttresses to interrupt the smooth planes or cast relieving shadows. The church proclaims itself to be Early English, or earlier, to be so devoid of projecting support. The lancet windows, singly or in pairs or as a triplet, confirm the Early English contention and it is only when one gains the interior and one sees the blocked Norman window high up on the north wall of the nave that its Norman ancestry becomes apparent.

The nave and chancel are roughly equal in size with a south aisle of such mini-dimensions that it can easily be covered by a minor extension of the nave roof. All these areas suffer, I fear, from Victorian floor tiles which effectively banish the aura of antiquity. The church was restored in 1892 and that, I imagine, was when the impropriety was committed.

Of the contents, the most remarkable must be the font, partly embedded in the aisle wall; fonts, I would have thought, are the least likely things to be stolen. There is also an iron chest, said to have come from one of the Armada ships. Embarrassing though it is to admit it, I failed to notice this treasure. Lesson one — re-read the guide before finally leaving the church. The monuments which monopolise the chancel, floors and walls, exclusively commemorate members of the Geere family; they provided vicars from 1738-1765 and from 1774-1831, a total of 84 years. Not bad for a father and son at a time when life expectancy was shorter than it is now. I doubt, though, if early retirement was then on offer, particularly in the remoter parts of any diocese. I hope the Geere family prospers still.

Such, briefly, is my impression of the innocent little church at Tarring Neville. I suppose it has no great thing or happening to attract the eulogies of the ecclesiologists or the historians. Nevertheless, it recorded a visitor from Annapolis, Md. USA ten days before my visit. Perhaps they were searching for their roots. One could hardly hope to take back a better memory of the mother country than that given by a country church like this.

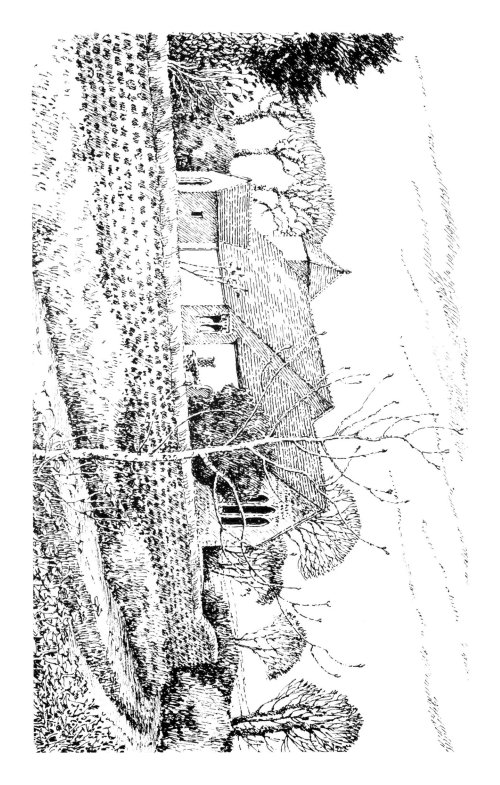

HERSTMONCEUX
All Saints

Wooded hill
(associated with de Monceux)

One finds this church, about a mile and a half down a dead-end lane, opposite the rather anonymous entrance to the grounds of the famous castle. The castle lies in a hollow, surrounded by a moat, whereas the church stands on a gentle slope that looks south and west for miles across the Pevensey levels. In the golden haze of a misty November day it was difficult to disengage one's eyes from the view to concentrate on the church which, I need hardly say, is very well worth looking at. Both are.

The name Herstmonceux derives from two Norman families. In 1131, the de Monceux, descended from the Conqueror, were granted the manor in place of the de Hestes who had previously held it. However, the next generation made amends by marrying a de Heste and combining the two family names in the following generation. Later still, the de Fiennes married into the estate, so to speak, and it was Sir Roger de Fiennes who began to build in 1440 the brick castle that still survives.

The church, most of it, preceded the castle by well over a hundred years. The oldest parts are the 12th century west tower and west wall of the nave. Apparently the tower formed the end bay of the north aisle which explains the somewhat lop-sided appearance of the church when viewed from the west. The tower is notable for the large, regular, coursed blocks, greenish grey, of sandstone I imagine, of which it is constructed. Here and there are tiles in occasional patches and in-between the blocks in place of mortar — an early form of galleting perhaps. It all looks to be in excellent condition and it is hard to remember that, broach spire apart, it is eight hundred years old. The rest of the church consists of a 13th/14th century nave, chancel and north and south aisles with a 15th century north chapel of red Flemish bricks added by the builders of the castle. At the same time they evidently renewed the east face of the chancel with the same attractive little bricks. The chapel is now known as the Dacre chapel, Sir Richard Fiennes (minus the 'de') having acquired the Dacre barony in 1457 by marriage. Accounts of this church are inevitably such as to make it all seem rather more genealogical than ecclesiastical — a consequence, I suppose, of its proximity to its famous neighbour. Sadly for them, the Astronomers Royal arrived too late on the scene to leave their mark on the church however much they may have left it on the estate.

It is inside that the aristocratic connections become most obvious and for which, like it or not, this church is chiefly famous. It is not a church with which egalitarians may easily empathise. We may all be equal in the pews nowadays but there is no concession to egalitarianism in the memorials here. Pride of place must go to the elaborate tomb chest of Lord Dacre and his son, Sir Thomas Fiennes. They are represented by the painted, recumbent stone effigies of knights in full (Italianate) armour, hands clasped in prayer. It is my contention that stone sculpture is better left unpainted; colouring may have been medieval practice but, dusty and faded now, the Dacre effigies look more like coloured papier-mache. Not fair on the Fiennes and not fair on the Lords Hooe, the original models, either. More ancient and equally untrue to life (knights on brasses always exhibit the same resigned expression and accentuated wasp waists) is the magnificent brass of Sir William Fiennes on the chancel floor. Perfectly preserved under its strip of carpet, the eyes seemed to look reproachfully at me when I reluctantly replaced the carpet and returned the memorial to its sepulchral privacy.

On the evidence of its carefully documented memorials and general state of well-being, this remote church, with its continued religious observance, preserved fabric and cherished contents, successfully maintains its integrity and function. In sad contrast, the hidden castle has lost its illustrious connections and descended to public auction (Daily Telegraph 13.11.91). At least such an undignified fate is unlikely to overtake the church, one hopes. There ought to be a law against that.

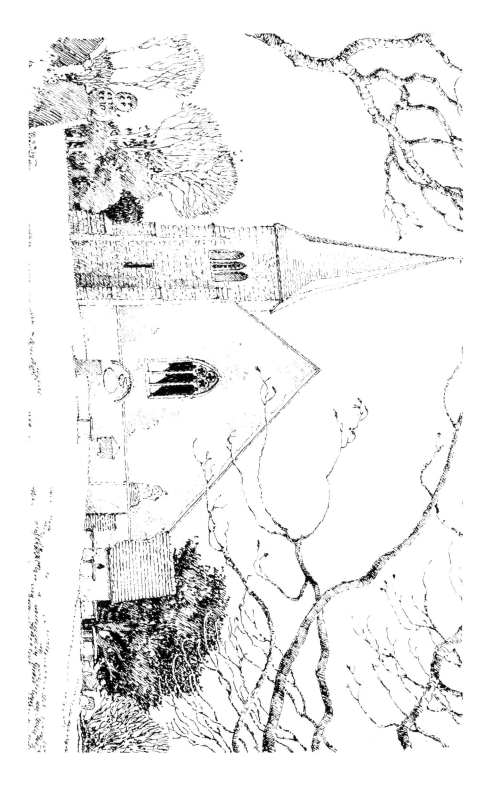

WILMINGTON
St Mary and St Peter

Wilma's farmstead

I suppose the most famous thing about Wilmington must be the 'Long Man' cut into the slope of Windover Hill, facing the church, so I will begin with that. It is the outline of a man, holding two staves, claimed to be the largest representation of the human figure in Europe. Pevsner says it is 'probably not of very great antiquity'. Others suggest it may represent the sun god, Balder, pushing back the doors of darkness; others again that it may be some sort of symbol of agricultural fertility but, if either of these, why on a north-facing slope? It is very subtle — perfectly proportioned when viewed from the ground below, elongated and thin if viewed from the air. Would stone-age man or iron-age man have been sufficiently sophisticated for such perspective management? But he did manage Stonehenge. There are burial mounds on the summit above, c1000 BC, and flint mines nearby, c3500 BC, and a dew pond below, all of which imply extreme antiquity. Each theory seems to contain elements of uncertainty; I subscribe to the prehistoric submission and marvel that it is still there.

Perhaps it was what drew the Benedictine monks from Normandy in 1088 to build their priory and church here; might they not have decided that a pagan figure needed confrontation by the forces of Christianity because confront it they have. The priory was suppressed in 1403 by Henry IV. At that time Henry was at odds with Owen Glendower and with that impetuous scion of the Percies, Hotspur. In his preoccupation, how did the king have time to suppress a small innocuous outfit like Wilmington Priory? Did he need the money or was it because it was French? The priory, as such, is now in ruins, part absorbed into a house, part remnants of flinty walling and part the skeletal frame of a transomed Elizabethan window (obviously post-the monks). If it wasn't for the church, one might say that Balder had won.

The issue remains unresolved. The church still stands, high above the sunken road that winds below Windover Hill, immediately adjacent to the vestiges of the priory with all there is of the churchyard lying to the north of the church. The only entrance now is through the north porch. The chancel that the monks built still serves as the chancel and the stone ledges on which they sat still line the walls. The space enclosed by the south chapel, or aisle, must be Norman too, that is where the monks came in, but its enclosing walls are 19th century. There is also a tiny north chapel, almost hidden by the organ; it now serves as the vestry but it is well worth a trespass to inspect the stained glass of its 'butterfly window'. This window depicts insects as a border to the image of St Peter; amongst others are the Camberwell Beauty, Large Copper, Appollo butterfly ('never recorded in Britain') and bumble bee. The church guide lists all ten specimens but does not relate the history of this unusually intriguing window. I don't think St Peter is known to have been an insectologist but the donor or designer must have been.

There are few memorials; two large ledger stones in the sanctuary commemorate 18th century vicars who each managed to live to the age of eighty — a testimonial to country air and a life of piety. In marked contrast to the modest 14th century nave is the sumptuous pulpit — Jacobean with sounding board and pagoda-like finial to crown. To be realistic, though, the centre of interest here must lie outside the church.

'Possibly older than the church', so it is said, is the venerable yew which overshadows the chancel. The yew, split at ground level, is still vigorous notwithstanding the supporting timbers. It is a monument to the tenacity of life and commands the attention of all who visit this church. It seems all of a piece with the enigmatic prehistoric statement on the hillside above.

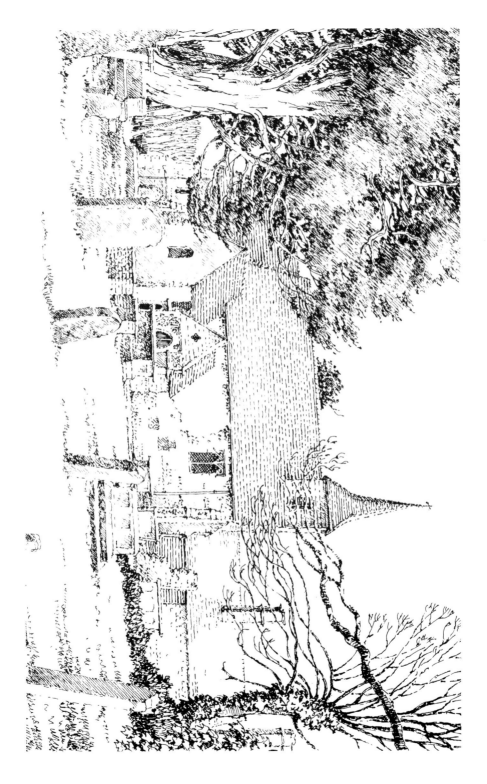

ASHBURNHAM
St Peter

Ash tree stream settlement

The parish church of Ashburnham can be found at the heart of the Ashburnham estate, surrounded by the ancestral buildings of the Ashburnhams; where, though, is the village, if there is one? Now there are no Ashburnhams left and the estate, but not the church, is a Christian Prayer and Conference Centre. One still may get an impression of sweeping parkland, fenced about by elegant iron railings from the famous furnaces of the estate, and watered by the ornamental lakes of the Ash bourne, but some of the romance of this great house has gone to be replaced by a faint air of institutionalism. It seems a pity but country houses of this size do appear to have become the dinosaurs of landed property.

In its heyday, the 17th century when most of the church was rebuilt, the buildings here, even or especially, the stables and the essential adjuncts like lodges, terraces and bridges were designed and constructed to discriminating standards; at Ashburnham, large sandstone, ashlared blocks, were used in the style of Wren or Inigo Jones — I may be mistaken, of course, but that is how it all seems to me, a beginner in such matters. More recent utilitation additions, which lurk behind the remnant of the main house, only serve to emphasize how standards have given way under the pressure of economics.

The church was here before the Ashburnhams if the evidence of the Pelham Buckles on the label stops of the tower doorway is anything to go by.* The tower is Perpendicular, i.e. 14th century, but the rest of the church dates from 1665 when Sir John Ashburnham, the friend of Charles I, rebuilt the church with similar materials and in the same style as the tower so that the whole now looks homogeneous. I wonder what was there before to displease the squire — neglect probably. Anyway, from this munificence he has left us a nave, chancel, north and south chapels and 17th century furnishings throughout — box pews, west gallery reached by a winding, domestic staircase (made by the estate carpenters, I would imagine) and Ashburnham iron railings separating nave and chancel and chancel and chapels. Iron work does belong here and very handsome the railings look. Unusually, there is no altar; instead a Jacobean communion table does duty — a relic of Puritanism possibly.

But of course, apart from its setting, what lifts this 'parish' church from the avreage are two Ashburnham monuments in the north chapel. One to the founder, Sir John, lying prone in full armour between his two wives on their table tomb, supported by their seven children kneeling as weepers — conventional if on the grand scale. The other, to Sir John's brother and the latter's wife, is a florid life-size tableau of the pair in life-like and death-like attitudes respectively. It probably ill behoves me to criticise the second memorial but I could not help prefering the traditional table tomb of Sir John to the theatrical effigies of his brother and sister-in-law. Other Ashburnhams, down to the sixth and last earl, are simply recorded by commemorative wall tablets — an abrupt descent from the histrionic to the matter of fact. Nevertheless the flamboyant sculpture in the north chapel attracts much comment and, in general, admiration. As long as it lasts, the Ashburnhams will be remembered.

My encounter with Ashburnham Place, as it now is, and the memorials in the church inevitably provokes thoughts of egalitarianism and whether that ideal brings benefit. Egalitarianism would not have brought us Ashburnham Place or church; egalitarianism and the last of the Ashburnhams has given us an institute.

* Arthur Mee says the Ashburnhams have been here from before the Conquest; why then the Pelham Buckle? Perhaps there was inter-marriage.

MOUNTFIELD
All Saints

One cannot help but approach Mountfield church with thoughts of the battle of Hastings in mind. From the churchyard, looking south across the wooded valley towards Battle, one can just about make out the ridge on which were assembled (deployed would convey an impression of control which Harold did not enjoy) Harold's host or fryd as the local Saxon levies were known. Raised in this time of crisis for the defence of the realm, this last Saxon fryd had mustered there that fateful October evening to await the onslaught next day of Norman William's acquisitive opportunists. As we know, the natives were unsuccessful in their resistance; many of the survivors must, one imagines, have fled across the low Mountfield ridge before all here was laid waste by the victors. There was no church then on the blood-soaked turf but it is believed that this place was sacred before the arrival of Christianity. At all events a church, this one, was soon built and recorded in William's Domesday Book — to make amends possibly for the post-Conquest wasting. What a turning point in our history it all was.

It was a small church which they built in those years after the Conquest — their nave is only 24 feet by 22 and the replacement Early English chancel, equally compact, is just 17 feet by 17. Early English also is the robust, dumpy two-stage tower. It is all happily simple and unpretentious inside. An unmoulded Norman arch, plus squints, separates nave and chancel; few memorials decorate the walls and the most primitive staircase at the base of the tower provides access to the single bell. I always rather enjoy the stark contrast between elementary stairs or ladders and the usual agglomeration of switches and fuzes which share the base of church towers, cheek by jowl. The ancient carpentry invariably looks more beguiling than the 20th century technology. Prone as the latter is to electrocute the unwary (or ungodly), I keep well clear.

There are wall paintings on the nave side of the chancel wall but far too faint to make out if one cautiously eschews the electricity. There is also a Norman font, tub-shaped of generous dimensions and bearing panels carved on the original stone surface hundreds of years later. It looks to be a companion piece to the solid, golden sandstone west tower and equally permanent. Two other companion pieces, it seemed to me, are the south porch and the lych gate at the western end of the churchyard. The great timbers that frame the entrance to the former are so old, 14th century, that they look like silvery, pitted and eroded coral. The lych gate, built commemoratively in 1912, follows the design of the porch with huge arched and pointed timbers. With luck they will last as long and look just as crystallised one day — unless they choose to widen the road which runs past. Fortunately it is only a winding country road.

In the porch, a botanical savant had listed all the plants found in the churchyard in 1987. There were 58 varieties including such little-known rarities as bugle, common mouse ear, common cat's ear, pignut, nibblewort, stitchwort (the greater and the lesser), burnet saxifrage, prickly sowthistle, smooth hawkbit and hairy tare and so on — lovely vernacular names even if one couldn't link a plant to any. The catalogue is an argument for allowing nature to flourish relatively unchecked in churchyards and emphasises how much lies under one's feet all the time, waiting only to be found. It is thus an inducement for local rather than distant exploration; in microscopic terms there is probably as much terra incognito in our country churchyards as there is at Tierra del Fuego, for instance. Mountfield makes the point very well.

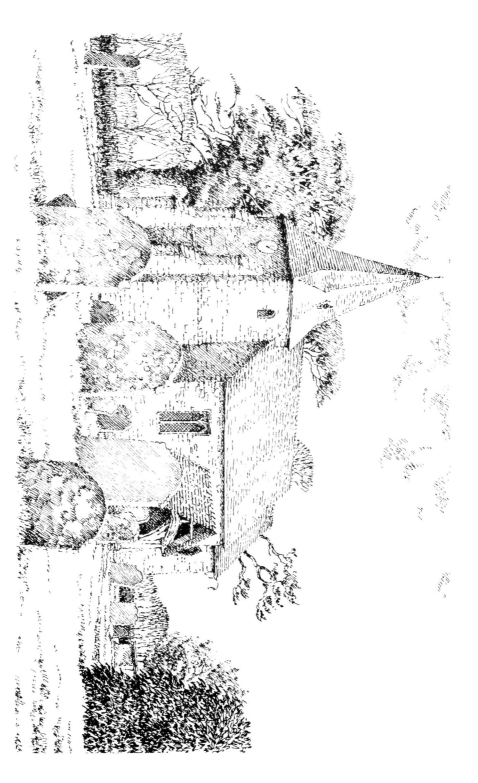

SALEHURST
St Mary

Willow wood*

"A big plain church in a desolate place" wrote Arthur Mee; he must have had dyspepsia that day. Certainly it is big, as befits a church built, I understand, by the Cistercian monks of Robertsbridge Abbey. And overlooking the Rother valley with Robertsbridge no more than a mile away, it is far from desolate. If one didn't know about the dissolved monks and the lack of a proper church in Robertsbridge, one might be surprised to find so substantial a church grouped with a house or two, a few cottages and one pub, the Salehurst Halt — a reminder of the railway to Tenterden which has followed the abbey into dissolution. Robertsbridge is no more than sensible to be content with St Mary's at Salehurst.

It is the tall imposing west tower, emblazoned with the arms of Culpeper and Etchingham, that engages the eye as one approaches down the lane from Robertsbridge — Early English in its lower ranges, it becomes Perpendicular higher up where the buttresses diminish and merge into the faces of the walls. As you go in, though, through the vaulted west porch, a semi-circular arch at the base of the tower gives a Norman impression. Evidently the monks must have taken their time, a century or so, to complete their tower. Its base, floored by a pavement of 12 17th century slate and cast-iron ledger stones, now serves as a sort of vestibule to the long nave. Very fine these memorial slabs are, infinitely superior and probably longer lasting than the Victorian tiles that pave the rest of the church. What has lasted even longer is the 13th century font, entwined with salamanders (mythical lizards), which guards the doors to the nave.

Once in the nave, the daunting impression created by the tower is reinforced by a nave of cathedral-like dimensions. There are north and south aisles, separated from the nave by identical arcades consisting of five octagonal pillars and two responds each, making six bays end to end. Bays, I believe, are much the same in size, 12 to 16 feet stepped out, whether in church A or church B. Here the six bays make a nave some 80 feet long. The octagonal pillars are Early English, as is the chancel, while the outer walls of the aisles are Perpendicular. Thus the only example of the Decorated style is the north, Wigsell chapel. It seems sad that the only element of this flamboyant style is so little regarded here as to be used as an unlovely lumber room in which the elegant cartouche memorials are confronted bleakly by the backside of the cumbersome organ.

There are Victorian clerestory windows — necessary I suppose because the Perpendicular aisle windows, uniform though they may be, do not admit much light. In one of these aisle windows, the stained glass is by the pre-Raphaelite artist Kempe. Kempe always signed his work by an inconspicuous wheatsheaf. It took me some time to find his signature but there it is, low down in the left-hand margin. Alexander Pope did not support such personal aggrandisement when he said —
> "Who builds a church to God, and not to fame,
> Will never mark the marble with his name."

I am on the side of Kempe; God may know who has done what, lesser beings are not so well informed and may need to be told.

The churchyard, sloping from north to south towards the Rother valley floor, is pleasantly unkempt; lots of long yellow grass half hiding table tombs in plenty and headstones indiscriminate. One is encouraged to explore to its outer reaches by narrow paths. Tucked away modestly in an obscure corner is a massive square block of inscribed stone; there, one can read, are interred the mortal remains of Alfred, 1st Viscount Milner, of St James and Cape Town. I felt, on that January day, as if I had encountered an old acquaintance. Milner was our High Commissioner in South Africa at the time of the Boer War and, unfashionably to-day, he wanted the map from Cape to Cairo to be coloured red.** Such an imperialist has been given a memorial worthy of his lifetime status although perhaps he might have preferred the foothills of Table Mountain to the homely Rother valley.

* Famous for cricket bats, made from these willows, says Judith Glover.
** I know all this because 'The Scramble for Africa', which my son gave me for Christmas, has just told me so.

66

ROTHERFIELD
St Denys

Open space where cattle graze

A splendid sandstone church on its mound in the middle of the village. It is a worthy successor to a wooden Saxon church of which no trace remains above ground but which, historically, is recorded in the will of the 'Duke' of the South Saxons at the end of the 8th century. What could be more romantic? It would be fascinating to put the Saxon version beside the present Early English cum Perpendicular church and compare the two. Saxon buildings soared and so does this church; lofty and precipitous, it must have absorbed some genes from its predecessor. At least that is how my imagination worked as I gazed up in admiration.

It has to be the western tower that is the most striking feature here. Built in the 15th century, it is Perpendicular in style with an inset octagonal spire that reaches 135 feet into the sky and dominates the clustering village. With its sandstone blocks set in ashlared courses, there are no external signs of deterioration despite 500 years of wind and weather, just a little discolouration here and there to soften the hard unyielding surfaces.

As one leaves the external for the internal, the swirling metal hinges of the entrance doors, all compatible with each other, whether it is the north porch door, the tower door or the blocked south door, alert a visitor's sense of the celtic past. These hinges may or may not be old; they are nevertheless well worth remarking. Through the substantial storeyed and vaulted porch, one finds oneself in a lofty nave supported by north and south aisles. There are box pews throughout, tiered at the west end like those in a theatre. The nave and aisles are three bays in length with late 14th century octagonal pillars to the south and round 13th century pillars to the north; so something like a century or more separates the two aisles. All this looks medieval enough but the chancel, which is Early English, looks more venerable still. Even loftier in proportion, its southern wall has been left rough-hewn and unplastered and one feels the masons might have been made to finish abruptly; as when they appear to have been dragging their feet unduly. There is a north, Neville, chapel with an embossed and panelled roof; as so often seems the case, entry is denied by the organ and its use as vestry. It ill becomes a visitor to criticise but it does seem that more use could be made of the bases of towers with chapels left as intended. The Abergavennys must be a tolerant family.

There is much good joinery here; the choir stalls are above average, the pulpit is particularly grand having been made for the archbishops of York (the guide explains that an archbishop's daughter married a rector of Rotherfield — part of the dowry, perhaps) and a font cover, dated 1533, bears the arms of George Neville, Baron Burgavenny. It rests on a metal stand beside the mutilated Norman font which now appears to serve as a temporary jardinière.

There are few memorials but much carpeting. If a book* which I was given for Christmas is correct in its contention, the underfloor of practically every parish church is a honeycombe of interments, with or without remembrance, Rotherfield will be no exception, I don't doubt.

In compensation for the lack of memorials on the walls are the paintings which cover large areas of the interior. They date from the 13th, 14th and 15th centuries and must therefore be contemporary with the aisles. One scene depicts St Michael weighing the souls of the departed — it can't be easy to weigh immaterial things, I imagine. It can't be easy to judge immaterial things either. Fortunately it is difficult to envisage immaterial things actually sinning and that's a consoling thought.

* Church Archaeology by Warwick Rodwell.

68

BUXTED
St Margaret the Queen

Margaret the Queen, of Scotland, lived in the 11th century and was canonised for domestic virtues by Pope Innocent IV in 1250. This church, successor to an earlier church, was begun in 1250 which may explain its dedication to a queen of Scotland, of Saxon descent, who as far as I know had no connection with this minor manor in Sussex and despite the fact that her husband, Malcolm III Canmore, invaded England four times. We are a forgiving people.

Entering this church, through the north porch, one is the cynosure of gaping gargoyles but welcomed more happily by the figure of a woman holding a churn; a pun it is said on the name of the family who built the porch in the 15th century, the Allchorns. Protection, one reads, is added by Carroll Security Alarm Systems; so is my house I am happy to say.

The rest of the church is earlier. Nave and west tower are Early English with a chancel rebuilt in 1292 by the rector, Sir John de Lewes. He it was, presumably, who ordered the very grand Decorated east window — grand in tracery, grand in glass. As with many churches, the arcade pillars between nave and aisles do not match, north and south, which leads one to the conclusion that the aisles were added at different times. There is also a south chapel, converted in 1800 to act as a 'park pew' for the Liverpool family. It has its own porch with a rarely trodden path leading to Buxted Place. Religious attendance seems to have waned in that direction.

The most conspicuous memorials here are five lozenge-shaped hatchments which are displayed at the west end of the nave. They commemorate the members of three families culminating in the 2nd Earl of Liverpool who was prime minister for 15 years from 1812 — longer even than Margaret Thatcher. Nearby, in a glass frame, are several fragments of brass; one piece, the lower legs of a knight in armour, was found in the rectory barn! Less loseable is the massive old oak muniment chest at the west end of the north aisle. It dates from the late 13th century and, although greatly eroded and pitted, the gothic moulding on its front panels still stands out faintly in relief. In its long life wars and strife have disturbed the peace but this old chest has survived trimphantly. The sinews of war are indeed represented here. A box of iron cannon balls reminds the visitor that Ralph Hogge, the iron-founder who made the first iron cannon, lived here in 1543. His house, Hogge House, at the entrance to the park bears a hog in relief on its north wall. I expect he had a cannon guarding his front door.

In the churchyard I was lucky enough to encounter a friendly parishioner who was meticulously edging the paths. Under his prompting I rolled back the chancel carpet to admire the six-foot brass to a 14th century rector, Britellus Avenel. It is unusual and worth the effort. My churchyard acquaintance also pointed out that I was sketching within a few yards of the headstone of William Wordsworth's brother, Christoper. The latter was rector here for 25 years and at the same time Master of Trinity College, Cambridge.* One thing I learnt from the Naval Staff College years ago was the paramount importance of getting one's aim right. How, I wonder, did the rector reconcile the competing claims of a country church with distinguished parishioners and a Cambridge college with potentially-distinguished undergraduates. Not easy before the advent of the motor car.

Immediately north east of the chancel stands the shell of a magnificent old yew. Said to be about 2000 years old, which would put it contemporary with the life of Christ, it is carefully propped now but still full of vigour. Who would dare to cut down a tree with such associations, with or without the edict of Edward I — 'ne rector abores in cemeterio prosternat'. Its not every day you can draw a tree like that, or rub shoulders with a Wordsworth, for that matter. Thanks are due to Edward I and an amiable churchyard gardener.

---

* I have since read that he was so politically-minded that, in a speech at Reading, he described the Bible as 'the most Conservative book in the world' with the Book of Common Prayer the 'next'.

Alone and embowered in the fields, Isfield church stands in a churchyard that almost seems a yew plantation. To the west, the once navigable Ouse meanders down to the sea; to the south, that formidable torrent the Usk finds its way down from Uckfield; to the east, a quarter of a mile away lies the village, ribboning north and south with the parsonage at its farthest extremity, while overall, across the stubble to the north east, like a stranded whale looms the grey bulk of Isfield Place. For the church connoisseur, this is a delightful and solitary composition; for the vicar and the parish, it seems rather as if the church wants to keep them all at arm's length.

It was of course firmly locked with a warning in the porch to the effect that — 'removable objects marked and photographed'. Quite right too. Fortunately for me the fields and streams round about are so idyllic that it is a dog-walker's paradise and two young men were able to suggest correctly where the vicar and the key might be found.

First impressions of the church from the outside are apt to be misleading. The top of the tower which welcomes the visitor from above the enclosing yews looks Victorian, as indeed it is; the belfry stage and inset spire were, in fact, added in 1893 to a sturdy base that was erected four hundred years earlier as one can verify on a closer inspection. The chancel is 14th century, so the guide tells one, but that large Decorated east window looks far too unblemished by weather to be five hundred years or so old. There has been some renewal around the window and that might support my amateur opinion. Little can be seen of the earliest 13th century walling at the west end of the south wall of the nave. Although largely masked by the modern porch, this section still manages to retain a single Early English lancet. Attached at right angles to the east end of this wall is the 14th century south chapel which may look somewhat unremarkable from the outside notwithstanding the carved heads supporting the gable parapet and a scratch dial that can scarcely ever see the sun now-a-days. It may be the pressure of the overhanging trees that dampens the critical spirit a bit here.

Internally though, the south Shurley chapel is anything but unremarkable; it is what matters here and what most people come to see and why that enabling key is so desirable. Here, in the small side chapel off the nave, roughly 12 feet by 15 feet, the Tudor Shurleys set out their stall, so to speak. Of what was there before, I can find no mention but probably the Shurleys have long had a claim on this little sanctuary. In chronological order of decease they are memorialised as follows: Sir John †1527 by a recess but brass lost; Edward †1558 by a recess with brass; Thomas †1579 by a recess with brass; and monumentally, Sir John †1631. The last lies in effigy between two wives (one a Shirley) on a rising tier (so that each figure may easily be visible) under an elaborate canopy and supported by their seven daughters and two sons. Sir John's and his family's biography are inscribed on the backing marble and one can read that, amongst other responsibilities, Sir John was a 'Justice of Ye Peace and Coram' — decorum, I imagine. A later Shurley, †1647, lies under the altar in the chancel. One couldn't object to that estrangement even if one was 'Lord Chief Justice of the Chiefe Pleases (? places) of Ireland. The Shurleys are all very cosy in their private chapel — elegant linen-fold panelling, poppyhead stalls, fire place and a squint for the squire or his lady to monitor the progress of the service. Succeeding Shurleys could no doubt doze comfortably there with their ancestors peacefully sleeping the long sleep of death around them.

Isfield church is memorable for one other memorial — the coffin lid of the tomb of the daughter of the Conqueror which has now been restored to Lewes from whence it found refuge here after the Dissolution. Gundrada must be thankful to have her property back but grateful that it was safely preserved here amidst the 'alien corn'.

Berwick church is famous in this part of Sussex. It stands on rising ground above the Cuckmere plain looking east towards the Long Man of Wilmington. This is haunted territory — prehistoric barrows and burial mounds abound while the Downs loom majestically east and west. So I can hardly be blamed for making my drawing of Berwick church from one such ancient burial mound in its churchyard.

The church is small and Early English, or rather was originally. Now, because of general disintegration followed by timely rescue, it is essentially Victorian an an earlier framework. That it has survived at all must be to the credit of the Revd Edward Boys Ellman, curate and rector here for 66 years from 1837 to 1906. On his mother's side he was a member of the well-known Kent family of Boys and, on his paternal side, he was descended from the developer of the strain of Southdown sheep, Ellman of Glynde. So the Victorian rector was well-enough endowed to be able to renew and endow his charge. And thoroughly he did it. In his time he restored the spire, rebuilt the north aisle, cleared away the churchyard turf which had built up against the south aisle windows, restored the east end of the chancel to its former foundations and thus left us the flint church that we find to-day — in apple pie order. He was also a naturalist and diarist of the stamp of Gilbert White; for instance here at Berwick he noted seeing the Dartford Warbler and the hoopoe. What an idyllic life he must have had, rebuilding his church, caring for and instructing his parishioners and observing all about him in this still delightful tract of country.

Mr Ellman may have left us the revitalised, flinty framework of this little downland church; others, more famous, have left us their imprint inside. It was Bishop Bell, bishop of Chichester, who apparently conceived the idea of linking art (with a capital A) to Berwick and for this he enlisted the voluntary services of the bohemian coterie who lived unconventionally a couple of miles away at Charleston Farmhouse. Like Mr Ellman in his tenure, there were no half measures about the work undertaken in the 1940s by Duncan Grant, Vanessa Bell and her son, Quentin. Virtually every vertical surface inside is covered with their paintings and the church is justly celebrated on that account. It might be considered impertinence for a casual visitor to offer criticism but I could not avoid a feeling of disappointment with the result. Notwithstanding the reputation of the artists, it seemed to me that quality had been sacrificed for quantity. Others, more sympathetic, will no doubt disagree.

To revert to the church proper, there is an elaborate Decorated Easter sepulchre in the chancel, a twin sedilia divided by a central column which is supported in mid air, so to speak, by a protruding corbel, and a modern screen covered with murals. The tower arch is semi-circular — Norman? — but no, inscribed above is 'ANO 1603' which my 'Notes on Sussex Churches' confirms was the date of its reconstruction. The aisles are two bays in length, ergo, one pillar supports an arch to right and left. But not with Mr Ellman's north aisle where a pair of twin pillars provide the central support — painted rather too garishly, I thought. The oldest object in the church is the font; made up before the Conquest of courses of shaped stone blocks, it seems to form part of the west wall. If I hadn't known it was a font, I could have taken it for a well-head. But then, I suppose, wells could be used for baptism just as effectively as a basin. After all, wells are often considered to be holy, especially in the West Country.

Drawn by the Bloomsbury set, my wife came to Berwick as well. After we had completed our sketches, we retreated to a lee in the churchyard for a picnic lunch. Very pleasant it was — the February sun shone, snowdrops flourished at our feet and, with no-one to disturb us, our thoughts were happily occupied with the little church and what may have been here before. The Long Man casts a long shadow hereabouts.

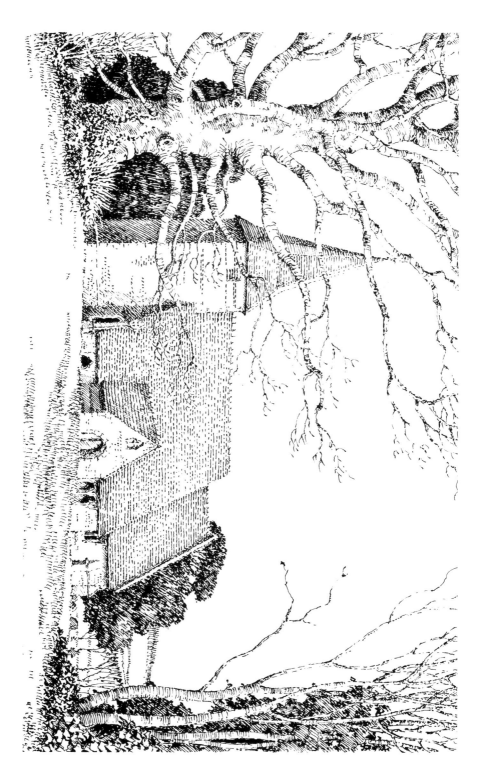

Framfield church or village may not have bothered the historian unduly but at least the church did attract the artist, Frederick Griggs, sufficiently for him to record it in 1903 when the old houses that line the cul-de-sac that leads to the churchyard looked much the same as they do to-day. It still presents the cosy appearance so ably depicted by Mr Griggs. By now, in these enlightened days I daresay the brief approach to the church is a conservation area.

The church has not enjoyed a tranquil life. There was a disastrous fire in 1509 which destroyed almost all except the north chapel and the tower. The church is thus now that rarity, largely Tudor, but to add insult to injury the tower collapsed in 1667. Replacement presented an insuperable financial problem for the parish; fortunately there are some grand houses in the neighbourhood and the family who lived in one, High Cross, came to the rescue in the 1890s and defrayed the cost of the present tower. It may therefore be Victorian but it was constructed with such restraint that it harmonises admirably with the rest of the church. So, after the tribulations of the past, when fire fighting was not as effective as to-day and when candles were more accident-prone than electricity, the church now looks reassuringly enduring.

Built almost entirely of dressed, relatively uniform, sandstone blocks, it consists of a four bay nave, narrow north and south aisles and a chancel with more or less matching chapels on either side. I say 'more or less' because the north chapel, which dates from the late 13th century and is the earliest part of the church, was locked and blocked by the omnipresent organ. A pity perhaps; one can't tell. The all-seeing Pevsner doesn't in fact bother to mention this antique chamber so maybe not. The nave is distinguished at ground level by a row of ledger stones* along the central gangway and enhanced, at roof level, by a range of painted bosses. Observing the height of the clerestoried roof one cannot help a feeling of respect for whoever managed to decorate those bosses amongst the lofty darkened roof timbers. Memorials, in the shape of wall tablets, seem mostly to have been placed above the arcade arches — in case we should be too inquisitive?

But not the engraved lists of the fallen in the last two wars which are at eye level at the west end of the church. Here, unusually, the numbers in the 1939-45 war equal, if not exceed, those lost in the 1914-18 war. What a terrible price these villages had to pay.

Externally, the most arresting feature of this church, it seemed to me, are the roofs of mellow, lichen-spattered Horsham stone. These great slabs grace even the commemorative lych-gate that acts as a full stop to the short approach street. What does not grace this particular structure is the graffiti scrawled by unknown hands on its white ceiling; if ever there was a case for the re-introduction of the stocks, vandalism in churchyards must be it. Vandalism, of a lesser order I think, is the removal of headstones from the graves to which they refer (there should be a law against it and there possibly is); here in the one-time county of iron smelting, there is a considerable stack of cast-iron headstones** piled tidily against the base of the tower. One wonders if there is a record of the graves from which they came in this extensive churchyard. I doubt it.

Enough of carping. Let me acknowledge that Framfield has a very handsome church of substantial proportions, typical of its county, which many a less-fortunate village can well envy. Neither the Tudors, nor the Victorian county sheriff or his son, spared their pockets over their resuscitated parish church. Would we do as much to-day, I wonder. Or rather, I don't, which is why all these country churches are so irreplaceable, Framfield as much as any.

---

* Apparently these 7 stone slabs were moved from their original settings in the chancel and north chapel; memorials surely aren't like shrubs which can benefit from transplanting.
** 'Stone' can't be the right word — grave marker would be more accurate.

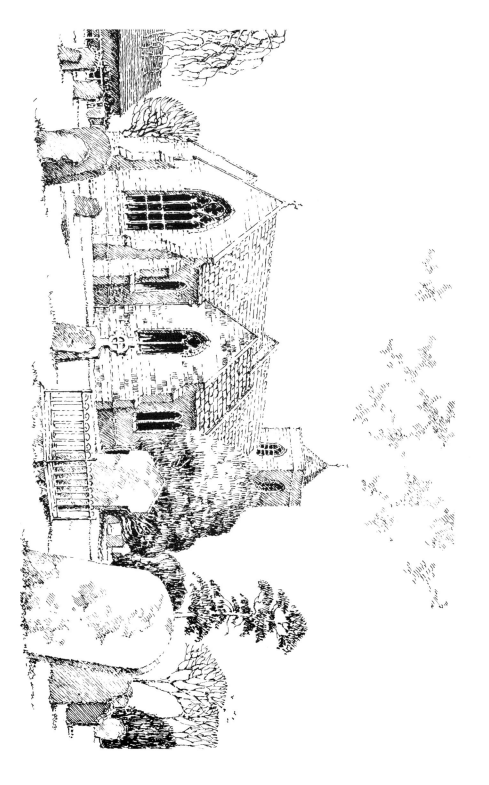

Set snugly in the middle of nowhere in particular, hard by Muddles Green, Chiddingly church is sufficiently anonymous for my three reference mentors, Pevsner, the 'Notes' and Mee, to omit any dedication. Nor is there a guide to enlighten the curious. But for all that, Chiddingly church and hamlet are well worth the effort of discovery — but a map is necessary for Chiddingly is fortunate enough to lie amidst unremarkable fields and copses that resound to pheasants as one negotiates the winding lanes.

There are two outstanding features to this church, both by virtue of their size. The first to greet the eye is the Perpendicular west tower with its stone spire that reaches 128 feet into the Sussex sky. There are few stone spires in Sussex and this one is joined at the top of its tower in a somewhat confusing way, set off by octagonal pinnacles at the corners. Stone spires must be heavy and the tower here, built strongly of large ashlar stone blocks, looks well capable of supporting the extra weight. When E V Lucas wrote in 1924, he found the spire bound with iron chains 'that suggest the possibility of imminent dissolution'. Nearly eighty years on, the chains have gone but not the spire. At the base of the tower, as label stops to the west doorway, are the ubiquitous Pelham buckles* — in good repair, too. The Pelhams lived not far away at Laughton but from the evidence of their insignia elsewhere, their reach extended far and wide in Sussex and beyond — in fact to Downing Street in the case of two.

The second outstanding feature of this church is inside in the south transept which was added to the church in 1612 so that another local family could assert their status. No half measures here; the high, blank wall of the transept is occupied by a colossal monument to Sir John Jefferay and his wife, both recumbent and flanked by the life-size figures of their daughter and son-in-law, she with one foot peeping out from under her skirt, pressing down on a skull to imply the defeat of death. It is all a bit overbearing but one might have expected as much from a Tudor Chief Baron of the Exchequer. Now-a-days the lords of the Treasury may be more circumspect in their display but they are no less insistent in their exactions. Sadly, modern monumental modesty will never engage the attention that Tudor ostentation now enjoys.

Less prominent beneath his unmarked coffin slab in the porch but possibly of more general benefit, the Revd John Herring, vicar here in the 1900s, is credited with the introduction of the potato, no less, into these parts from Devonshire. It is difficult to envisage a diet without the potato; his reverence deserves his prime position in the porch which incidentally was being done up when I was here.

In the nave are box pews and an elegant pulpit with an inlaid sounding board overhead. Any vicar would be glad to deliver a sermon from that eminence. One such, Thomas Eades, has secured his place in history as a 'non-juror' and in the process lost his living. A commemorative tablet records —

'He was suspended in the Dutchman's days,
Because he would not walk in their strange ways.'

The Dutchman was William of Orange; at his coronation he automatically became head of the Church of England and, by Act of Parliament, all the clergy were called upon to recognise him as such. Most did so but some could not bring themselves to swear, amongst them the then archbishop of Canterbury and, of course, our Thomas Eades. The arguments for swearing allegiance were well rehearsed by Macaulay and seem to me (from reading his history) to be finely balanced; but not the consequences. Indeed Macaulay went so far as to compare the convictions of the non-jurors with the superstitions of the ancient Egyptians who 'Worshipped cats and onions'. Onions may be good for one but Macaulay had no intention of flattering those who were prepared to suffer hardship for the sake of their principles.

* See Wartling church for the origin of these emblems.

Considering that the mortal remains of two prime ministers, one bishop, a duke and three earls lie below the chancel of this church, it is surprisingly unpretentious in ornament and simple in design. It is, or was, the church of the Pelham family.

There is a broadish but aisless nave; Early English originally with a lancet window on either side, now supplemented by windows with Perpendicular tracery. Its walls look to be of rubblestone covered with peeling and discoloured rendering which conveys an authentic impression of long-term weathering. The west tower of orderly sandstone blocks comes next chronologically, and is genuine Perpendicular; it is genuine Pelham, too, with emaciated buckles as label stops to the west door above which, in the spandrels, are two worn stone shields where my imagination encouraged me to make out a shadowy pelican.

There must have been a medieval chancel to complete the structure of this church. To-day, one's attention is inevitably focused on the 18th century replacement chancel below which repose the thirty or so members of the Pelham family. They gave themselves a very graceful appendix to the nave in which to await the Last Trump; meticulously squared flint stones in regular courses are augmented at the corners by diagonal buttresses with crocketed pinnacles as finals to lend a touch of distinction. On the south side, they included a priest's doorway, outlined by an ogival stone ribbon of quatrefoils. Very pretty it looks in a quiet way — with such a family there was felt, no doubt, little need for vulgar display.

So here we have a compact little church built of four different materials — ashlared sandstone tower, rubblestone and flint walls, topped by slate roofs — extending through three different architectural periods — Early English, Perpendicular and early Gothic.

Inside, the restraint is continued. It is rather barn-like in the nave with tie-beams stretching across from wall to wall. On one are perched two iron helmets dating from the mid 1500s and mid 1600s; both look rusty and very diminutive and are carefully inaccessible. Facing the entrance is a prominent memorial to the fallen of both world wars which comprehensively obliterates all internal evidence of a north doorway opposing the still functional south. One idiosyncracy here that you rarely see elsewhere is a complete list of the churchwardens from 1681 to 1951; it is much grander in appearance, if not in status, to that devoted to the incumbents.

So to the 18th century chancel where one might expect the restraint would be less observed. But no; it is true that there are three large ledger stones in the sanctuary, on one of which rests the solid oak altar table. They commemorate Pelhams. There are two austere wall tablets, side by side, remarking the lives of the 6th and 7th Earls of Chichester, father and son, who died within eight days of each other. Two stained glass windows in the chancel are dedicated to the family but of the other thirty or so individuals of the family there is no obvious trace so far as I could see. Nor is there any indication of the existence of a vault below (it was sealed in 1886). It is all rather 'let us lie in peace in our church', I felt, which makes one seem somewhat intrusive even to write about it or them.

And that is the impression one receives here. Having come the week before from Chiddingly — only about three miles distant as the crow flies — where the Jefferays are exhuberantly ostentatious with their monumental extravaganza, the difference in attitudes is striking. The Victorian Pelhams seem to have preferred to rely on the record of history for their claim on immortality. They could well be in the right. The written word has a way of outlasting the graven image and the Dictionary of National Biography might be the more permanent memorial. It is undeniable though that churches are more ornamental than the DNB. One may consult the latter, many do, but we all admire a country church and its surroundings even if the inscriptions in the churchyard are often now indecipherable.

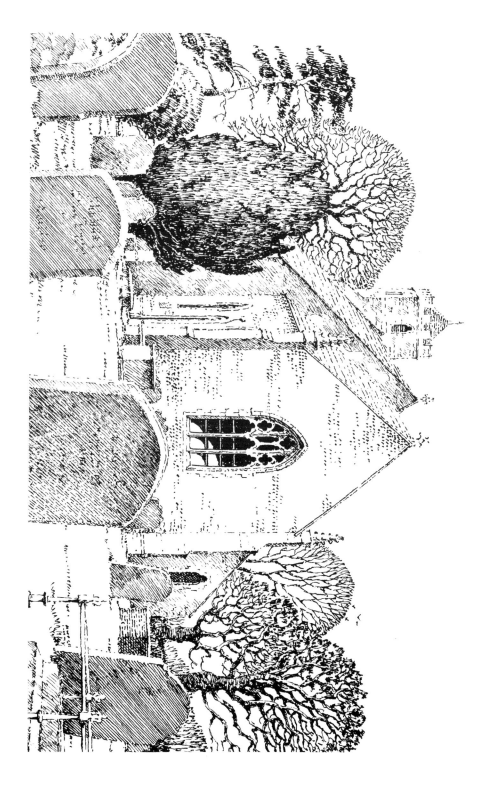

ALFRISTON
St Andrew

Alfriston is something of a honeypot for trippers, even in mid March. Fortunately, they mostly seem to infest the medieval inns here which, I would imagine, are Alfriston's second proudest boast. As a consequence, the church which stands apart, separated from the village street by a strip of green, the Tye, is relatively undisturbed. Although less well attended, the church is Alfriston's proudest boast, I would maintain, and indeed it is quoted in the guide as the 'Cathedral of the Downs'.

It stands on a slight mound, overlooking the winding Cuckmere, in a circular churchyard which suggests earlier pre-Christian occupation. And that is hardly surprising observing the proliferation of barrows and tumuli in the vicinity, not to mention the inscrutable Long Man on the opposing hillside. The church is in the form of a Greek cross, that is with all four arms of the cross of equal length although in Alfriston's case the nave and chancel are of two bays each whereas the transepts are only one bay each thus leaving a crossing area of one bay square, above which rises the massive central tower. Such dimensions do make the church seem rather mathematical but also indicate that the church was completed in one, single building campaign without later additions (except for a south porch) or subtractions. It must have been a fairly monumental undertaking for the locality in 1360; no great lord or prince of the church is known to have been connected with Alfriston then — smugglers later, but they were more interested in rum than redemption — so why a parish church of such noble proportions and such careful construction with everywhere flints squared and uniform. There must have been some major guiding hand here but whose and why? Everything has a cause. If one could job back far enough from antecedent to antecedent cause, one ultimately reaches the First Cause which some call God. Since my references are unable to offer a proximate cause one may be content with the First Cause as a sufficient reason for Alfriston's church. And no bad reason when one comes to think of it.

Inside, there is a great feeling of spaciousness. This impression is emphasised by the empty space under the tower which separates chancel from nave and provides an occasional stage for the bellringers on which to ring their changes. The tower above is supported by four pillared arches, unusual in that the columns consist of concave flutes. Concavities presumably diminish strength — hardly the sort of effect one wants when carrying a substantial weight. However, the columns are manifestly up to the job; nothing has moved for 600 years and that must be an endorsement of medieval architectural practice and mathematics.

In the chancel, on the north side, is an Easter Sepulchre notable for its moulding stops; on the south side a triple sedilia, the design of which Pevsner castigates as 'very odd and rather perverse'. It seemed conventional enough to me. One should remark on the windows which, being put together when the Decorated style was giving way to the Perpendicular, combines the characteristics of each. I think one needs to be a bit of an expert to appreciate the full subtlety of these particular examples of transitional tracery.

Considering the majesty of this church, there are virtually no memorials to commemorate local dignitaries. In compensation, there are accomplished sketches of the church and its interior by the Sussex artist, S H Grimm, signed and dated 1787. Naturally, there are no visible changes to the church since then although the topiary yews which decorate the churchyard were noticeably absent when Grimm sketched. The churchyard is better for them but the church might perhaps look more starkly impressive if left to stand alone on its grassy knoll as it must have looked when newly built. It was clearly meant to impress, still does, — but who? The Almighty, perhaps, who has the keys to heaven.

CHALVINGTON
St Bartholomew

Ceaffa's farmstead

One finds this demure little church at the end of a lane in the middle of flat farming country inland of the Downs not far from Alfriston. The garden of Chalvington Manor abuts the churchyard wall to the north and other substantial houses, probably with agricultural interests, line the short lane down to the church. It is the sort of place where, on an ordinary day, free-range chickens cluck, the occasional dog will bark and rusty corrugated iron will clang in the wind but no-one moves. I had little doubt, though, that I was observed by someone as I prowled around the churchyard peering at this and examining that. Quite right, too.

The 13th century church, of appropriate size to its remote rural community which does not run to a village shop or pub, is small and simple — just a nave of 37 feet by 27, a chancel of 21 feet by 15, a modern north porch and a wooden bell turret topped by a tiled broach spire. The external features that characterise Chalvington are the tiled gable ends, east and west, of the nave, the weathered rendered walls resting on flint plinths (these latter didn't look to be 13th century to me) and the side chancel windows with their flattened hood moulds. And it is not often that one sees small triangles of stained glass at the apex of the nave gable and at the bottom right-hand corner of the bell turret. I can't imagine what the point of these minute lights can be — certainly not illumination. An engaged bell turret, like this one here, is always a sign of a church with limited pretensions lacking wealthy patrons; insufficient tithes to attract the bishop or benefactor results in inadequate funds to build a tower. The wonder is why there is a church here at all and that is why one is prepared to travel miles to revel in these rural backwaters.

I was disappointed but not surprised when the venerable church door refused to yield to my efforts to manipulate the latch. It gave me time to admire the door, co-eval with the church I understand, to reflect on the provenance of the ancient, eroded timbers in a corner of the porch and to identify the small fragments of Norman zigzag above the arch of the doorway. (How come Norman masonry in a 13th century church with no known predecessor?) When, later, I had finished my rough sketch, I was surprised, pleasantly this time, to find the church door had blown open in the wind; it had not been locked after all and I had merely been cack-handed.

The interior is restrained and, as one might expect, there is not much room for display; poppy-head pews but very few monuments with only one large, lozenge-shaped, hatchment to command attention. The church leaflet makes good the lack of memorials by dilating on the registers of marriages, christenings and deaths which were started in 1538 under the threatening injunction of Thomas Cromwell. These registers are of sufficient historical importance now to be kept by the County Archivist at Lewes. One can understand that precaution but I wonder at what stage an everyday register is promoted to the status of historical document and kept out of harm's way where it probably gathers dust. Perhaps xerox offers a more satisfactory answer.

I thought I recognised an iron bracket for an hour glass on the wall beside the pulpit. Imagine the tortured feelings many a church goer must have suffered when a prolix parson reversed the glass to give himself a second hour. In the heyday of the hour glass and the hatchment there was no competition from the media and, in fact, the sermon could as well have been regarded as a relief from a week of toil as an improving homily. No preacher would be allowed an hour glass to-day; we need time to get to the supermarket.

The churchyard is enclosed by a well-found waist-high brick wall pierced by strong wrought-iron gates, east and west. There is the expected quota of headstones still with room, I would say, for plenty more but with an inadequate supply from hereabouts to fill it. In the distance, the silhouette of the downs hauntingly limits the horizon and speaks of the timeless past. Strange to think it was all under water once.

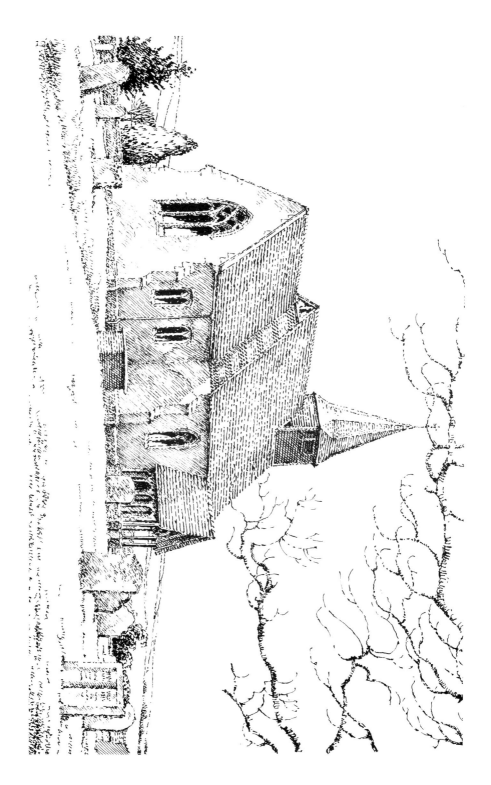

FOLKINGTON
St Peter ad Vincula

Folka's farmstead

'Ancient and rustic' says Betjeman. Rustic is absolutely right; at the end of a lane to nowhere, in company with two grand old houses and at the boundary wall of Folkington Manor, Folkington church is rustic without a doubt. Bosky, too, I would say, with a sloping churchyard carpeted with primroses and surrounded by trees that lead away westwards to Windover Hill and the Long Man. As I sketched, the only sounds were the murmurings of the birds about their springtime nesting and the musical clatter of the hoofs of the thoroughbred horses from the manor's stables. The 20th century did seem remote and hardly represented by the car which had brought me here. But without the car how many strangers could ever come to admire this country church. And well worth coming to see it is; I daresay Betjeman came by car.

Nor can it be other than ancient either, if the lancet windows on each side of the chancel are anything to go by. And so they are, being confirmed as Early English by the church leaflet which dates the church from the mid-13th century — far older than the few houses which form its scattered parish. This is a tiny church, just nave and chancel (forgetting the Victorian vestry to the south and porch to the north), two equally wide cells which run together without distinction apart from the small break in the roof line. Inside, the separation is less apparent although a study of the exposed roof timbers should reveal where chancel begins and nave ends.

With three houses of quality in the immediate vicinity it is not surprising to find the interior of the church well furnished and eloquent of enduring local wealth persisting from generation to generation. Persisting also are 18th century box pews from the midst of which springs an 18th century pulpit. All the side windows have clear glass so that the effect in this restricted interior may be one of lightness and space. It is no doubt to reinforce this clarity that the insides of the box pews are painted white as well. The walls are liberally faced with handsome hanging monuments and wall tablets and the chancel floored by particularly fine black ledger stones. Text boards of the Commandments, the Creed and the Lord's Prayer line the walls at the rear of the nave where the organ has its presence and the light is subdued. The texts are no longer meant to be read, it would seem; I expect they were more prominently displayed in the days before we all had prayer books of our own. Perhaps the ancestral memorials have displaced them.

The first recorded rector is one Gervase who held sway in 1226 (when Henry III was on the throne and French affairs loomed large — Gervase was probably of French extraction); another rector to emerge from the rank and file of the list was Thomas Brett who was deprived of his living in 1689 as a non-juror.* One wonders to what extent the obstinate Thomas was influenced by or did defy the lord of the manor here. It cannot have been easy for him and for countless other parsons in like-isolated livings.

Only one thing disappointed me at Folkington. In the church leaflet mention is made of an alms box made from wood taken from H M S Benbow but, depsite a vigilant search, I could find no trace of this box. I don't know how many ships of the Navy rejoiced in the name Benbow (after the admiral who laced rum with water and therby invented grog and lost his leg in action) but there may have been more than one ship of that name. I would like to think that the alms box at Folkington was made from the wood of the battleship Benbow in which my father-in-law served at the battle of Jutland in 1916.

* See Chiddingly for enlightenment if needed.

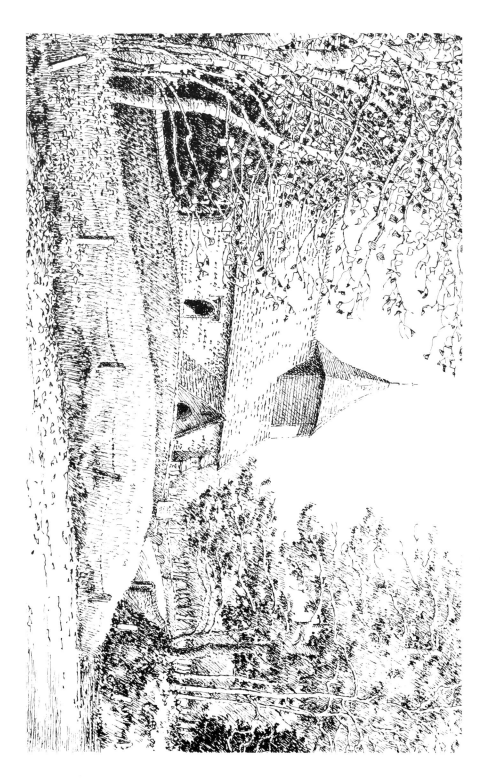

'The Poor Knights of Christ and of the Temple of Solomon', (thus the Oxford Dictionary
of the Christian Church which never fails one) or the Templars as we more briefly know
them, were established here at Shipley and St Mary's was their church or preceptory. Seen
from the south, it could almost be a fortress on the road to Acre and not a parish church
beside the stream of the Adur in the placid heart of Sussex. The Templars seemed to have
made sure that they had militarily orientated architects here as well as abroad in Outremer.

Their church presents a considerable conundrum to the amateur ecclesiologist, even when
armed with knowledgeable reference books. Disregarding my experts and indulging in my
own opinion for the moment, I identified the long nave as displaying predominantly Saxon
characteristics externally — that is to say, lofty and narrow, lacking in buttresses and with
that Saxon exemplar, rough and ready, double-splayed windows. My 'Notes on Sussex
Churches' says 'the nave was entirely rebuilt about the middle of the last century and a north
aisle (unfortunately — my word) added'. In that case, all I can say is the nave was rebuilt
in the Saxo-Norman style. The great, precipitous tower, longitudinally central, is early Norman
and was built by the Templars in 1125 (if that date is correct, the Templars must have got
here to Sussex very smartly after their formation in France in 1118 by Hugh de Payens —
a wise move on their part but hardly consistent with their professed aim of protecting pilgrims
in the Holy Land). The west doorway, although ordered with Norman zigzag moulding is
slightly pointed and thus would seem to mark the transition from Norman to Gothic. There
is a range of styles here sufficient to give anyone the chance to be right or wrong or at least
to pontificate. What can confidently be remarked upon is the skill of the medieval masons
who managed to erect such a ponderous tower using only smallish, undressed, non-uniform
stones. Bound by iron reinforcing cramps, their work has stood for eight hundred years and
looks good for a millenium or two yet. Mee says the walls are about nine feet thick and that
may have something to do with it.

At the time of my sketch the church was under rescue with the interior almost completely
swathed in green polythene sheeting as a protection from repairs to the roof timbers. However,
in spite of all the evidence of work in progress, the Norman atmosphere conveyed by the
great semi-circular tower arches could not be entirely banished. As is usual with Norman
work the arches carry elaborate moulding but, as is also usual, on the nave side only.
Presumably this emphasis on the west front is no more than a recognition of an east-facing
congregation and clergy.

The memorials inside were either covered or taken down. Pevsner mentions only one; that
of the recumbent figure of Sir Thomas Caryll, his wife and daughters. They could only be
glimpsed in their Elizabethan glory under a loose corner of the polythene. Still, a lack of
memorials to divert the eye serves to remind one of an austerity that is appropriate to the
selfless aims of the warrior knights who worshipped here.

This exploration of Shipley church was combined with a picnic with two friends who had
been married here forty years before. Without them we would probably not have gained
admittance to a vicarless church, closed to the public. As always, those working in the church
were only too ready to discuss their work — the consequent danger being a tendency to invite
one to examine the upper, vertiginous recesses. As two retired and aged naval officers, we
might have found that embarrassing.

Standing in a corner of the south porch, beside the Saxo-Norman doorway, is a large plum-
coloured stone — a Sarsen stone possibly. It may seem incongruous to find something with
pre-Christian overtones in close association with a Christian church but it was a pope, I believe,
who advised his early missionaries to build their churches on sites that had been sacred to
their pagan predecessors. So that dark stone from the Tertiary geological era which lies in
the south porch is in all probability the prior tenant here.

ALCISTON
Dedication not known

Aelfsige's farmstead

I think it is fair to say that in the Middle Ages the clergy had all the brains. Or, if not a monopoly, they had the education to make the best use of the brains which the good God had given them. So it is not surprising that the monks of Battle Abbey picked on Alciston for their granary. Most of the land immediately north of the Downs is poor, I was told by a lady arranging primroses around the font for Easter Sunday, but here at Alciston under the lee of Firle Beacon it is very good. Evidently the monks found it so for, next to the church, they established the most enormous tithe barn, 170 feet long, dwarfing the church in size and in the abbatial economy. They didn't intend to starve even if the laity had to make do with tares and thistles.

The church is small and engagingly unpretentious. It could be described as two celled without a chancel arch to separate the two vital sections essential for any complete church, however diminutive. It has Norman origins, vide a Norman window, and a Saxon forerunner has been identified underground, but now what one sees is mainly Early English with later windows added. It was strange, I thought, to find the porch and all the windows, lancet and Perpendicular, on the north, east and west sides leaving only one low-side window on the south. There are traces of a blocked arch on the south side of the chancel which might have constituted a window before the chancel was shortened. But that doesn't explain the absence of south-facing windows to-day. It is a fact that the walls of the garden of Court House Farm, which includes the remains of the monastic establishment in its rambling extensions, run close alongside the southern side of the church. Possibly one party did not want to be overlooked by the other. Nevertheless, a low-side window such as the one here, is popularly supposed to be there in order to allow external access to the services within from without; it is the 'without' that is so circumscribed by the adjoining garden wall as to make the window almost redundant. It presents a nice little conundrum to reflect on as one wanders around the churchyard and contemplates the ancient flint and rubblestone walling and the harmonious surroundings. It is almost as if the church has turned its back on its grand neighbour. There must be some reason; perhaps it was the loss of the granary to lay hands and the departure of the monks that provoked the cold shoulder.

That the church is lovingly looked after is obvious, from the clear white-washed walls of the chancel and nave to the polished pews and the stencilled organ which came from Berwick church, a mile away. It is one of the smallest organs I have seen and, for once, does not intrude clumsily. There is a rustic simplicity to the interior which is emphasised by the red-brick floors and the primitive scaffolding that supports the bell turret and its two bells; one as old as 1380 exhorts the patron saint of bell founders to 'pray for us' ('us' being the bell ringers, no doubt.)

There is in the porch a framed history of the church embellished on its margins with attractive vignettes of particular things of local interest. Without its prompting I would never have spotted the faint scratch dial beside the blocked priest's door. Nor would I have known that the ruin in the paddock below the church to the west was what remains of a medieval dovecot or that the nearby duck ponds had once been fish ponds for the monks. Because, I gather, the village is still largely in the hands of one landlord it is quite unspoilt and has an air of secluded peace — proof even against the multi-coloured anoraks of hikers heading past the church for the Downs. Who could object to sartorial vandalism in the spring?

Alciston is a place of contrast though. Not far away in the shadow of that oasis of medieval religion, architecture and agriculture, the church and tithe barn, a young man was spring cleaning his car, that epitome of the technology of the 20th century. The car is utilitarian, short-lived and a mixed blessing. The buildings are beautiful, remarkably permanent and transcendent in purpose.

When I ascended the narrow lane to Jevington church, past the old rectory and accompanied by an eerie chorus of peacock calls, I knew what to expect. Nor was I disappointed, envious though. This is the most delectable little place in a valley within the Downs where one could be very happy to end one's days. It ought to be writ small on the map, though, so that few can find it — says a selfish thought. But it is difficult to avoid such a self-centred attitude as one surveys the ancient flint church in its churchyard across the path from the Monastery Field where the monks from Flanders once held sway.

The church was locked but my disappointment turned to relief when three friendly ladies drew up in a mini to open up and replenish the Easter flowers. Always open hitherto, they said, recent vandalism had caused a change of policy. We all agreed that the re-introduction of the stocks would be a good thing.

The stocky west tower is the main feature of interest at Jevington. It is Saxon, at least up to its belfry stage. The evidence for its provenance are long and short quoin stones on the north east corner and a herring-bone course or two, not very obvious but there all right. There are also the remains, in the shape of irregular voussoirs of Roman tiles, of one blocked window north and south. The voussoirs do not look entirely reliable now and that may explain why the windows were blocked. Below are two narrow windows which looked to me to be of Norman design — 'of much later date' says the guide. The bell apertures, once round-headed and with a central turned shaft, have been restored and might now be described as Saxo-Victorian. To judge from photographs of before and after, the Victorians would seem to have superimposed a pointed-arch dripstone to protect the original round-headed Saxon opening. This may not be an improvement but it clearly is a preservative. They also apparently inserted oeil-de-boeuf openings above the bell apertures — to let in the birds? Which they do.

Inside the nave, the tall, narrow arched doorway to the tower looked Saxon to me though the smaller replica doorways on either side are said not to be authentic. What is certainly Saxon is the sculpted figure in relief, rescued from elsewhere, that now adorns a wall and confronts one on entry.

The church guide puts the date of the tower as 900 to 950 AD. One of the flower ladies, a keen local historian, put the date as far earlier — about 700 AD, if I understood her correctly. Her chronology is based on the legend of St Lewinna, a young girl martyred here about then whose remains were aparenetly kept in the church until removed (stolen in 1058 by an unprincipled monk named Balgerus — Sussex Archaeological Collections, Vol. 1) to the monastery of St Winoc in Flanders. Fable has it (SAC again) that Balgerus hoped to improve the status of his monastery by the possession of holy relics. If true, and the dedication to St Lewinna of the lost monastery in Monastery Field would seem to be corroborative, then there would have been a church here long before 900 AD.*

After the tower, the rest of the church is relatively recent being Early English and only 700 years old. However its lasting qualities may not prove as persistent as those of the tower if the south wall of the nave is anything to go by. This wall, of squared blocks as opposed to the flints of which the rest of the church is built, leans alarmingly and is only held more or less upright by two substantial buttresses. It is always a matter for surprise that the Saxons managed so well without buttresses.

As well as enormous antiquity, this little church enjoys the most captivating surroundings. To the north, behind its high flint wall, one glimpses the mellow red roofs of Jevington Place, to the west, the fields give way shortly to the encroaching Downs; to the south lies Monastery Field and to the east the land falls away to the village before the Downs press in again on the road which runs down the valley to Friston and the sea. Once heavily populated in prehistoric times, to-day this magical place seems to belong as much to the spirits of the past as to its present, scanty population.

* SAC Vol. 1 again, for the third time, suggests uncertainly and to the contrary that the bones of St Lewinna may have rested at Lewes before removal.

St George

Brede provided my first encounter, in historical terms, with Canute in East Sussex. Apparently, in 1031 (so says the church guide) his wife, Queen Emma, granted the manor here to the Abbey of Fecamp, the monks of which responded by building the first church in 1180. They evidently took their time as well as their tithes. Not much of the work remains so that now this church is almost entirely Perpendicular and certainly English — which is not to decry Canute who was a very great man in his day, if a foreigner.

It consists of a nave and chancel, north and south aisles, a south chapel and a west tower, the whole ranging from 1180 (the south aisle arcade) to mid 15th century (the west tower). In fact the tower that we see to-day is the second; its Norman predecessor being off-centre in what is now the baptistry at the west end of the south aisle.

The south chapel is more properly known as the Oxenbridge chantry-chapel. Here memorialised (or rather was before her brass was stolen from her tomb recess) was a female Oxenbridge. However, to make good the loss, the brasses of Robert Oxenbridge, †1487, (he, legs and two feet only) and his wife, Anne, †1493, have been attached to the backing of the recess. Very medieval this despoiled tomb now looks, as it should, having stood in this church since the Wars of the Roses. Tudor and grander is the effigy of their armoured and armigerous son, Sir Goddard Oxenbridge, †1531, recumbent on his decorated tomb chest. One of this family was reputed to have had an appetite for children; it can't have been Sir Goddard who, although known locally as the Brede giant, was on the staff of Cardinal Wolsey and should therefore have had no occasion for such behaviour.

Considering the modest village in which it stands, this church bears an unexpected stamp of quality. The proximity of Brede Place must have had a lot to do with this distinction. For instance, Sir Goddard caused the south chapel to be built and other owners have no doubt contributed to the church's upkeep and embellishment. It is now virtually an artistic gallery as well as a place of worship, mausoleum and village heirloom. In no order of merit there are a pair of cheerful paintings of the church by the Victorian water-colourist, de Paris; an appropriately sombre set of Stations of the Cross by Sir Thomas Monnington, PRA 1966-76; and a tall, carved oak figure of the Madonna and Child by the sculptress, Clare Sheridan, who lived at Brede Place and from whence came the oak. A towering, Gothic font cover, a blackened 17th century carved chest and a large oil painting furnish the baptistry but of the celebrated wooden cradle of Jonathan Swift there is no trace — stolen in the godless 1970s. A cradle does seem to have been an oddly utilitarian object to keep in a church but then the Dean did write an 'Argument to Prove the Inconvenience of Abolishing Christianity' as well as 'Gulliver's Travels'.

In the north aisle, there is a window depicting St Lewinna who, says the church guide, was buried at Selsey at the other end of the county. Lewinna must have exerted a powerful post-mortem influence along the Sussex coastal strip so many claim her mortal remains; the Sussex Archaeological Collections suggest her bones may have rested at Lewes while the flower ladies of Jevington confidently confide her bones to their church until abstracted by the monk from Flanders. For what it is worth, I am on the side of Jevington.

In my sketch I could not ignore the clock face set clumsily in the bell aperture in the tower. There is a sundial on the exterior of the south aisle, no doubt scratch dials elsewhere and we all have watches. Even without the tower clock, there can be little excuse for being late in Brede unless it might be the hospitable inn across the road.

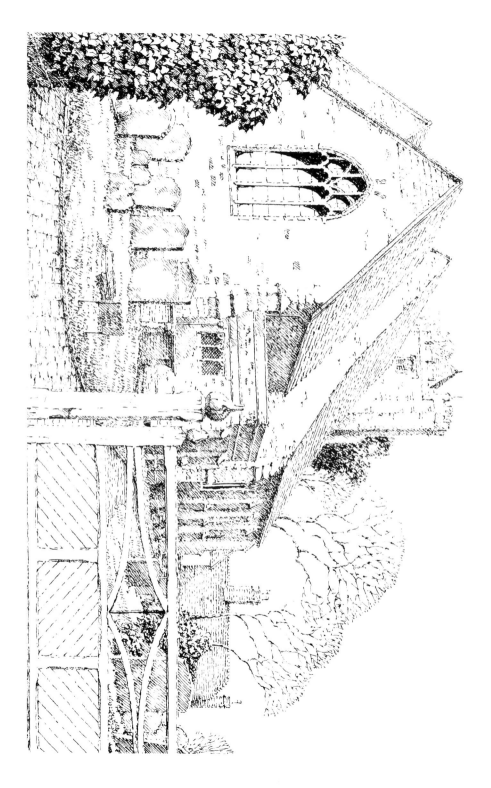

At a junction on the outskirts of its long straggle of a village (by the time I had found the church, I had forgotten where the pub was!) one finds All Saints beyond a handsome, sad but welcoming, lych-gate. This is the memorial put up by a couple in memory of their two sons killed in the Great War. If the ghosts of that war could speak I wonder what they would say to their present-day successors. They would not ignore the country churches in which they are so eloquently commemorated. Nor, to be honest, do we; the churches are far better cared for now than they were before the Victorians rescued them. As they did this church in 1885, two years before Queen Victoria's golden jubilee.

The confirmation here is inside where three nice watercolours dated 1868 and 1878 depict the church with no sign of the present south chapel; one shows the remnants of the stocks (where the lych-gate now stands) and another bears that well-known quote 'where heaves the turf in many a mouldring heap'. The caption is apt for this extensive churchyard is rather field-like containing headstones set more or less at random. It is surrounded by a ring of ivy-clad, aged and twisted, sweet chestnut trees with in the distance on the skyline the spire of Northiam church. As I sketched, the cuckoo occasionally cuckoo-ed invisibly and a jay jarred nearby. It was all very rural, undisturbed and entirely enjoyable to be there.

This church originated with the tower, which is 12th century, and the dominant feature. Its windows are Norman but the church guide suggests that the few courses of herring-bone stonework about fifteen feet above the ground might be of Saxon origin. One wonders what, apart from the decorative aspect, can be the point of this pattern of building — because point there must be. My own layman's explanation is that, just as the hips of a hipped roof are provided to offer resistance to the lateral sway of parallel rafters, so courses of stones laid in opposition are similarly hoped to achieve longitudinal stability in a wall-face. Buttresses do the job too and here at Beckley they found it necessary to support the tower with two enormous diagonal buttresses.

After the tower, the rest of the church is relatively traditional medieval-cum-Victorian. One idiosyncracy is the insertion of dormer windows on either side of a roof that embraces nave and aisles. It is noticeable that the south-facing dormers are more elaborate than their poor relations on the north side. One can find a comparable north south split inside with the corbel heads which support the western arches of the arcade. The southern is modern, serene and benign; the northern is intentionally malicious in expression and must be the sort of thing that prompted M R James, himself a clergyman's son, to compose his chilling ghost stories.

The church guide refers to this latter head and another by the term 'Jack-in-the-Green'. Sir James Frazer, in his study of primitive customs, 'The Golden Bough', has much to say about 'Jack-in-the-Green' and Tree Spirits. The medieval version of Jack, the vernal spirit of vegetation, was usually a 'chimney sweep who walks encased in a pyramidal framework of wicker-work, which is covered in holly and ivy and surmounted by a crown of flowers and ribbons'. That sounds harmless enough but I think the grotesque head in the nave more accurately represents the pagan concept of the tree spirit which, in human form, suffers death the moment signs of decay appear. Hardly the way to encourage a successor to foster regeneration. As a practice it seems reminiscent of the execution of Admiral Byng — as the French sardonically put it — 'pour encourager les autres'.

Such penumbral thoughts, inspired though they may be by the corbel at the west end of the nave, are far removed from the air of peace and tranquillity that pervade Beckley church and churchyard. Perhaps after nightfall, though ... who knows what imagination might conjure from out of the old oak chest in the aisle.

Eorla's farmstead

Towards the end of May, anywhere in the country is delightful and nowhere more so than Arlington church and churchyard. It is — where it has been for a thousand years — near the banks of the Cuckmere river, north of the Downs on the site of a vanished Roman village. One needs a map to find it. With the trees in leaf, butterflies on the wing and cow parsley in flower, one can understand what the poet was on about; he might even have had Arlington in mind.

The church stands at the end of a tiny lane together with a house or two and a pub. Largely screened by trees as one approaches, it looks normal enough — 13th century let's say, Decorated and Perpendicular in style with a spire that has warped with age. Past the trees by the south porch, one realises, especially if briefed by Pevsner, that one is confronted by a Saxon church or at least by a Saxon wall. Most obviously pre-Conquest is the small window, splayed externally and headed by an erratic semi-circle of pink Roman tiles — from the lost village? The wall itself is rough old flint, interrupted by two Perpendicular windows and the ghost of a blocked arch, with at either end Saxon quoins of long and short (horizontal and vertical would be more descriptive) stone work that says Saxon emphatically. For once there is no ambiguity even if, here and there, rosy Tudor brickwork has been used to make good the gaps.

The opposing wall of the nave, which would have been Saxon too, has gone to be replaced by the north aisle arcade. Here one does encounter a hint of ambiguity. The north chapel is Norman as the dog-tooth moulding on the impost of its entrance arch confirms. One would expect a circular arch to 'spring', as they say; instead the arch is pointed which postpones this particular feature to that shadowy realm between two architectural styles, the Transitional. Actually, the guide says the tower is also Transitional. Its wooden door, and the two other doors of the church, are all distinguished by identical iron strapwork hinges, presumably made by the same hand or anvil. All three, with their sinister serpent-head ends, have the look of the culture of the fearsome Vikings, I thought. I daresay I an quite wrong but those hinges, so distinctive, have surprisingly not qualified for professional comment.

There are, I counted, 5 stone coffin lids, 4 fixed vertically here and there inside and one as a threshhold beneath the arch, between chapel and chancel. Originally, the guide says, they paved the chapel where countless feet and supplicant knees eroded their foliate crosses. The Victorians may have saved our ancient churches, as they did here in the 1890s, but in the process they invariably ripped up the old stone floors and effectively banished much of the atmosphere of austerity and other-worldliness that properly belongs to a medieval church. If one wished, and was able, to confer a benefaction on a church what better gift than a stone-flagged floor in place of Victorian tiles. Then at Arlington the coffin lids could resume their rightful place in the chapel and be knelt upon once more. If the money ran to it, I would bring back the ejected box pews — just a few — and leave the rest of the nave free for standing room so that it could again be dignified by the elegant inscriptions of the now proscribed ledger stones.

The church guide says that in the 15th century the church kept 30 cows to be rented out to local farmers in exchange for beeswax to 'supply lights for the shrines'. It can't have been easy to strike a balance of cows against beeswax and one can see the difficulty when, for instance, a farmer did not have enough beeswax to justify the rent of a cow. What was the church to do? Go without what beeswax there was or rent out the cow uneconomically? Such problems of barter are what money was invented for. Here, at Arlington, where the churchyard is ample and the money supply may have been thin, why did the churchwardens not keep the bees themselves and thus avoid the difficulty of equating bees with cows.

BEDDINGHAM
St Andrew

Derivations, like the one above, do serve to remind us of what things were like in the distant past. Here at Beddingham it was, I gather, once all floodland from the Ouse with the mound on which the church stands an island of dry land amongst the water meadows. Now, after drainage and with the Glynde Reach canalised to run past under Mount Caburn, it is all more like sheep pasturage which, in fact, is what the churchyard evidently becomes upon occasion.

Nor does musical Glyndebourne, a couple of miles away, allow itself to be forgotten either as a poster in the porch, offering a sweepstake to 'win a night at the opera', attests. What a reward for coming to this church — two tickets for Cosi fan Tutte. Not that one needs a reward for coming to St Andrew's. Had one the strength, it would be a rewarding double to admire the church and then to climb the 500 feet to explore the iron-age hill fort on the summit of Mt Caburn. The view from the top must be stunning and even Beddingham's substantial tower will be temporarily reduced to panoramic insignificance.

I was content with St Andrew's. The west tower is, of course, far from insignificant. Perpendicular, it dates from 1540 and is made of flint and stone, set in a chequer pattern still distinguishable in patches. Its apertures are small, buttresses reliable and its weather vane rides high on its small tiled cap. It is bulky and stalwart but it will not outlast the embanked fort on the hill above.

Before the tower was the nave. At ground level only its corners remain, the rest having succumbed to arcades when they threw out the north and south aisles in the 15th century. Presumably there was a well-tried procedure for inserting arches without demolishing the whole wall and that, from the hewn-out appearance of the arcade soffits, is that they probably did here. The pillars must present a problem — how to support the weight above without distorting the fabric either up or down. It can't be easy but the short cylindrical and octagonal pillars here look well up to the job. They are Transitional and Early English, the guide says, with square abaci adorned with heads at the corners. Combined with traces of wall painting on the arches and an unrestored floor of matt, plum-coloured tiles, the nave now has an atmosphere of simple austerity and antiquity, undisturbed by later alterations or additions. Only the pews, which one can reasonably describe as utility, are out of keeping. A pity but they do remind one that this is a parish with a very modest population and which is linked to West Firle where the money is, and stays, and the grander grandees are. A spartan chancel confirms, I think, where the centre of gravity now lies.

As well as architectural details, the guide gives a potted history of Beddingham. Apparently in Offa's time, there was a monastery here briefly from 757 to 796. It is not unlike Jevington in that respect. It is also not unlike Jevington in that Beddingham supposes (or rather reports without too much conviction) that that infamous monk from Flanders came here looking for the relics of St Lewinna. He might well have done. After the Conquest, the advowson of this church was given to the abbey of Grestain in Normandy and one can easily understand that the suffering native Saxons would not have had too nice a regard for the property of an absentee landlord. Perhaps they hid Lewinna's remains from all acquisitors so that now no-one knows for sure where they were held and all can advance their claim as the original hosts with an equal plausibility. It was a sort of early scorched-earth policy by the dispossessed. I would like to think I would have done the same.

HORSTED KEYNES
St Giles

Horse place (of de Cahaignes)

It was a typical day of the English cricket season when I came to Horsted Keynes; ten tenths cloud, intermittent drizzle and with the Test Match being rained off at Edgbaston. But although it was near impossible to sketch out in the open, the church is well worth a visit regardless of the weather. If one's sketching is restricted, there will be more time to admire the architecture and to reflect on the why's and wherefore's that attend any church with a long history.

Horsted Keynes is one such. Essentially it is a Norman church with a central tower between nave and chancel and, once, transepts either side of the tower. Their roof lines, high up, are still visible externally and the Norman arches that gave on to them still stand on each side of the crossing. These early transepts have been replaced, on the north side by the vestry, and to the south by the 14th century Lady Chapel. A third Norman arch, simple and robust, supports the east face of the tower and opens on to the Norman chancel. Within the chancel one finds the best of the memorials; elegantly inscribed wall tablets enriched by coloured armorial bearings. There is also a large coffin slab from elsewhere, anchored vertically as is the current fashion, against the wall. But pride of place must go to the miniature effigy of a crusader. This sculpture, which was found in 1838 amongst some lumber by the then vicar, reposes in a recess that looks to have been made for it but might alternatively have been the Easter Sepulchre — a nice which or what to ponder over. Small figures as opposed to life-size, are generally supposed, I believe, to have been used where the heart rather than the corpse of the deceased was interred. In this case, the heart is said to be that of a knight of the time of Henry III who died in the Holy Land — probably one of the martial de Cahaignes, the family who were granted the manor here by William de Warenne after Hastings. Contemplating this miniature, one can't help wondering how old our knight was when he met his death, absolved of his sins and with his passport to heaven secure. Anyway, full marks to the vicar who restored him to his rightful place on earth. May he in turn have been the vicar's sponsor in the hereafter.

The church was restored in 1884 when it was enlarged by the addition of a north aisle. The floor everywhere is handsomely flagged except under the silvery grey oak pews where wood has been substituted. It is always a pity, I think, to sacrifice fitness for comfort. After all, this church does possess a very decorative set of embroidered hassocks to ease the bones.

Outside, south of the chancel where for a time there was a chantry chapel, one finds the memorial to Robert Leighton, Archbishop of Glasgow from 1670 to 1674. He must have been one of the last, if not the last, bishop in Scotland as in 1638 the Glasgow General Assembly voted to 'sweep episcopy away' and, in 1690 the Church of Scotland finally reverted to Presbyterianism. He is better at Horsted Keynes.

With so tall a spire, the church presents problems of perspective unless one can withdraw sufficiently to reduce the angles. My search for a drawable view took me to the outer reaches of the churchyard where mown lawn gives way to long grass. Here, in a secluded hedged plot, I found unexpectedly the Macmillan family memorials. They are discreet — a cross with Celtic overtones and two low granite headstones almost ostentatiously bare of title or decoration to proclaim worldly success — just names and dates. Is it a genuine modesty that disdains mention of high office or a pride that one is above such things? No politician can be modest, especially one who has risen to be prime minister, so I conclude that it was a form of inverse pride in the case of Harold Macmillan. His interment here adds lustre to the church; perhaps the church guide, when there is one, will make good the deficiency. I hope so.

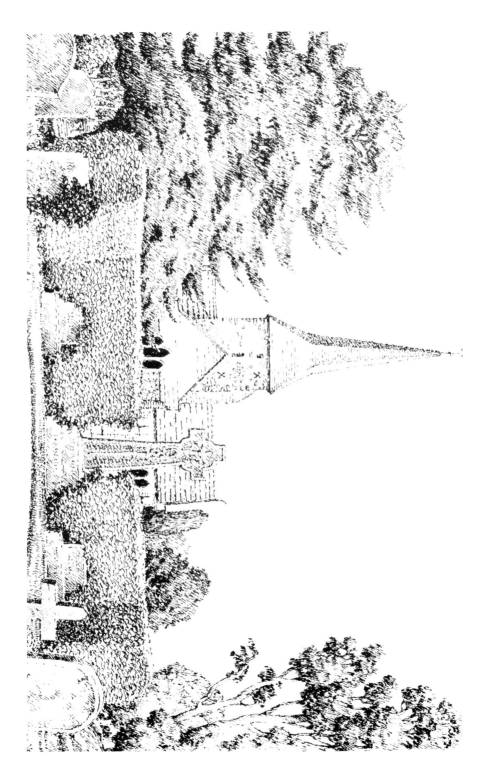

Another ancient Sussex church deep in the heart of the empty countryside where in June the air is heavy with the scent of elderberry flower, the grasses are long and busy with the gatekeeper butterfly while, unseen, the cuckoo calls intermittently. It all seems so innocent of man and yet it was man who built this church nine hundred years ago.

One finds the church at a fork in the lane with Church Farm inconspicuously beyond and a couple of cottages some way before. The ground slopes up to the church tower, then down away to the wooded east where the tower of Fairlight church is silhouetted on the ridge on the far side of the valley. Guestling Green is nowhere to be seen but nevertheless the churchyard is looked after, paths mown and the lych gate in a proper state of repair. And, considering the relative isolation, to my very great surprise the heavy, double-skinned oak door inside the porch gave way gracefully. It was more than I felt I could reasonably have hoped for; and there is a detailed guide to supplement Pevsner. 'Alleluia' seemed an appropriate comment at the time.

The dark, golden sandstone church consists of a nave (what remains after the additions, 11th century), west tower and north aisle (early 12th century), north chapel (late 12th century), chancel (13th century), south chapel (late 13th century), south aisle (14th century) and south porch (modern); a graduated production extended over a period of 300 years. Such is the church in which the chancel is longer than the nave and all except the stone walling is in fact recent after a disastrous fire in 1870; unquenched because apparently 'it took some time to find the horses for the fire engine'. Sensible horses.

Notwithstanding the fire, the origins of the church are still extant and confirmed by the Norman windows in the tower, the west doorway with its Romanesque semi-circular arch, and more impressively by the internal doorway to the north chapel. Here, the arch, resting on half-round responds, consists of at least four orders of roll moulding and one of the tell-tale zigzag which, being unweathered, are all in prime condition. The fire was less kind to the two principal memorials in the church which both look as if they have been under artillery, rather than incendiary, fire. That in the chancel commemorates by effigy John Cheney, †1603, and his wife; their children were casualties of the fire but at least one tiny skull (for a small son 'who didn't grow up') remains. The memorials in the south chapel, the Ashburnham chapel, are naturally those of members of this family. The most prominent, and most damaged, is that to Adam Ashburnham, †1597. In fact, like Ashburnham church itself, Guestling church is virtually a mausoleum, inside and out, for the Ashburnhams. Like this church, they are survivors; I noted two as members of the current Guestling Parochial Church Council. Perhaps that is why everything here is so well cared for.

The north aisle houses a most interesting relic, kept in a glass case from inquisitive hands. It is Volume 1 of Foxe's Book of Martyrs, a much quoted book in the history of the Reformation in this country*. I have often wondered about it and about Foxe and here it is — open halfway at page 454 where the text is concerned with 'The Ploughman's Complaint of the Abuses of the World' — no small matter and no small book. It was written between 1556 and 1559 by John Foxe, an exile on the Continent from Queen Mary, as a panegyric for the Protestant martyrs of that reign. There were several in Sussex but none, so far as I know, from Guestling. Foxe came into his reward, prebendall stalls, in Elizabeth's reign; the martyrs one hopes are enjoying their's now.

* In 1571, it was ordered that a copy of Foxe's book be placed in all cathedrals (says Professor Owen Chadwick); many parish incumbents followed suit, among them Thomas Staffer, rector here from 1566 to 1572.

Hamsey Old Church must be on the edge of redundancy. It stands, as it has since the 12th century, on a slight mound in an oxbow formed by the river Ouse above Lewes. To reach it, one has first to pass through Hamseyplace Farm (16th century and Stella Gibbons' Cold Comfort Farm, if ever I saw it) where, in a cowshed, the key of the church is reputed to be found. Of course, one only learns of this when one has reached the church some distance further on.

The church is a miracle of unaltered survival since the last major change in the 15th century when the strong west tower was added to the Norman nave and the elegant Perpendicular east window was put in. I say Norman nave because there is an undeniable Norman arch between nave and chancel and also a couple of Norman windows remaining. The rest of the windows are lancet which supports the alternative contention that the church was built in the 13th century by the de Says.

The tower is splendid and dominates the meadows around, blue with the newly-fashionable crop of linseed when I was there. Solidly built of stone, whereas the rest of the church is rendered flint, the tower is now defenestrated after the bells had been taken down. It is an oddity that the interior faces of this structure are resolutely unfinished and pitted with put-log holes. I suppose there is no more reason for scaffolding being on the outside than the inside but the latter is unusual, I am sure.

The church is wonderfully spare and atmospheric inside — no electricity, no pulpit, no lectern and no movables; in 1347 a chalice was stolen by a parson from St John sub Castro in Lewes! There are few pews, some of extreme antiquity and discomfort. There are memorials though — hatchments in the nave and wall tablets in the chancel to members of the families of the successive local squirearchy. One memorial precedes them; a chest tomb under its canopy in the recess in the north wall of the chancel. Argument surrounds this important feature. It is known as the de Say or Founder's tomb but Robert Chapman, writing in 1865 in the Sussex Archaeological Collections, considered its mouldings too recent to be ascribed to the 14th century. He said it is Tudor and attributed it to a member of the Lewknor family, probably he who was 'Groom Porter' to Edward VI. There are similar chest tombs of the Lewknor family elsewhere in the county, says Mr Chapman.

He also commented unfavourably on the state of the church in his 1865 report — it was, he said, 'so far dilapidated as to be unfit for worship'. That must be why the Shiffners, the last of the squires here, had their 'elegant modern church' built close by at Offham. How could they abandon a church where their ancestors lay in serried ranks? To-day there is no dilapidation. Even the barn like roof timbers have been treated to the extent of invisible reinforcement by steel girders and the roofs re-covered with clay tiles in place of much of the sandstone Horsham slates which did duty before. Cared for as it obviously now is, Hamsey Old Church could grace the valley of the Ouse for generations to come, can we but rely on our descendants and their descendants.

The Almighty, or one of his lieutenants more likely, was on my side when I came here to sketch. Locked, naturally, with the key hidden in that cowshed, my visit fortunately coincided with the arrival of the local organiser of musical evenings here who had come to check his arrangements. He was surprisingly accommodating and my intrusion was not in the least resented and the finer points of internal put-log holes and the invisible reinforcement of beams were happily discussed as we wandered within this Sussex time capsule (if I may be permitted such an awful cliche). I am sure the musical evenings will be a sell-out*. What more enchanting way to spend a summer evening than listening to the Elizabethan songs of John Dowland in this venerable place. The Tudor Lewknors would surely agree.

* I have since learnt that the concerts raised £1,000 for the upkeep of the church.

FRISTON
St Mary the Virgin

Furze farmstead

Friston is one of those small churches without a village. I doubt if it ever had one and since 1688 it has not had its own vicar either. That it stands where it is, just aside from the Eastbourne/Seaford road with its relentless traffic, is due to one Fritha, a Saxon landowner who established his 'tun' or farmstead here; a pity he couldn't foresee the traffic. Later grandees, notably the fertile Selwyn family, have ensured that the church is worth coming to see — and to preserve, one must add.

Fritha's church may have been made of wood, it probably was, but later Saxons in the reign of Edward the Confessor graduated to stone, the evidence for which is still present over 900 years later. The stone used is flint although now there seems to be rather more mortar than flint which, incidentally, is a sign of antiquity, I believe. The quoins are of dressed stone, some of sufficient substance to suggest they were put there by the Saxons who had a penchant for large stones. One can still see, beside the south porch, some of the voussoir stones of their original south doorway and, close by, their tiny slit window.

The general plan is compact, as it should be for a church without a village — a small nave, a smaller chancel and a modest Victorian north transeptal chapel plus, of course, the south porch now embowered with rambler roses like any cottage. Inside lies the interest; ancient grafitti in the porch (difficult to relate the faint scratchings to what they are said to represent), a segmental chancel arch (that is an arch made from the chord of a circle) and two matching arches, north and south in the chancel, leading to nowhere. Behind the altar is a third arched recess necessitating a reduced east window above. Over all, the centuries-old oak beams arch across to support the tiled roof and tiny timber belfry. It is all very cosy in here, designed for a limited but historically choice congregation.

Apart from the intimate architecture, it is the Selwyns that one comes to see, as presumably did the two entrants in the visitors' book before me — one from Dusseldorf, the other from Frankfurt. In the Stuart days of the pomp of the Selwyns, Eastbourne must have needed a day's journey and London was a far-away place, little known. Lack of a village to-day need no longer result in isolation and the church was, to my surprise and relief, unlocked and open to all comers.

To return to the Selwyns from this cosmopolitan digression, first chronologically are the brasses of Thomas Selwyn, †1525, and his wife, †1562, which now hang by the Saxon window; the next a stone 'rather forlorn' (which I failed to see); and thence to the transferred memorials in the transeptal chapel. That on the west wall consists of the kneeling effigies of another Thomas and his wife; immediately between them are their three babies on a pillow, identially wrapped in swaddling clothes, and finally as a dado to the composition, their six kneeling daughters, hands uniformly clasped in prayer. It is a monumental piece. Opposite the group, on the facing wall, is a large marble slab copiously inscribed in Latin, commemorating Francis Selwyn and his wife and their children. The latter add up to 7 sons and 8 daughters — a total that makes one wonder how so numerous a family could ever die out and leave no further generations to populate their church.

For a church that stands on the hinterland of the downs, only a mile from the chalk cliffs of the Seven Sisters, I suppose one should not be surprised to find a simple wooden cross in the churchyard briefly marked 'washed ashore'. It seems rather sad to be so anonymously buried, but if it has to be, Friston is no bad place in which to lie. 'AB' also intended to be anonymous, no doubt; was he in charge of the well-kept churchyard in his day, one wonders.

Even in summer one can understand why Friston church has such a snugly diminutive belfry, barely topping the roof line. The wind must blow across the Downs from the sea with ferocity in winter — as the wind-blown trees acknowledge.

IN MEMORY OF AB
WHO LOVED
THE VIEW
1938

Well insulated from the busy road where this runs down to Rye, Playden church stands undisturbed in a large haphazard churchyard of assorted trees. Dominant in this oasis of calm is the church's axial tower, placed on the centre-line between nave and chancel. This tall, almost exaggerated, spire is very sharply broached and, I would imagine, is a later addition to the work of the 13th century masons. The church guide thoughtfully contains an illustration of the complicated timber frame needed to stabilise such an elongated structure. Viewed from the east, it is said ominously to be 'out of the perpendicular'. A further idiosyncracy to strike one on first acquaintance is the series of triangular buttresses that support the huge catslide roof which encompasses both nave and aisles. That the buttresses are necessary is evident inside where the aisle walls seem to be unable to withstand the thrust of the roof without assistance. There are in total six supplementary buttresses on either side; they were added in the 17th century when presumably the catslide roof replaced separate aisle roofs. Although valleys between roofs often lead to trouble, so also do overarching roofs of the dimensions of this one here. Let's hope the buttresses continue the good work of the last three hundred years — there's not room for any more.

The internal architecture is equally interesting and liable to misinterpretation by such as myself. It is the arcade and tower arches that pose the problem. The nave is four bays long with semi-circular Norman arches for three on either side but completed at the west end by pointed arches. So one might conclude, as I do, that the west end of the nave is an afterthought. But the central tower, said by the Sussex Historic Churches Trust to precede the nave, sits firmly above pointed arches. My own conclusion, for what its worth, is that the Norman arches came first but before the tower and west end could be completed, there was a change of master mason and the new man had the latest ideas and incorprated them here by his pointed arches. I expect the Trust is in the right but, in that case, it does seem to put the cart before the horse.

As always with central towers, the lack of an external stair turret presents problems of access to the bells. Here they have solved it by a precipitous, primitive ladder arrangement in the crossing. Its date is uncertain, maybe 17th century, but anyway prior to the three bells above. There was apparently a fourth but this, being cracked, was generously bestowed on East Guldeford where possibly it is the only bell*. Other woodwork of note are two medieval screens, both in my opinion more remarkable for their extreme antiquity than for their elegance. Pevsner describes one as coarse — rustic and rudimentary would be my description. Playden is after all only a modest parish, still without a shop, and the screens are honourably old.

Except for one window, all the glass in the church is clear. One in the chancel is engraved to serve as a memorial to a naval officer who lost his life in HMS Barham when she was torpedoed and blew up in 1941. About 1800 others perished with him; this window, with its ship's badges and silhouette of the battleship, could be said to be their memorial too.

Near enough to cast its shadow on this window is a large, branching tree which I identified, rather uncertainly, as a willow oak. At its base are attached some large, sinister, parasitic plates of fungus. They reminded me of a recent newspaper report (July 1992) about a fungus that is destroying the forests of Ponderosa pine in Washington State, USA. This fungus, most of which is underground, extends as one individual over an area roughly equivalent to four London parks, is 1,000 years old and is still growing; it sounds very alarming. At Playden there is fortunately St Michael for protection; in Washington State there cannot be many parish churches, with their dedicated patron saints, which may account for the devilish growth there.

---

* Apart, that is, from the small, non-operational bell which was liberated from a wrecked coastal vessel.

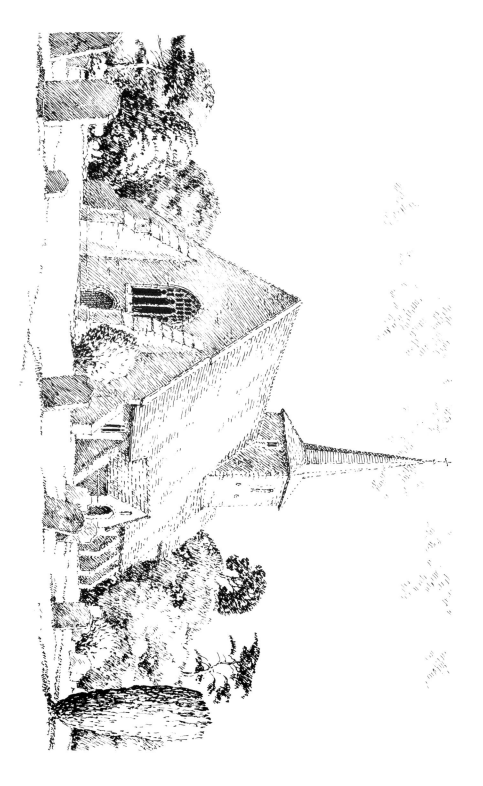

Ripe is an attractive little hamlet, centred around a crossroads in the level farmland between the Ouse and Cuckmere rivers. At its eastern approach the church, with a Perpendicular tower that can bear comparison with any, stands sentinel.

And that tall tower with its Pelham buckles as label stops to its western doorway is the essence of St John's as far as I was concerned for the blank outer porch door was firmly and anonymously locked. Entry within by the unauthorised was clearly not popular. It is mistaken, though, to become upset at a locked church with no hint as to where the key may be found. No doubt Ripe church is open when its parishioners want it to be open and locked when they don't; the expectations of some passing Tom, Dick or Harry (such as your author) must take second place to security against vandalism and theft. If that results in the denial of admission, the fault lies with a lawless society and not with officers of the parish. As a policy it may not reflect the ethos of the Church; it is nevertheless realistic and a disappointed deprivation must be an acceptable price to pay for preservation. Such was the homily I read myself as I struggled with some nettles to peer through a nave window. The nettles stung all the same; they are guardians too. What's more, they are always 'en poste'. The ubiquitous nettle is the plant most actively hostile to humans. They seem like John Wyndham's Tryffids, only less mobile, although they do spread in their own good time — remorselessly.

To return to the tower — it presents an uncompromisingly confident air of consequence. Less than a mile away to the east, little Chalvington's weather-boarded bell turret may seem more appropriate to the rural situation; the grandeur of this tower here could owe something to those Pelham buckles, I don't doubt. One could hardly imagine the 15th century Pelhams putting their signature to anything less. Above the door, in the spandrels of the doorcase, are two stone shields. One bears a 'bend sinister', the other a 'bend dexter'. These charges, my little Observer's Book of Heraldry tells me, are 'ordinaries the simplest and oldest charges and the most important' — another explanation, maybe, for a tower that seems somewhat extravagant for a church on the edge of a rural hamlet. Not least for an excluded sketcher, the tower has a clock with a particularly melodious chime to mark the quarter hours.

The rest of the church, nave and chancel, precedes the tower, being Decorated with a very flamboyant east window. The other windows are more modestly Perpendicular from which one infers reconstruction when the tower was added. The walls are uncoursed rubblestone for the nave and flint for the chancel, rendered on the south side, bare on the north — all in marked contrast to the orderly rows of dressed blocks that make up the tower.

From what one can see of the interior through the clear glass of the nave windows, there seems little to get excited about. I could just discern some sort of open gallery at the base of the tower, for a choir perhaps, but was denied a sight of the recess beside the chancel arch. The purpose of this recess seems to have puzzled Pevsner from which I think one can take it he got inside and didn't simply repeat an earlier commentary — as I have been obliged to do.

One can't, or shouldn't, leave Ripe without sparing an admiring glance at the several handsome houses that constitute the village, one of which appeared to carry the famous buckles in its porch doorway. Especially rivetting is the front facade of The Old Cottage with its storeyed porch, jetties, carved figures, ornamented fascia boards and noggin brickwork between the black timbers. Surely it qualifies for inclusion in any Sussex gazetteer of historic timber-framed buildings. I am very happy to include it in my amateur's gazetteer of some east Sussex churches.

WESTFIELD
St John the Baptist

This church, at the southern end of its extended village not far from Hastings, is chiefly remarkable for the outsize buttresses that were found necessary to keep it upright. The ground here is not marshy or low-lying so why such elephantiasis waxed is not clear to the uninitiated. The buttresses are concentrated on the west tower and the south facade. The tower is Norman but the church guide hints that it is a Norman superstructure on a Saxon base of insufficient dimensions to support the extra weight. The interior dimensions are approximately a modest 9 feet square. With the buttresses not far short of 9 ft square attached to walls of over 3 feet in thickness, the net result is a tower that consists more of clasping stonework than it does of space inside. In the immortal words of Field Marshall Montgomery they do seem to have 'over-egged the omelette' in the 13th century. Could there have been some sort of ground instability rather than lack of confidence in the Saxon masonry to provoke such insurance. It can't have been the dynamics of swinging bells because the first came in 1350 and the second not until 1698. Three similar gargantuan buttresses are distributed along the southern side of the church; these are dated as 17th centiury which does rather suggest that the 13th century alarms were repeated four hundred years later producing much the same reaction. Strangely there are no buttresses on the north side, all of which tends to give this little church a very distinctive, if lop-sided, identity.

Forgetting the buttresses for a moment, if one can, the lych-gate must first secure the visitor's admiration. It is a monument to Victorian craftmanship — an open tiled roof supported by king posts and carved angels that would grace the rafters of any nave. It is followed by a brick path lined with topiary yews that lead one to the 14th century porch. Here one meets another minor masterpiece — a blackened door proudly dated 1542 (two years after the execution of Thomas Cromwell, that scourge of surplus ecclesiastics. A celebration?).

Within the door, one is immediately reminded of the church's Norman ancestry by the arcade of three Norman arches which announce the north aisle. The arches rest on cylindrical pillars and are flanked at the responds by elegant foliated columns. Very handsome and substantial it all looks. The north aisle beyond is, it turns out, Victorian; ergo the Norman arches are, too. However it is appropriate that the latter should be Romanesque for the arch to the chancel is genuine Norman. This is supported by capitalled columns, moulded on the nave side, plain on the chancel side, and flanked by a squint on either side. Who could pierce an ancient wall and install unmatching arches to a new aisle when confronted by this majestic chancel arch. Foe once, evidently, the Victorians were not opinionated and bowed to compatability.

Although there are no memorials to trouble the antiquarian (as they say of the scorer after a batsman has failed to score), they did, the Victorians again I presume, place a few churchyard headstones as paving by the chancel arch to make good the absence of ledger stones — a praiseworthy effort to which the departed could hardly object. Overhead, the chancel ceiling is comprehensively coloured as are the organ pipes on their concave plinth behind the silvery oak choirstalls. Both matching decorations successfully contribute to the embellishment of this important part of the church. But then a church so carefully buttressed externally deserves the return of the compliment inside.

Such are my superficial observations after only a couple of hours or so at Westfield, much of which was spent gazing across the long grass that covers most of the churchyard; where incidentally the local WI took the trouble to record such botanical familiars as lords and ladies, bluebell, celandine and cuckoopint. I am all for long grass.

A brief acquaintance like mine makes one wonder how long the Pevsners, the Betjemans and the Mees of the reference books also spent with their quarries as they progressed magisterially around the countryside to pronounce on the highlights. Which, of course, never failed to include the village church. I am all for them, too, needless to say.

PLUMPTON
St Michael and All Angels

Plum farmstead

For many, I fancy Plumpton means steeplechasing in winter; for those living locally, Plumpton probably means the Agricultural College but, for me, it means a compact flint church, under the lee of the Downs, enclosed within the territorial compass of the College's Horticultural Division.

The church sits snugly by two spreading sycamores and a little iron gate. It is old and small; a 12th century nave, a 13th century chancel and west tower and a Tudor porch complete its basic essentials. To the unpractised eye, the tower looks the most antique. It is supported at the west end by two large buttresses — that to the north fairly obviously an addition with a line of quoin stones marking the original edge of the tower; that to the south seems to have grown organically with no junction apparent. Both in fact are 14th century reinforcements. Other buttresses, especially those on the north side where the nave wall leans visibly outward, are roofed with tiles which almost disguises their function.

There is a considerable aura of charm to the rustic appearance and situation of St Michael's so it is quite understandable that conscientious efforts should be made to preserve the integrity of the medieval fabric — indeed one might say its cretaceous fabric, since most of it is composed of the petrified fragments of sponges that 100 million years of geological compression have turned into iron-hard flints. Nevertheless, attention must be paid to the insidious effects of even a few years of damp and, while I was there, two young men were laying brick gulleys, digging trenches and soak-aways and uprooting, unavoidably, several old headstones in the process. Their excavations to channel their drainage laid bare much of the foundations which, to my surprise looked exiguous, not to say virtually non-existent. In effect the church seems to squat squarely on the Sussex turf like a plump partridge, anchored only by gravity. I have often wondered how deep buttresses go; now I know — more or less nowhere.

Although this church, shaded by its two great sycamores against a backdrop of the steep slope of the Downs, is evocative enough for anyone to be captivated by its weathered appearance, it is the interior which is probably the more important from an antiquarian point of view. The key is therefore a necessity and fortunately the Horticultural Department's shop will come to the rescue, as it did for me.

A pleasantly unassuming, windowless, little brick porch, eminently suitable for a population of less than 300 when it was built, leads one to an equally spartan interior with no architectural feature dominant unless it is the one remaining Norman window, the last of four, high on the north wall of the nave. A curiosity which I failed to observe are the box pews now said to be lining the ceiling of the nave. They would be better on the floor where their replacements are distinctly pedestrian. But what arouses the interest of the scholar, and everybody really, especially those with good eyesight, are the wall paintings shining fitfully through the whitewash. They were discovered by Eric Rouse FSA who thoughtfully provided accomplished water-colour reproductions; these latter now hang framed by the chancel arch so one can see what the Anglo-Norman frescoes looked like in 1955 when revealed under layers of coloured wash. Nearly 40 years later the most visible remnant is the pink scroll work that decorates the inside splay of the Norman window. Money is now wanted to restore the paintings although, when that is done, can one then be sure that one is looking at Anglo-Norman work or a 20th century reproduction. I think I would prefer to rely on Mr Rouse's water-colours with the originals left untouched in their barely-perceptible antique purity.

Now, with the recent protection against rising damp, harsh and garish though it may look until weathered, this church should be secure against decay and dilapidation; all that is needed is regular attendance to air the interior but that might be the most uncertain factor of all.

When I descended on Westmeston, the rain also descended, without the hoped-for intermission. Rain, however slight, makes sketching impossible unless there is some sort of shelter. At Westmeston, the 14th century porch offered the essential protection, hence this close-up of the north doorway. Although hardly panoramic, it is a very nice little porch with timbers that would not disgrace the ribs of the Victory.

One cannot, though, get an idea of the whole church from an interior view of a porch, however impressive its members may be. The church, to be exact, consists of a chancel, south aisle and nave topped by a simple wooden bell turret at the west end. The north wall is Norman and the west and south walls are 14th century like the porch. Apart from the quoin stones, all is flint, covered by patches of rendering. The windows are a mixture of lancet and Perpendicular but mostly look new as the Victorians were very much at work here in the 1860s. The fearsome feline head that projects as a waterspout between chancel and vestry looks like their handiwork it is so undefaced. The roof is part tiles and part Horsham stone, sliding down over the aisle to kiss the churchyard turf. There is no sign of dilapidation or neglect except perhaps in the case of some cast-iron grave crosses which lie about forsaken; sepulchral iron-work never enjoys as much respect as stone, in my experience, especially railings around graves which so often seem to have been a target for re-cycling. Railings, the Churchyard Handbook tells one, should be 'retained and kept painted'. They may also be listed as 'being of special architectural or historical interest' — provided always that they have survived.

The interior is resolutely Victorian; pews, floor, arches*, unblemished plaster, stained glass and memorials all look, in the words of Pevsner, 'over restored'. One could not disagree with that verdict when one has come to see the wall paintings and find they no longer exist. Fortunately, they were imperishably recorded in 1862 by the Revd C H Campion in the pages of Volume XVI of the Sussex Archaeological Collections. He carefully exposed all of them from under coats of yellow, white and blue wash. They consisted of texts and figurative paintings, including the Scourging and the Crucifixion and they covered most of the nave walls. The paintings were mid-12th century and the texts early Reformation, Mr Campion concludes. He cautioned then against their loss; they were, he said, 'the books of the unlearned'. Now they are no more except in the pages of the Collections.

Memorials are few; three pavement slabs in the south aisle and a couple of wall plaques. My imagination was caught by that to a vicar who died in Milan 'after a long and painful illness'. It reminded me, quite unfairly, of Trollope's the Revd Dr Vesey Stanhope who conducted his Barchester diocesan duties for 12 years from the seclusion of Lake Como until summarily extracted from there by Mr Slope. Reality is restored by a splendid Victorian bale-cum-gabled chest tomb in the churchyard. It can't be overlooked nor, presumably, did the Cripps family intend it should be.

A notice in the lych-gate tells the visitor that the churchyard here is a wild-life conservation area upon which no weed killer or chemical fertiliser (I expect there have been sheep) has been used since 1103 — a very precise date only to be questioned by the over-scrupulous. The church in its churchyard stands at a sharp bend in the road. Immediately opposite to the south west looms Ditchling Beacon while to the south east, planted in 1897 to commemorate Queen Victoria's Diamond Jubilee, is a plantation of spruce firs descending the slope of the Downs in the shape of a conspicuous V.

What a pity it rained; and how sad the paintings have not survived. The Revd Campion would have been disappointed and so was I.

---

*   According to Mr Campion, the chancel arch in his day was 'small, semi-circular and constructed of rubble without quoin stones'. To-day it is large and hard-edged Victorian Gothic.

EAST CHILTINGTON
Farmstead of Cilta's people

Dedication not known, by me or Pevsner apparently

One finds East Chiltington with difficulty. It is in the middle of nowhere, inconspicuous and rather by itself; felix East Chiltington.*

As befits its rural situation, the church is small and simple, just a nave, chancel and stumpy west tower, set at the end of a lane leading to a distant farmhouse. There is one large house, unobtrusively screened, and an elegant lodge at the farm gate. In the latter, to my good fortune, lives the churchwarden.

The nave of the church is Norman, vide a typical window beside the porch and north and south doorways, the former now blocked. The tower is 13th century (put-log holes still unblocked) and the chancel Decorated where it hasn't been renewed. When I was there, they were 'out of the history' but not of inscribed dates — for instance, the central of the three substantial tie beams that hold the walls together is dated 1669, the pulpit 1719, the lych-gate 1913 (its timbers are the next job for the resourceful churchwarden) and the lords of the manor and previous churchwardens held office for 125 years from 1854 to 1979.

Of the confined interior, it seemed to me that the most noteworthy feature is the solid and handsome screen separating the nave from the tower base; there is no such grandeur between nave and chancel. The chancel and tower arches are pointed and would look, from their crisp moulding, to result from the 1890s restoration. There is only one memorial, that to the lords of the manor, otherwise all is prim and proper but not exactly spellbinding in human terms. One fears to describe the domain of the lords of the manor as bucolic tranquillity but that might not be inaccurate or convey a false impression. I hope I do not do East Chiltington an injustice but peace and quiet must be the keynote here.

Perhaps as a result, this little church turns out to be more interesting externally than internally. For one thing, there are no windows on the north side, nor any sign that there ever have been, which is unique in my experience. My acquaintance the churchwarden drew my attention to the brownish stonework which I had taken to be sandstone. It was, he said, known locally as winklestone or more properly Sussex marble. At close range, one can see that the stones consist of a mass of consolidated winkles or small snail shells, presumably laid down when the Weald was in one of its submarine phases. Reference to Alec Clifton-Taylor's 'English Stone Building' discovers no mention of winklestone; marble, he says, contains no fossil traces so winklestone and marble are not synonymous. He does say, however, that in the Lower Chalk (and we are here in the lee of the Downs) there are some 'compact beds which contain tiny fragments of shells and other impurities . . .' So maybe that is what winklestone is. It is fascinating to contemplate these rough stones, laid down by deposition 100 million years ago, erected by the Normans nearly 1,000 years ago and still of service to-day.

Around the churchyard runs a low, intact flint wall. Charles Lyall, the Victorian professor of geology who taught us what we stand upon, and Alfred Wegener, the German whose theory of continental drift explained how what we stand upon came to be as it is, would have had no difficulty with fossilised winkles and sponges supporting a Christian church. But possibly Archbishop Ussher, who calculated the age of the earth as 6,000 years, might have taken exception to such disturbing theories. Still, it is not fair to disparage the archbishop; he did flourish in 1600, long before geology had come to question truth as revealed in the Bible. Rightly or wrongly, we could do with a few of the archbishop's certainties to-day in our scientific age of uncertainty. At all events there is durability in winkles.

* Daily Telegraph, 29 December 1992 — Not so felix apparently; the threat of increased sand quarrying has caused upset locally.

WESTHAM
St Mary

West water meadow

The name Westham must derive from the fact that here were once the low-lying meadows that watered the western gate of the Roman fort of Pevensey. The church of St Mary now stands on its meadow in its nice village corner within bowshot of the crumbling walls of the fort's outer bailey balancing its opposite number, St Nicholas, at the eastern entrance to the castle. The approach, though, from Polegate is an awful warning against living too close to the south coast in the 20th century; with luck, before too long the ribbon development will have gone leaving the church and the Roman walls untrammelled again in their glory.

After the Romans, the next recorded occupants of the fort, 500 years later, were Normans almost immediately after the Conquest. They first built their own fortress, as a keep, within the Roman walls and 'very soon' this handsome and substantial church at the western gate — why not inside, I wonder, there is plenty of room. What remains of their church building is the south wall of the nave, cobbled in herring-bone courses with shingle from the sea shore, above and below a string course. Above the string is a trio of Norman windows and one Perpendicular window where the fourth previously let in its modicum of light. It is we who need light now — to read the printed word. Unlettered faith can manage without. Below the string, the wall is blank as is the south doorway. Not far away, deep in the grass, lie four inconspicuous stones at the four extremities of an imaginary cross. They are, the guide says, plague stones marking the site of a pit for the communal burial of victims of the plague — a plot, the guide continues, where the old sexton was reluctant to dig. Who can blame him.

Still standing rather bleakly beside the Norman nave is the Lady Chapel to which is still attached a fragment of walling that once constituted an apse to the southern transept. Pevsner suggests that originally the Normans built a cruciform church here with north and south apsidal transepts and an apse to the chancel. However, about 1300, all this was changed with the addition of a north aisle which effectively eliminated the north transept and left us the distinguished Perpendicular facade that I have attempted to reproduce. It was then that the four-square tower, with its chequered pattern of stone and flint, was attached at the west end to loom benevolently over the cottages beyond. The apses have all but disappeared, as they have almost everywhere else; no doubt they smacked too much of Continental architecture at a time when England was striving to assert its own native genius.

Inside, the impression is of empty space more appropriate to a castle stronghold than to what must have been a tiny hamlet when the church was building. Of the memorials, the most prestigious is the altar stone on its huge carved oak table in the Lady Chapel. Apparently, until rescued by a vicar who noticed its consecration crosses, it was used to pave the floor of the church and had, as well, done duty in the 17th century as a gravestone for another vicar, †1602. He must have been a Puritan, certainly an iconoclast. On the chancel floor are two stone coffin lids with foliate crosses; they are described as 'Ecclesiastical Stones', recovered from elsewhere and one of which was also appropriated for a gravestone. They can't have been too scrupulous in the 17th century if their cavalier treatment of other people's memorials is anything to go by; we are more cautious to-day. Indeed, I doubt if we would go so far as the Victorian vicar who happened on Solomon's Temple in Jerusalem while it was being excavated. In passing, he took the opportunity to rescue a fragment of the temple stone, which had 'fallen off the back of a barrow', I dare say. This piece, two inches square, smooth to the touch, now rests encased in onyx in the splay of one of the chancel windows. All stone is old but this piece in Westham church, itself 900 years old, must have been in use 3,000 years ago. It is odd and fascinating to find an Old Testament fragment from the first national shrine of the Jewish religion proudly preserved in a Christian church. To-day we might call it ecumenicalism. The Revd Howard Hopley was ahead of his time.

CLAYTON
St John the Baptist

Clay farmstead

Clayton church has been lucky. Standing immediately under the north slope of the Downs, it can only have been saved from extinction at the hands of the London to Brighton railway by the tunnel almost directly below. Of this monstrosity one is blissfully unaware as one contemplates this little Saxon church from across the winding lane that follows the contours of the slope back to Lewes.

What confronts one initially is the handsome lych-gate — Horsham slabs resting on solid oak timbers, king post in arrangement. It dates from 1919 and is the village memorial to those who fell in the wars of 1914 and 1939 and, more recently, the 1982 campaign to recover the Falkland Islands. The memorial does the fallen and the village credit.

Beyond, tall and lean, rises the 900 year-old church. Its walls are austere and plain, flint under limewash rendering with only a few irregularly placed windows and a neat gabled porch to distract the eye. There is but one buttress to the whole church to emphasise what reliable builders the Saxons were. Above, are roofs of Horsham slabs replaced towards the ridges by clay tiles plus, as a western finial, a simple shingled bell turret. Nothing to get excited about one might think but, if the height of the nave and chancel do not give pause for thought, the interior of the porch certainly should. Here, a detached, arched tie beam and low, round-headed doorway really do give the feel of stepping into the past. (Next-door Westmeston has a strikingly similar porch). The church guide makes the interesting point that 'Saxon doorways were usually straight-through with no rebates to combat draughts.' On the basis of that definition, the guide concludes that this doorway is Norman. If that is the case, as the guide suggests, the Saxons must have had access through an earlier doorway. Yes indeed, and probably opposite, where the entrance to the vestry now is.

Past the doorway, one steps further into the past, some of which has been preserved, some eradicated. Eradicated were the box pews and west gallery as a framed water-colour of 1890 makes clear. Gone also are the north and south transeptal chapels as traces of their arches affirm. Gone, too, or rather blocked up and hidden by memorial wall tablets are two Norman windows in the chancel. Nevertheless, these changes, old and new, cannot banish the atmosphere of extreme antiquity that pervades the tall, narrow nave. To that we are indebted primarily to the faded paintings that cover the walls and also to the great chancel arch about which there seems to be no chronological ambiguity. Pevsner puts it at 11th century; so does the guide and my 'Notes' say Saxon as do the others and all agree that it is pre-Conquest. As the guide declares 'it has a dignity of design' that impresses the spirit not to mention its evident age that concentrates the mind.

And all around are the famous paintings of figures in fugitive outlines. They cover the upper parts of the north and south walls of the nave and the chancel arch. They are said to reflect Byzantine influence — if so, they infer a remarkable spread of culture from the Mediterranean to 11th century Britain. Equally remarkable, they were only discovered in 1895; think of all those years when they lay unobserved under coats of limewash in this unassuming little church in its quiet hamlet under the Downs. (Did the discovery post-date the railway?) The central feature of the paintings, above the arch as is appropriate, is the Doom or Day of Judgement. The uncertain outcome of such an awful occasion must explain, I think, the sad and apprehensive look on the faces of those depicted. Their painters plainly dreaded what might befall some, or even, themselves.

The continued, lingering presence of the Day of Judgement on the walls here, as elsewhere in other fortunate churches, seems to confirm Kafka's eschatological comment on the Day — 'in reality it is a summary court in perpetual session'. That is a sobering thought, as presumably these wall paintings were always intended to convey.

124

WEST GRINSTEAD
St George

West green place

South of that crowded ribbon of road that horizontally bisects Sussex, in the peace of the prosperous country that lies about the upper reaches of the Adur river, one finds West Ginstead church. There is no village, just a few grandish establishments and some cottages across the river; why then a church here? It is Norman in origin which, I feel, confers some sort of association with the ruins of Knapp Castle, once the stronghold of de Broaze, administrators of the Rape of Bramber after the Conquest, and a hunting lodge of King John. The Normans have long gone but their church remains, a monument to their faith and the staying power of religion, albeit now of a slightly different persuasion.

Externally, the evidence of their building is found in the crude herring-bone courses west of the celebrated 15th century porch. I can't remember anything quite so rough and ready. Further evidence is found on the south side where a mutilated Norman doorway once gave access to the south aisle. We are lucky to see this doorway, I suspect. The rest of the southern facade, including the tower and its pilasters, is submerged in a heavy coat of cement which effectively conceals what lies below — more herring-bone possibly. Nevertheless the grey uniformity of the rendering cannot suppress the strength of the 13th century tower, its idiosyncratic double-broach spire or its unusual position between aisle and chapel.

Inside, one, or rather we, were greeted by that incense of old churches, the odour of damp and centuries of use; eyes closed, one would infallibly sense that one was standing in a medieval church. This church consists essentially of two equal parallel compartments, the north comprising nave and chancel, the south, the aisle, the tower and chapel or 'Manorial Burying Place'. We shall come to the last in a moment but first one must remark on two things. Floors are important everywhere, in churches as much as anywhere. Stone flags, as here mostly, are better than wooden boards, ledger stones are an improvement on plain flags and armorial stones better than those of simple textual inscription. Regrettably the use of ledger stones seems to have been discontinued; except here where lies a new one dated 1979 — hurrah! Similarly pews are better than chairs in a church and box pews better than bench pews, even those with carved bench ends. Here the pews are identified by the name plates of local houses. I wonder did any non-resident ever presume to sit in one of them.

But to anyone of an antiquarian bent, the south half of the church is most stimulating. In the chapel one finds two immense, low chest tombs complete with canopied brasses, virtually all intact. Their dates are 1395 and 1441. One of those portrayed, Sir Hugh Halsham, is recorded on the rolls of those who fought at Agincourt. Even then, there was a secretariat (clerical no doubt) efficient enough to enforce feudal obligations and record their satisfaction. Our equivalents to-day are conscription and campaign medals. In the aisle, the memorials are no longer medieval (although there are a couple of brass indents in the paving) but more sculpted, life-like or overbearing; in particular that of Sir William Burrell, †1796, the antiquarian grandee, thwarted by death. He is commemorated by a grandiose conception from Flaxman that, if not altogether as successful, is at least arresting. Sadly, a figurative Merrik Burrell, †1787, is so damaged that what Pevsner describes as 'a kindly perriwigged face full of wrinkles' no longer exists to look down on the aisle. There is, what cannot be overlooked, an ancient chest, hollowed out of a solid baulk of timber, which must be older than all and co-eval with the remnants of wall painting in the nave. For a church without a village, it is all rather remarkable and a monument to the lords, down the centuries, of Knapp Castle.

We had a picnic here with old friends of 50 years or more. Watched from a safe distance by the suspicious local dogs but by no more, so far as one could tell, one half expected to see King John, with his hunting party, or William Burrell, with his note book, come into view. We could have offered them a glass of sherry.

126

If it wasn't for the Gage family, I fear that West Firle church would be something of a disappointment. It shouldn't be. What could be more promising than a downland village, under Firle Beacon to be exact, through which there no longer runs a through road and which is protected by an ancestral park.

And furthermore, St Peter's is a church to which the 12th, 13th, 14th, 15th, 16th, 17th and 20th centuries have all made their separate contributions. The walls should be pure history but, as one looks at the adamantine flints and ublemished pointing of the south aisle, it might also be mistaken for Victorian rather than the 15th century work which the guide says it is. The handsome, open, leaf-strewn south porch, of the same period, does look its age and one might be tempted to sketch just that. The tower, substantial and heavily buttressed, is part of the work in the 13th century and undoubtedly does present a commanding aspect as one approaches from the west. Its buttresses may match, north and south, but they are separated by the lapse of 300 years. The north, Gage, chapel which is dated as 16th century looked to my unpractised eye to be the oldest part of the church but one can't argue with the guide. What is genuinely old is the north doorway which, since it bears the marks of a scratch dial, must have come from elsewhere where the sun can strike. So much for the exterior of a church, dark with the unyielding flint, that shows little sign of the wear and tear of centuries of weather. Perhaps the Gages, who have been here since the 15th century and still are, saw to it that maintenance was timely and adequate. The tower buttresses could be a case in point.

Through then to the interior, as much Gage territory as is their park. The spacious nave consists of four bays separated from the flanking aisles by identical octagonal columns above which are identical small, round clerestory windows. The ceiling is dark and boarded and, together with the low aisle windows, creates a rather sombre and commonplace effect, commonplace in archeological terms that is. Perhaps unremarkable traditional would be a more polite description. However, any mediocrity should be thoroughly dispelled by the north chapel. Before one can even enter, one encounters three Gage brasses against the chapel wall, either side of the doorway. They date from 1476; the earliest being that to Bartholomew Bolney through whose daughter the Gages came to acquire the estate. After Bolney, the Gages have held undisputed sway in their chapel. They are interred under three bulky altar tombs, two of which carry brasses on their surface, difficult to make out against the diffused light from John Piper's colourful window. The third tomb, dividing the chancel from the chapel, is a magnificent elaboration of polished, gleaming alabaster. On it lie, in conventional attitudes, Sir John Gage, †1556, and his wife Philippa. She has the luxury of a cushion for her headrest; he a more spartan pillow of rolled-up platted matting. Sculpted matting is apparently customary in Dutch monuments (the sculptor was Dutch) but it does present the problem of inscribing the pattern where a chisel can only reach with difficulty. The whole arrangement is so outstanding that its sculptor can hardly have expected it to escape notice and admiration and close scrutiny. Indeed, I don't doubt he regarded as much as his due.

The Gages rest in style here at Firle but the status implied is not always a bed of roses. For instance, Sir John when Constable of the Tower was obliged to preside at the execution of his kinswoman, Lady Jane Grey. His son, as High Sheriff, was one of those who condemned the Sussex martyrs to the stake. High office has its rigous as well as its rewards as this chapel at Firle and history remind us.

If Arthur Mee is right, the Gages have yet another memorial to add to those brasses here — that delicious plum of theirs, the greengage.

PYECOMBE
The Transfiguration of Our Lord

The essence of this little church on top of the Downs is simplicity. There are no unnecessary frills or extravagant embellishments; economy of design and resistance to change seems to have been the guiding principle over the years so that now the church looks much as it must always have done — low to the ground and unashamedly unpretentious.

It stands in a hamlet, once famous for shepherd's crooks, where two major roads lead north from Brighton over the Downs to fork across the Weald either side of the church. The roads and their traffic are growing but, with luck, Pyecombe should remain undisturbed and unseen by the travellers. Only the roar of the traffic will trouble this island of tranquillity but some of the magic of the Downs is bound to be further dissipated here — for instance, by the construction of the four-lane highway which now appears to be lapping against the Plough Inn. Fortunately for the church, it does stand on an unviolated eminence, actually vertically above BR's Clayton tunnel. How blessed is Sussex that the Downs have prevented the spread of Brighton inland but how disastrous for the coast line.

Enough of these cantankerous complaints about the unavoidable pressures of population. Let us return to the church and the septuagenarian pleasures of nostalgia which is what country churches are about, almost as much as religion these days. This one consists of no more than a brief chancel and nave, supported at the west end by a squat tower and entered through a plain, utilitarian north porch which still bears the rough bolster marks of its 14th century masons. The walls, thick as they should be from their Norman origin, exhibit unknapped flints with plenty of mortar externally, and, internally, plenty of whitewash. Buttresses are few; two large ones to prevent the tower disengaging from the nave and two to prop the modest walls of the porch. The windows speak their age — Early English lancets for the chancel and square-headed Perpendicular for the nave. Pevsner seems to suggest that they are all 19th century replicas but they don't look it. What does look a fake (not said in any perjorative sense) is the east window of the chancel — handsome, round-headed, shafted, Norman in appearance but unmarked by time and hinting at the 1897 restoration. The stonework around it looks unmarked as if there had been no re-fenestration. What can have been here before? The guide is silent.

Inside, all is austere and compact and the simplicity is very evident. Two things stand out where the rest is unassuming. The first and most striking is the Norman chancel arch ('unmoulded, on the plainest imposts' says Pevsner but entirely in character with the rest of the church, say I) flanked on either side by lesser, modern arches like fore-and-aft squints. The second thing, but possibly the more important, is the 12th century lead font. Lead fonts, after the alleged depredations of the Puritan soldiery, are in short supply. In the whole of England there only remain some 40 and here, in Sussex, Pyecombe's is one of three (like the wedding guest!). Pyecombe's treasure, drum-shaped and moulded in relief in intricate scroll work, sits on a stone pedestal and is capped by a Victorian carved pyramid. The 17th century pulpit also deserves mention; satisfactorily permanent but not overbearing. One hardly needs a sounding board to address a dozen or so pews, even though they do have poppyhead finials.

I enjoyed attempting to reproduce that interesting-looking tree in the foreground. Despite removing a leaf and consulting my tree encyclopaedia at home, I could not identify it with confidence. A form of hornbeam is my best guess. Might I here put in a plea for churchyard trees to be labelled or for a chart identifying the more unusual specimens to be displayed in the porch. Is that too much to ask? Churchyards are important, too, and someone might enjoy doing it.

It is not easy to concentrate on this church with the immense bulk of the Roman walls looming at one's back. The Romans built their fort of Anderida, one of several in the south east, in 300 AD but left one hundred years later in 410 AD. In came the Ancient Britons to be slaughtered later that century by the invading Saxons. In their turn, the latter were ousted by Norman William (not quite yet the Conqueror) in 1066. He rested here in this Roman fort for seventeen days before pushing on to Hastings and his destiny — our's too. Later still, the Normans built their own castle within the ample enclosure and later again the castle was fortified with pill-boxes against yet another invader*. One can hardly ignore so historic a place.

In due course, the Normans built a church, Westham, by the western entrance to the Roman fort to be followed, almost a hundred years later, by this one at the eastern entrance. Why, one wonders, were neither built within the fort where there is ample room and where sheep now graze in safety. Why, indeed, are there two churches separated by no more than a stretch of walled grass. Inevitably, an element of competition must develop between the two; competition is said to be beneficial in economic terms but history, I think, suggests it is harmful in religious terms. Nevertheless, both churches have survived, albeit with the loss of a chapel or two, and both look to be well-enough equipped to last for another millenium given the will of those who live here.

To come now to St Nicholas, they must have raided the beach, rather than the Roman walls, when they came to build it in the reigns of John and Henry III; to my amateur eye the walls seem to be constructed almost entirely of rounded pebble stones, interspersed here and there by square blocks, green sandstone, if I read the guide correctly. The pebbles have withstood the passage of time so well that the whole edifice now appears silvery and Victorian, as in fact are the bell stage and spire of the tower. George Gilbert Scott should never have been allowed his over-sized bell openings.

As well as the tower, the church consists of a nave, north and south aisles and an exceptionally long chancel — plus porch and vestry. The impression inside is cavernous; high ceilings lit by clerestory lancets, rows of varied arcade pillars, stone-flagged floor and the long vista of the chancel. So long in fact that, in the 17th century, part of the chancel was blocked off and used as a store for coal and contraband. Rescue came in 1875 when Archdeacon Sutton was appointed vicar and rented the chancel for 1d a year! In gratitude, the archdeacon's 50th wedding anniversary was celebrated by a marathon peal of bells and the installation of a memorial tablet at the base of the tower. Beside it, in a corner, stands an iron spiral staircase to the bell chamber. I would not care to attempt this contraption; it has an even tighter spiral than those intimidating stone staircases that ascend the stair turrets beloved of Kent churches. It would, I am sure, excite the admiration of any interior designer intent on saving space — even where there is room to swing several cats, as here.

Monuments are few — two stone coffin lids in the south aisle and three brasses, all of which I failed to see. One cannot miss, though, the recumbent figure of John Wheatley, †1616, beneath his pediment of black marble. Evidently not a sailor himself, he paid for one ship from Pevensey to oppose the Armada. So, he has got his memorial. There are two fonts; one looks Victorian and one is said to be Norman. The latter, which boasts an elaborate pinnacled cover (presented 1864), must be the operative article. Being Norman, it predates the church; Arthur Mee reports foundations of a church and an old font in the Norman keep in the castle so possibly that is where St Nicholas' font comes from. So, also, there was after all a church within the Roman walls. Now there are two without.

---

* The Romans obligingly left behind some of their substantial catapult ammunition; no occasion having arisen to test its efficacy, it is still preserved here as good as new.

Most of us have heard of Winchelsea and some of us have visited this unique little place and those that have can hardly forget the church, or what remains of it. As a town, or rather a still-born, embryonic town, Winchelsea is an oddity, to say the least. What we see to-day represents an ideal lay-out for a medieval town, commissioned by that Plantagenet tough, Edward I (they were all tough — had to be) after the first Winchelsea down on the strand had been drowned by the sea. It was intended that the second Winchelsea should continue as an important seaport but again the sea had its way and the harbour became unuseable. So the town, on its cliff above, ossified and it was only the successive seaborne raids by the French in the 13th and 14th centuries that disturbed its peaceful decline into genteel inactivity.

The extent to which the church suffered at the hands of the French is not, I believe, established for sure. What is beyond doubt is that it did suffer but enough still stands to create an impression of indestructible nobility. Broken shattered walls and blocked archways and defoliated windows now serve to emphasize the majesty of what might have been.

In Edward's day, when religion was all-important and faith assured, the church was naturally accorded priority in planning and here, in Winchelsea, St Thomas was given the central square of this grid-plan town for his church and churchyard. They do it justice. At a respectful distance, of a much later date, stand the comely, white-painted houses that now comprise this charmed relic of the past. In their midst rises the grandeur of what was intended to be the chancel and side chapels of a major church; these remnants now constitute a church which, without benefit of its nave or transepts, is still entirely adequate for its function and congregation and is a major ornament of East Sussex. It is a commentary on the history of its region and a compliment to that long-defunct monarch, Edward I, †1307. Would that we could do as well to-day. I hope I will be forgiven if the above sounds rather a purple patch but really what else can pay adequate respect to so splendid and tenacious a survivor.

As it stands, now, there is no trace of the planned or original nave although the jagged stumps of walling and arcade pillars, currently acting as buttresses, suggest that there was indeed construction to the west. The admirable church guide speculates that the nave may have reached to where a sundial stands by the churchyard wall — a distance of some 55 yards, roughly paced. With such a nave and its glorious aisled chancel, Winchelsea's church in its pomp could well have been the grandest edifice between Chichester and Canterbury. It might still be.

Externally, the glory may have been wasted; inside it survives, enhanced even. Initially, it is the opulent, glowing effect of the stained glass in the huge windows that fills the senses. In the afternoon sunlight (or in any sunlight for that matter), the effect is stunning. Ranged beneath the aisle windows are elaborate, canopied tombs; three on the north side bear the marble effigies of a young man, a lady and an armoured knight, cross-legged with his right hand vigilantly clasping the hilt of his sword. On the south side are two stone effigies of the Alards — crusaders both and Admirals of the Western Fleet. The elder, Gervase, clasps the replica of a heart in his hands, his grandson, Stephen, holds his hands in that typical attitude of prayer, piety and penitence which is so unmistakably medieval. All five are marvellous but why just them? Did they have no distinguished descendants? Amongst all this splendour, a small ledger stone, in a prime position, to a young girl who died aged 7, strikes a salutary balance.

However, what with the magnificence of the windows, the gabled sedilia and the medieval effigies, and the flow of tourists to admire, one feels, unfairly perhaps, that the religious element may be somewhat overshadowed. But then, if the Devil has 'all the good tunes', why should God not have the best buildings?

BARCOMBE
St Mary the Virgin

Barley field

Somehow I had expected Barcombe church to be run-of-the-mill without much to get excited about. My 'Notes' are brief and laconic; Pevsner is as much concerned with Shelley's Folly — a mile away — and Mee is unreliable in his assessment and pre-occupied with an infant's grave. So Barcombe hardly promised the enchantment it delivered. What I found was a low-lying, unpretentious little flint church in the company of a few attractive tile-hung houses, including the Court House, a Sussex barn, a large pond and undulating fields stretching away without interruption to the Downs about Lewes. It was exactly as one hopes to find a country church, and fortunately for us, so often do.

It is not a large church; just chancel, nave and south aisle with a west tower that fails to reach the roof line. One can't help wondering whether the roof of the nave was raised to accommodate the Victorian widening of the aisle long after the tower had been built. In fact, pace Mee, the nave is Norman, the arcade pillars a mixture, the chancel and tower 13th century while the aisle dates from the restoration of 1879 which was when, presumably, the east window was transformed from square-headed to pointed — not to its benefit, I would say. One 'improvement' that earns my accolade is the row of redundant headstones which are now embedded flush along the south and west walls of the church. they range from 168?* to the 1860s and their assembly as part of the church fabric seems a vast improvement on lining the perimeter of the churchyard when removal from their proper graves is undertaken, for whatever improper reason. Anyway full marks to Barcombe.

The interior is basically as simple as the exterior — a low three-bay arcade of 13th and 14th century arches, upright now but leaning rather oddly before the restoration if an illustration in the church guide is to be trusted. The box pews have gone but remain in the shape of a bookcase; similarly, one of the old chestnut tie beams of the roof, bearing the date 1682 and the names of two churchwardens, now constitutes part of this utilitarian piece of furniture. It is rather endearing; recycling we call it to-day.

Although there is one large wall tablet with 'two abundant caryatids' (why are female caryatids always load-bearing while their male counterparts, Atlantes, are generally less employed? It seems unfair on the ladies.), the memorials in this church are essentially a Grantham celebration. The earliest is a mellow stained-glass window, bearing the Grantham arms, dated 1657, which was brought from Lincoln in 1889. The second is modern; an engraved glass screen at the tower base. It commemorates two Granthams, †1978 and 1986. Souls, being immaterial and hence difficult to depict, the sculptress substituted somewhat ethereal shapes ascending heavenwards to suggest a heavenly hereafter for those concerned. While I was admiring this work, an amiable lady doing the flowers suggested I might find it interesting to have a look at the Grantham graves in the churchyard. She rather inferred the Granthams might still be turning in their graves.

So off I trotted to a distant reach of this extensive churchyard. There I found a longish line of grey Grantham headstones, simple and compatible and weathering well. Next but one to Sir Alexander Grantham, one-time Governor of Hong Kong, stands a large black marble headstone on which are the words, picked out in brazen gold lettering, 'In eternal memory of kind Mother and Grandma Mann Fung Chong †1978'. The churchyard here is large and unpeopled. What can have possessed someone to intrude a total stranger amonst a row of family graves. It looks like an expression of political or parochial spite. I would not like to have such an impertinent act on my conscience or made permanently public.

Happily, not even a mischievously placed black marble headstone, with gold lettering, can spoil the elegiac rusticity of Barcombe church and churchyard.

---

* The two earliest memorials inscribe the letter N thus И — the work of a 17th century dyslexic stonemason?

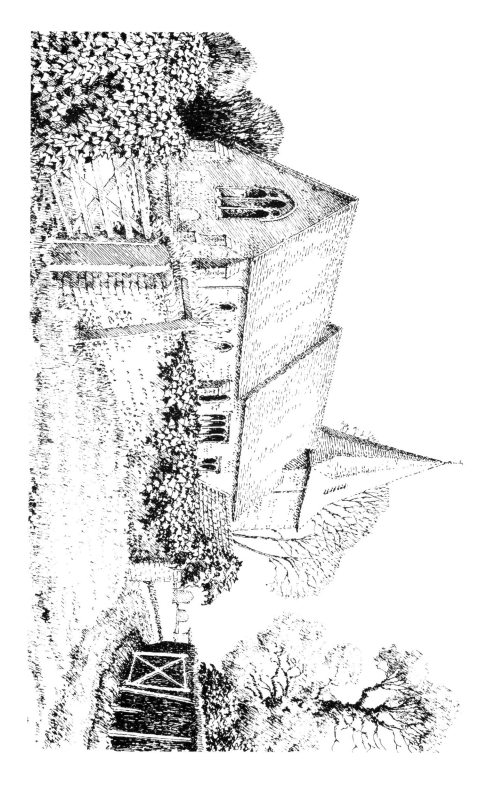

To-day, Kingston village seems to the visitor more like a suburb of Lewes than the country village close under the Downs which it is. The Street, which runs up to the slopes beyond, is still traditional enough, though, to satisfy the purist and here one finds the church. The rest of the houses that make up the village look to be modern which, when one comes to think about it, is what most villages are now-a-days. Happily the Street has managed to preserve its time-honoured identity relatively free of the 20th century and this is where one also finds the timbered pub, the oddly-named Juggs.

The church, consisting of nave and chancel and a seemingly-undernourished west tower is old; 14th century for the nave and chancel, possibly older for the tower. It doesn't look it. The church was badly damaged in the 19th century by lightning, says the guide, and it could be the extensive resulting reparation which gives it such a Victorian stamp. The unknapped flints which compose the walls seem scarcely touched by weather, the gable parapets are orderly and complete, the window tracery crisp and the roofs sound and obviously rain-proof. Even the antique tower looks recent (to the unsuspecting eye) with little or no sign of the patching that one might expect.

The repairs were carried out in 1874 at 'the sole expense' of the Revd John Goring of Wiston, the 'largest landowner in the parish'. One would like to know a little more about John Goring.* Wiston is miles away on the far side of Steyning near Chanctonbury and amounts to little more than Wiston House and the church. Pevsner makes much more of both than he does of Kingston. Was the generous Goring less true to his roots, one wonders, or perhaps Kingston's need was greater. He must have enjoyed the sort of disposable income that few are lucky enough to enjoy to-day, certainly few of the clergy. But also he may not have had a family on whom to bestow his largesse. Kingston was lucky to receive its lightning strike and John Goring his inheritance before fiscal redistribution really got underway. One might almost say that the inheritance taxes have proved as much the enemy of the Established Church and its properties as has secularisation.

The interior is as plain as the exterior seems unweathered. While they were about the repairs, all the monuments, if there were any, were swept away. Only a plaque to John Goring and two to those who perished in the Great Wars survive. The churchyard, though, is not bereft of its due quota of ivy-covered chest tombs and toppling headstones so there probably was a clean sweep within the church. There must have been other worthies to extol besides the benevolent parson; they are lost to us now. The new brooms also dealt comprehensively with the original flooring — now one is dazzled by coloured Victorian tiles arranged in various distracting patterns. There remains the eagle lectern, beloved of evangelists, but no sign so far as I could see of the old chest which so attracted Arthur Mee. Fonts do have a marvellous record of survival notwithstanding the 17th century objections of the Anabaptists and the 'improving' zeal of the Victorian restorers. Kingston's font is simple but solid and would take some removing, even by a lightning bolt.

In summary, although this flint church may give little away about its past parishioners or benefactors, its straightforward structure would seem to have remained faithful to its original plan. The large vestry to the north does look to be a recent excrescence but can easily be ignored by the church enthusiast however important it may be to the vested clergy.

The church was open but empty on the rainy day in which I attempted my sketch. Two ladies, exercising their dogs, passed by the Tapsell gate but otherwise nobody moved. The pub, though, was crowded.

* Later I learnt from the Victoria County History that in 1853 the Revd J Goring also paid for the rebuilding of Albourne church. The Goring family interests, liberality and resources must have been extensive and deep.

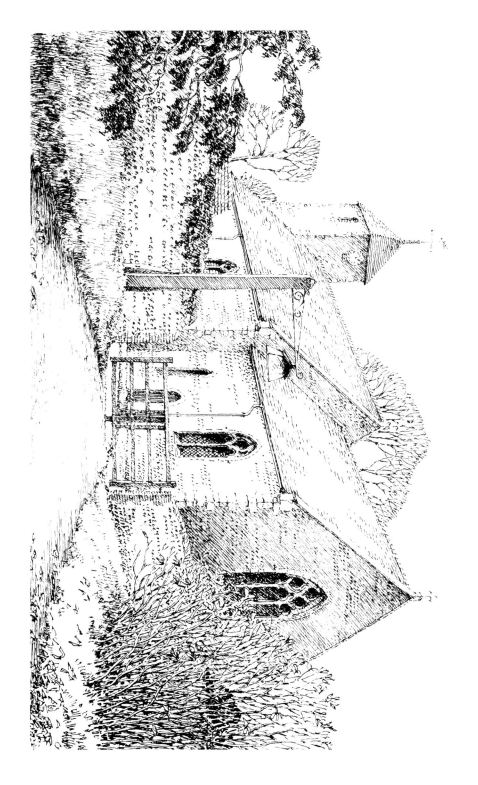

ICKLESHAM
All Saints

I don't think that Icklesham church has half the fame, say, of Winchelsea or Pevensey although it would seem to be the oldest and is far from negligable. William the Conqueror, who landed at Pevensey, would have passed along here on his way to Dover and probably noticed, and possibly prayed in, the Saxon church that then stood here. Part of its walling still remains beside the curious hexagonal west porch.

For a church which, with apologies to Icklesham village, one encounters at a nowhere-in-particular halt on the way from one important place to another, Hastings to Rye, All Saints is surprisingly grand (it surprised me). To stand in its truncated nave, surrounded by eight cylindrical pillars supporting six Norman arches must convince anyone that Icklesham ranked high in the minds of its founders, perhaps in memory of a famous victory. They didn't intend the church to be overlooked or patronised. Each of these pillars is capped by beautifully carved foliage — all subtly different; just imagine the gratification one must get if one's lovingly carved stonework is still admired 800 years later — as I have no doubt it has been all through those 800 years. One can understand why the returning Crusaders should have felt impelled to scratch their small thanksgiving crosses on these pillars. Its a wonder they aren't more defaced by later pilgrims but, no, they look virtually as good as ever.

The chronology of this church and its lay-out is rather confusing. The excellent guide puts the nave arcade as the oldest part, that is after the remnant of Saxon walling, followed by the north and south aisles, mid-north tower and north chapel as circa 1150 and hence also Norman. Pevsner, on the other hand, puts the tower with its stone-rib vaulting and Norman windows internal as well as external, as the oldest part. In fact, he says the tower was part of a cruciform church which certainly confuses me.

The equally long chancel and south chapel, being 14th century and 200 years later, are slightly offset. However, true to their Norman predecessors the blank arcading in the north chapel is faithfully reproduced in chancel and south chapel, 'in spades' actually. The north chapel is unaesthetically occupied by the hind quarters of the organ, as north chapels so often are, while the south chapel is rather bare of furniture and memorials. It is said that this is where the lords of the manor were buried and one 20th century 'lord' is remembered in most elegant lettering on a soapstone plaque. It feels like silk to the touch.

Like any medieval church, All Saints was periodically restored, on one occasion by Samuel Teulon in 1849. He has been characterised unflatteringly as 'a rogue architect' whose churches were 'domineering, details coarse'. One wouldn't think so here although the parish evidently did in 1920 when Teulon's tower parapet was removed and the cap replaced in its original state. What disposes me in Teulon's favour are the corbels by which the nave roof is supported above the Norman arcade. These eight corbels, all different and deeply undercut, represent I was informed, the leaves of the vine, oak, ivy and rose. I assume the corbels are his as is the similarly carved font. If only Mr Teulon had stopped at the roof and perhaps the porch and left the flooring alone. Black and red diamond tiles are not the same thing as flagstones and ledger stones; one makes the church, the others spoil it — as I am afraid I repeat all too often.

A church like this, which seems so obviously to sit astride the Conqueror's all-conquering sweep through the south east on his way to the throne, tends to provoke reflections on the might-have-been or nearly-was. If Harold had won, as he almost did, what then? No Norman churches but more Saxon. Would that have been better or worse and would there have been more or fewer? We may no longer build churches a patch on either but at least we do look after what we have got; a modest measure of approval, then, to a Gothicist architect and this secular age.

It is not often, I think, that a Victorian architect builds a replica medieval church tower which is what, on the face of it, happened here. Ringmer's flint tower, four square and unbuttressed, is the product of Ewan Christian and its foundation stone was laid by Mrs Agnes Christie in 1884 as one of the many benefactions by that famous family. I was interested to read in the church guide that Mr Christian's tower rests 8 feet deep in the ground on foundations 6 feet wide — no wonder neither buttresses nor plinth were necessary and that it stands so perpendicular.

The remainder of the church is genuine; 14th century arcade pillars and aisle walls, slightly later chancel and north and south chapels, square-headed Perpendicular windows for the aisles and four-centred Perpendicular for the gable ends. Left in situ by Mr Christian's restoration are some of the Horsham roof tiles although it would appear that the roofs were raised in the past if the brick courses above the dressed sandstone blocks are anything to go by. So much for one amateur's brief observations (helped by the guide) concerning the architectural details about which I am sure there is a great deal more to be said.

It is, though, the memorials and benefactions that stir the imagination here. It was pouring with rain when I arrived, the church was locked (nearby Beddingham had recently been stripped of movables even down to the chairs in the nave, I was told) and the augurs not encouraging. Fortunately the rain relented after a while so that I could sketch, damply, the vicar came back for his lunch and I obtained the massive key. The augurs were wrong.

So to the north chapel, bereft of pews and chairs as in my opinion it should be, where one finds a memorial to a 17th century vicar whose daughter married a certain John Harvard who went on to found Harvard University. Exposed on the floor is a very handsome black ledger stone commemorating a 'truly pious and most ingenious young lady . . .' Ingenious seems an odd adjective for a daughter who created the Stapley Charity. Perhaps she had problems in those patriarchal days; anyway her Charity still survives. Opposite in the south chapel, now also bare and bereft of its squire's pew, are the memorials to the Springett family. The daughter of one, a contemporary of Mistress Harvard, Gulielma Maria Posthuma, married the Quaker William Penn who founded the State of Pennsylvania. These 17th century girls, brought up in the gentle Sussex countryside, must have had steel in their fibres to be able to confront and help civilise the New World wilderness. They deserve to be remembered on both sides of the Atlantic. The other memorials in these chapels may not commemorate such intrepid characters but they are worth a second glance all the same.

Below the central gangway of the nave lie the Snooke family. They are not so much famed as remembered for their connection with their nephew, Gilbert White of Selborne, who came to visit them at Ringmer and, in due course, to adopt their celebrated tortoise. At this stage of my exploration I was joined by the post-prandial vicar who pointed out, what I had already missed, the splendid carved-limewood eagle that makes up the lectern with its widespread wings. It was, though, the organ above the west gallery that most aroused his enthusiasm. It is, he said, probably the most powerful village organ in England, is insured (1992) for £250,000 and has its innards installed in the tower. Once it was powered by a motor cycle engine, now by something better that is housed in the puzzling stone structure which forms part of the churchyard wall, hard by the Christie's tower. There is also an elegant, versified and sculpted but anonymous, wall tablet in the south aisle. I read elsewhere that it commemorates a young ensign — whose privacy I shall respect — but why the anonymity?

To digress from the church for a moment but not its 17th century parishioners, is it not remarkable that a somewhat unremarkable village in Sussex should have produced what can only be described as two of the founding matriarchs of the United States of America. They were brave in their lives and fortunate in their spouses.

WADHURST
St Peter and St Paul

Wadhurst is ironfounder's territory and nowhere is this more apparent than on the floors of Wadhurst church. Here one finds the iron tomb slabs that commemorate those industrialists of the 17th century and their families. There are some 30 slabs ranging in date from 1601 to 1771. They are very black, generally long and narrow, with the details raised in relief — as they would be coming from foundry moulds. The identification is mostly brief in content and crude in elevation, frequently simply initials and date — eg. TB 1647; occasionally there is a coat of arms and more detail but on the whole they are, or seem, more terse than ledger stones on which the incised lettering is so elegant. There are, as well, 7 of the latter to make the point. The whole flooring is quite remarkable and dominates the church (if that can be done at ground level). I have seen nothing remotely like it in any of the numerous Sussex churches I have sketched. What is also astonishing about them, as much as their proliferation here, is the fact that 'during the recently completed excavation (1859) no human remains have been found under any of the slabs. Here is a mystery'. Indeed.

This concentration of iron tomb slabs, spanning a period of 170 years, provokes an elementary calculation. There are, I think some 14 different surnames displayed here; if there are approximately 6 generations in the period covered and each generation produces, at the very least, one member to carry on the family tradition, then there should be 84 slabs if the will to persist with commemoration continued. Why then only 30 slabs? Cast-iron slabs cannot be added to in the manner of the versatile ledger stones; once cast, the die is cast, so to speak. Admittedly, existing slabs could be replaced by new ones incorporating subsequent members of the family but I don't think that this was done to any great extent. It is a constant puzzle to me that families which go to the trouble to commemorate one individual, permanently and expensively, seem happy to forget the rest. Of course, if all were remembered in stone, church interiors would long ago have become overrun and unduly secular. Perhaps the clergy objected and that may be part of the explanation.

Appropriately enough, Wadhurst's unique collection is housed in a very grand structure although practically all the construction had been completed by the time the iron-founders started their profitable industry. The Normans were here as the first builders and the west tower stands to their credit. It has been much patched over the years as the many shades of Wealden sandstone testify. And added to as well as the buttresses and slender broach spire confirm. In its way this 124 feet high tower and spire is as spectacular, vertically and visually (even after the gales of 1987) as the iron slabs are horizontally and historically on the floor below.

As well as the tower, the Normans naturally had a nave and chancel. The nave was expanded in the 14th century into a nave plus north and south aisles with a complete substitution in the case of the chancel by a disproportionately long replacement. The aisles differ in their width and in the roof arrangements, the south being generally grander, more patronised by the iron-founders for their slabs and, in the 15th century, dignified by a handsome storeyed porch. The latter is vaulted and lined with hanging wall tablets (one to a child aged 9) and furnished with silvery-oak benches on either side (one to a child aged 10). It is a distinguished entrance to a notable interior.

One can become so pre-occupied here with cast-iron slabs that much else is overlooked. It would be misguided, though, to miss the tall glass and wrought-iron screen at the base of the tower. It is dated 1957, only 700 years younger than the structure of which it now forms an important feature. In fact, the tower with its later buttresses, spire, windows and stone staircase has throughout its life been an example of organic development in stone. But then, so have almost all churches and that is part of their fascination.

Hartfield may have left no mark on history so far as I know but then history in the shape of great events or prominent people has left no trace on Hartfield. Can that be such a deprivation? We may all like to bask in the impress of history but we are not so anxious to suffer its more uncomfortable proceedings. Hartfield seems to have escaped the latter.

The village lies between the youthful Medway and the northern limit of the Ashdown Forest, athwart a minor road that runs south across the forest. This is a very agreeable tract of countryside and Hartfield has a very agreeable church to grace it.

The church is a warm golden brown in colour with sandstone walling that seems consistent throughout despite development through the 13th to the 15th centuries. I did notice a brief hint of herringbone work in the north wall of the nave which supports the contention of the church guide that there was a church here at the time of the Domesday Book. The present version consists of a 13th century nave, 14th century south aisle and chancel and a 15th century tower plus the inevitable modern additions — here a vestry which does not offend the rest. The whole construction is harmonious, comfortable and suggests continuing local prosperity over the years.

My visit to sketch took place six days before Christmas. Appropriately, I was welcomed inside by lively music on the organ and by a seasonal wreath of ivy, roses, apples and pomegranates over the south doorway; otherwise, apart from the temperature, it might have been any season of the year. I could admire and sketch undisturbed and without disturbing.

The interior is spacious with walls liberally adorned by memorial tablets and with floors flagged with stone. The nave is four bays long and here one encounters a conundrum. Normally, bays are equal in length with about 16 feet separation between the pillars that support the arches. Here the eastern bay is noticeably larger than the others — why? The guide speculates on the reason. It might, it is suggested, be as a result of reconstruction after a fire. Alternatively, if there was no fire, it might have resulted from conversion in the 17th century to suit Prayer Book services in which the altar played a reduced role. The chancel arch seems to have gone at the same time. It all seems rather drastic for a change in liturgical practice and therefore I favour the fire theory as a more plausible explanation for such a major structural alteration. Another hare is raised by the depiction of the chancel in a framed water colour dated 1874. In the painting, the east window is shown as four-centred with the flattened arch that is so eminently Tudor whereas, in fact, the chancel window to-day is manifestly pointed and Perpendicular. One wonders did the artist, who was clearly competent, complete his painting at home and rely on an uncertain memory. Although the Victorians were active in restoration in the 1860s, there is no sign of reconstruction in the east wall or mention in the guide. Faulty observation would be my verdict; not guilty myself, I trust.

Change continues to the present day but more by way of improvement to the furnishings (kneelers, for instance) than by alterations to the basic structure. It would appear that the urge to develop is exhausted with Hartfield church settling comfortably into mellow old age. So it is with many village churches where change is now largely confined to moving headstones to make way for the mower. Not a good idea in my opinion but I don't have to cut the grass.

The churchyard here is ample and free of trees shading the church so that an unobstructed view can be obtained from any direction and all are good. My view is dictated by a desire to include the little Tudor cottage that forms half the lych-gate. This miniscule cottage, once a retirement home for employees of the de la Warr estate, was home in the 1800s for a family that included 7 children. It must have been akin to a bird's nest with the older ones pushed out to make room for the later arrivals.

NEWICK
St Mary the Virgin

New farm

New Year's Eve, 1992, brought me to Newick to find the church open with the Christmas decorations still in place. The most decorative, I thought, were the candle staves attached to each pew end and entwined with ivy. When the candles were lit on the night of Christmas Eve the effect must have been entrancing and surely created an atmosphere of mystery and celebration. I would like to have seen it all.

One's introduction to this church begins with the west tower which confronts the visitor at the end of the short tree-lined approach avenue. The tower is impressively solid and four-square; not particularly tall, golden brown in colour and capped by an inset tiled roof; It was built in the early 15th century, says the guide, but the west doorway is Tudor and therefore a later 16th century modification. This doorway is surrounded by a rectangular hood-mould which is stopped on either side by substantial, matching carved heads. Although the years have weathered these heads in their Tudor caps, they said Sir Thomas More and Richard Cromwell firmly to my imagination. Had this been the Continent Martin Luther would have sprung to mind; as it is I will settle patriotically for the two Englishmen, saint and reformationist and executed, both. There are more carved heads adorning this church as kneestones to the gable parapets but too far above ground to be easily distinguished or to encourage fantasy. Here and there amongst the sandstone blocks of the tower are what looked like anomalous blocks of greyish stone. They were, I was informed by a lady attending to the notices in the porch, an example of economy in the 1920s when cement was used to make good erosion in the soft sandstone. This cement is now proving defective and providing even more of a problem than ever it was intended to solve 70 years ago.

The present church owes much to its Victorian rector, Clement Powell, whose office ran from 1885 to 1915. Almost immediately after his induction he decided that the Norman nave and 13th century chancel were not big enough (Newick has always been a large parish, I imagine); accordingly the nave was lengthened and the chancel taken down and re-erected at the end of the extended nave — to remain Early English in intent if not in fact. At the same time the original north aisle was lengthened to comply with the enlarged nave. The work was done with great sympathy for the past and, although the genuine Norman walling and its window are fairly obvious, the rest is compatible and does not suffer unduly by comparison.

As the enlargement was so much the concern of the rector, the reconstituted chancel was not neglected. Far from it; it is richly decorated internally — black and white diamond tiled floor, a blue patterned tiled dado around the sanctuary, a stencilled flower pattern above and a painted wagon ceiling. The Revd Powell's family were squires here and had the advowson; Clement was patently not going to be content with the second rate and he had a first-class architect to see that he got what he wanted. The result is well worth their efforts and an argument, dare one say it, for elitism.

The churchyard is expansive, and has expanded, to contain one rarity for me, a large spreading cedar tree, of Lebanon presumably. From their provenance cedars should be but aren't as common in churchyards as yews are. There is a prolific range and number of memorials in the long grass — tomb chests, coping stones, headstones and one indecipherable rusty-iron dead board. They demonstrate, I regret to say, how our taste has degenerated since the 18th century. It must be something to do with 'progress' and 'technology'.

NORTHIAM
St Mary

Hay meadow

The inside of a car in a saturating drizzle may not be ideal for sketching anything. In the case of my visit to Northiam church it was the only solution. Actually, the church is so hemmed about by old walls and old houses that a churchyard view is virtually impossible and a car is the safest place from which to conduct operations when in the middle of the road. So the weather proved irrelevant if uncomfortable and inclement.

The most prominent and first feature to greet a visitor is the west tower. This is said to 'probably have Saxon work'; it certainly has plenty of Norman work at the lower levels. At its base, internally, are rounded arches at each cardinal face; above, externally, are three-bay blank arcades north and south, and the sandstone walling at that stage is rough and ready. The enormous north west buttress is Perpendicular as, I imagine, is the balancing south west octagonal stair turret. Which offers the stronger support I have no idea but surely both are needed to prop the 15th century stone spire. The combined effect is dominant and dominates the village street which runs past well below.

The nave and aisles are unexceptional but unremarkable. Beyond all is Victorian Gothic; a large chancel and similarly large chancel aisles providing space for a squire's pew on the south side and, on the north, space for the organ. In the process, unfortunately, the 15th century Tufton chapel has disappeared. These recent 'improvements' are rather spartan, redeemed only in my opinion by the Carolean panelling and rails around the altar.

This enlarged building has been, essentially, the church of the Frewen and Lord families which contributed to its upkeep and provided rectors over a period of some 300 years. Two Puritan Frewens are particularly remembered here; one rejoiced in the name of Thankful — the altar rails are his; another was christened Accepted — he accompanied the unfortunate Charles I to Spain and lived to become Archbishop of York at the Restoration.

Not surprisingly, the main interest then, apart from the tower, inevitably lies with the Frewen mausoleum. This substantial adjunct was added as a north transept in 1845. Externally, east and west, it is enlivened under the parapet by a frieze of eighteen stone heraldic shields. Internally, the walls are hung with tablets, some elaborate, others more retrained, of those interred therrein. Light comes in all the colours of the spectrum from the east window in which glow the coats of arms of, I imagine, the collaterals of generations of Frewens. The simplest and most recent memorial is that to an admiral of my time in the Navy. I have always watched my step when in the presence of admirals and so must take care what I say in the presence of this one, benign though he was. One maxim the Navy enforces is that all things have a proper place and, especially in a ship, should be kept there. The admiral, therefore, would be less than happy, I think, to find his family mausoleum used as a stowage for miscellaneous pink armchairs. Upholstery and sephulchral memorials do not go together.

The Frewen memorials, in many cases, must antedate their mausoleum and consequently will have come from the body of the church which now looks rather bare and bereft as a result. The lack of memorials, as a matter of policy and as a reflection of the times we live in, is one reason why modern churches, however well designed, do not have the atmosphere of their predecessors. Northiam church has a long history but with little evidence of it away from the mausoleum; if its carpets could be removed to reveal the ledger stones and brasses that must lie underneath, a greater sense of piety and historical perspective in village terms might be restored.

Carpets and churches don't go together either, in my humble opinion. Fortunately carpets and armchairs don't have the lasting qualities of stone. Nor do we.

150

St Margaret or St Giles*

Having read up Dallington church before coming here to sketch, I was not expecting too much. In the event I was pleasantly surprised; it was a mild, sunlit January day (that helps) but the credit should really go, not to the balmy weather, but to the beguiling hamlet that is present-day Dallington. Just a few nice old houses closely lining the lane that makes up the village street with the church looking over their shoulders from above. It is all rather off the beaten track and eminently rural.

To reach the church from the lane one climbs up behind the houses towards the tower — as I have tried to reproduce. Nothing else is immediately visible so one can concentrate one's attention on the substantial 15th century masonry which makes up an imposing Perpendicular tower, well supported by buttresses and constructed of regular courses of sizeable blocks of dressed stone, presumably sandstone. It has an air of permanence that the two S shaped iron retaining clamps do nothing to dispel (although they will split the stone one day). Above is a stone steeple; no doubt stone steeples represent a considerable architectural achievement but they rarely look as comely as shingled spires, generally being stumpy as is this one. Probably a tall stone steeple would be too heavy for most towers and that's why they are stumpy. Dallington's tower is dignified by a battlemented parapet on which are displayed two stone armorial shields and two Pelham Buckles**.

After the tower, all is Victorian. There was, of course, a medieval church to accompany the medieval tower but in the 19th century the Earl of Ashburnham's architect (retained to resist rebuilding) felt obliged to report that 'the walls are crumbling to dust, cracking and giving way at all points'. Presumably this condemnation did not include the tower. At all events the Earl, and patron, failed in his defence of the original 14th century church and the then incumbent won. The nave and chancel were demolished in 1864 to be replaced by a new nave, north aisle and chancel, all in the best Decorated Gothic. The addition of an aisle necessitated an arcade between nave and aisle; here the architects seem rather to have let enthusiasm for the Gothic to go to their heads. Particularly obvious and florid are the overlarge capitals of the octagonal pillars. They may not be beautiful but they do confer a certain idiosyncracy on a Victorian rebuilding. Inevitably, in the course of the work down came the memorials, away went the squire's pew and covered was the floor and lost was the memory of those who lie below. Now, by good fortune, there are a few wall tablets on the north wall of the aisle with dates that take precedence over the rebuilding. Apparently, the church guide informs one, some few tablets were found in the belfry this century and it is these survivors that now dress the walls. What a pity about those lost and how unfair on those they commemorated.

We all desire a modicum of immortality. Offspring are the most reliable method, lapidary inscription another but if neither are available something else must be devised. Here, Miss Adelaide Tatham, daughter of the 'reconstructed' vicar, found a solution by compiling in 1886 the 'Parish Records of the Parish of Dallington, Sussex.' No great matter the worldly might say; but Miss Tatham is remembered and quoted to this day. I salute her as a Victorian spinster and as a tenacious daughter of the rectory; she retained her attachment to the past while her father, rural dean and prebendary, was forced to relinquish his in the face of crumbling walls.

* Dedication uncertain. St Margaret would seem to be prior but was supplanted by St Giles in the 17th century. Dedications are not easily changed and require consecration by a bishop in the first place. St Giles has the field to-day, whether with episcopal approval or not is unclear.

** It would be tedious to rehearse the significance of the Pelham Buckle whenerer it appears in East Sussex; see Wartling for a brief enlightenment.

Hellingly must be one of the rare places where the church is almost upstaged by the churchyard. Here the church rests in the centre of a circular Saxon burial mound which is bounded on three sides by a brick retaining wall and on the fourth, the north where the levels equalise, by a cluster of tile-hung period cottages that front directly on to the churchyard. One might almost say the churchyard takes the place of a private glade or park for the fortunate inhabitants of these cottages. There are four low entrance gates, garden gates they seem, connected by brick paths which converge on the central church. These admirable paths consumed 8,450 bricks, the church guide declares, and were laid by unemployed labourers in 1824 — an early form of 'workfare' and one which could well be adopted to-day for the benefit of a great many churchyards and of the many (1993) unemployed. Within this magical circle is supported a stand of several tall and slender conifers; by some miracle they have survived more or less intact the storms and tempests of the winters of the late 1980s. Amongst them, soothed by the sighing of the wind, lie the departed natives of Hellingly. Or is it we who are soothed by the rustling branches above as we wander amonst the ancient headstones? Very likely both. For a Saxon burial to have survived is a matter for congratulation; for it to have developed into its present elegiac condition without the intrusion of the 20th century is remarkable and a further matter for congratulation. Short of a hurricane, an unharmed and unchanging future looks assured.

To come, belatedly, to the church, it consists now of a nave with north and south aisles, the latter 15th century, an Early English north transept and a Norman cum Early English chancel and, last, a Georgian west tower. The chancel still contains two Norman windows on the north side — conventionally narrow externally, splayed and elaborate with shafted capitals on the inside. On the south wall are two Early English lancets, a low-side window and the trace of a priest's doorway. The eastern face of the chancel, which figures so prominently in my sketch, looks undeniably restored with ashlared stonework in its upper courses but with rougher iron-stone blocks from its past in the lower. It is noticeable that, whereas the aisle windows are comfortably low and cottagy, if Perpendicular, the chancel windows, earlier in time, are close up under the eaves and intended only to admit light rather than prying eyes. The solid west tower, also ashlared and rather severe, was built in 1836, the last year of the reign of William IV but Georgian all the same. Previously, there had been a wooden bell-turret described as 'a mean wooden spire'. Either this became decrepit and unable to carry its six bells or somebody decided the situation demanded something better. Down came the old, up went the new, at a cost of £866 and with sufficient speed for the accession of Queen Victoria to be commemorated by the installation of the clock the following year.

One gains access, not as one might expect (as I did) via the north porch, but directly into the south aisle — why have a porch and not use it? There must be a reason, for as it is, one now arrives directly in the aisle, wet and dishevelled if raining. To judge by his comments, Pevsner's interest inside is particularly aroused by the eastern respond of the north arcade — a cluster of unexplained columns — but most people's attention will be directed to the four foot long 15th century brass in the chancel. To-day it is uncovered and unprotected for all to admire but it is strange to read that it was only rediscovered in 1869 restoration; where can it have been meanwhile and where is her Devenysh companion. Deep under the indifferent Victorian tiling somewhere, no doubt; memorials are meant to be observed and remembered, preferably in their proper places, would say the memorialists, I am sure.

Hard-by but invisible from the churchyard is a notable Tudor timber house, Horselunges Manor, from whence originated the dimpled lady on the chancel floor, it is thought. All three, manor, church and courtyard have aged with grace and dignity and are a dowry from the past in the quiet Sussex countryside — preserved in aspic one might almost say and all the better for that.

NEWTIMBER
St John the Evangelist*

Newtimber church lies under the lee of Newtimber Hill, sandwiched in a quiet stretch of the countryside below the Downs between two widely-spaced busy main roads. The tower does rise a trifle conspicuously across the fields but I doubt if those speeding by have time to notice it. Nor, indeed, is it likely to attract the idle populace and so I was lucky on the Maundy Thursday when I came here to find someone else at the entrance to the path that leads across a paddock to the churchyard. He had come to tend the family graves, he said, but he knew where the key was being kept while the organ was under repair and, in due course, when he had finished his task and I had finished my sketch, he enlightened me. Others may not be so lucky in their timing.

The key was to be found at Newtimber Place, a marvellous old moated house, mansion to be exact, in which had lived the lord of the manor who built the church in the 13th century. Without that all-important key my day would have been less than complete; as it was I saw all there was to see with a patient guide to inform me. But then, happily for us church enthusiasts, churchwardens are likely to be patient with those who come to admire their churches and ask the obvious questions which they must have endured many times before.

The church is small and mainly Early English with lancets on either side to prove it. Externally, the fabric is almost entirely submerged under a sandy-coloured rendering of pebble dash giving a somewhat bland Victorian appearance. This is saved by a genuinely Victorian west tower, built in 1839, which displays a singularly idiosyncratic decorative aspect as one approaches. The whole structure is classified as Grade II** to-day — in Grade I surroundings, I would say. In the 18th century, when Grimm sketched the church, it looked quite different, much more rustic and without its distinctive west tower; more in keeping with the fields around really.

Inside, an overall coat of plaster and whitewash creates a spartan atmosphere which, together with the pebble dash outside, succeeds pretty well in obliterating any vestiges of the medieval church that has served a rural community here since the Domesday Book was compiled. Maundy Thursday and no flowers contributed to the lack of colour, of course. The walls are now dominated by the hanging memorials of the successive families from Newtimber Place — the Newnhams in the tiny, bare north transept, the Osbornes at the base of the tower and the Buxtons in the nave — some beautifully inscribed. As always when trying to make out inscriptions, I had that feeling that Dr Johnson was looking over my shoulders**. There once was a screen dividing the minimal nave from the chancel; to-day it is all straightforward and all that remains of the screen lies beside the font — a representative moulded section of what must have been quite a massive structure. Simplicity is the keynote here, often likely with an aisleless nave.

In spring, the churchyard was full of clumps of flowering primroses with only the distant roar of the Brighton traffic to compete with the chaffering of the birds. A survey of this churchyard was undertaken some ten years ago by the Countryside Survey, I was told, and over a hundred species of plant identified. As well as consecrated burial places and reservoirs for wild flowers, churchyards have also become refuges for wild life. Before coming here I read in E V Lucas's 'Highways and Byways' that he had counted a dozen adders basking in the sun one afternoon on the slopes to the south. Fortunately for me, the sun was not out on the morning when I was there so I could sketch undisturbed. Still, after all, adders deserve a refuge too so who should I be to resent or disturb them.

* Or that other St John, the Baptist, as Pevsner has it. I always tend to regard Pevsner as in the same class as the Pope so it is a comfort to find him occasionally fallible.
** After re-reading this piece, I cannot resist including Johnson's famous comment —
'In lapidary inscriptions a man is not upon oath'.

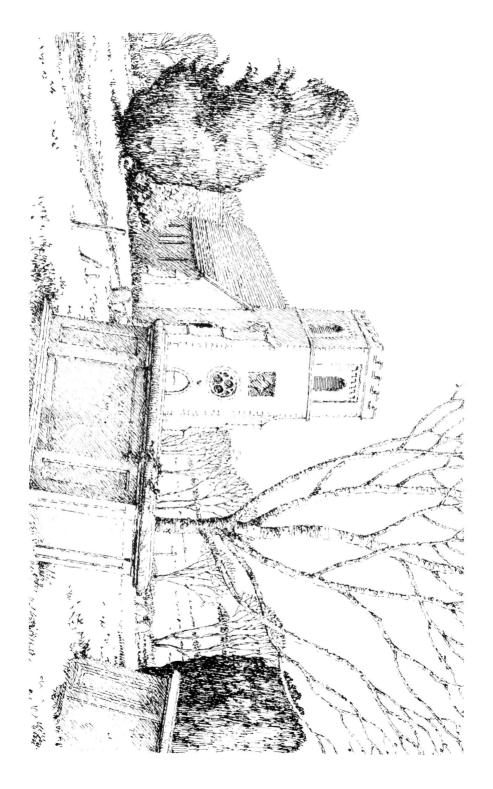

Standing on its ridge overlooking the Rother, St James's church, Ewhurst, continues to look down across the valley to its near contemporary on the other side, Bodiam Castle, as it has done for 600 years. The church is the senior in origin, being 12th century, whereas the castle dates from 1385. It is a salutary commentary on the relative staying power of religion and the secular to note that the church remains true to its purpose while the castle's intended role has withered and degenerated to no more than a tourist attraction, however majestic it may continue to look. One up to the church, even if it may attract fewer than the castle but, then, tourists are not always an unmixed blessing — unless one has a financial interest.

The Norman element in the church is most obvious in the tower and its west doorway. This entrance exhibits a conventional semi-circular inner arch, succeeded externally by a slightly pointed arch springing from foliated shafts to suggest late Norman in date. As some protection from the ravages of weather it has been given a much more recent, shallow, open, gabled porchlet. The tower itself, solid and square and glowing with ironstone blocks, barely reaches the roof line of the nave. Above, a shingled spire, oddly shaped, that must have been as difficult to construct as it is ungainly in appearance, reaches uncertainly to the sky. 'Twisted' says my 'Notes' — intentional, say I more politely. But why? It does few favours to the Norman tower on which it rests.

Norman traces persist in the arcade between nave and narrow south aisle where square-cut pillars and round arches seem, at least to me (there was no guide to amplify Pevsner's brevity), to have been cut from an original external nave wall. The church has a Decorated north aisle as well, much larger than the south, giving the interior an unbalanced look. In fact the whole church is asymmetrical with the tower noticeably offset from the line of nave and chancel. Again one wonders why.

What is there in here to remark on especially? First the font; substantial, simple and 13th century — what did they have before? Next, a somewhat open screen intervening between the chancel and an altar that is almost Calvinistic in its austerity — a far cry from Rome and pre-Reformation England. There are oil paintings in abundance and a painted wooden chandelier of ostentatious presence in the nave gangway. And last, but not least, a small brass at the west end of the north aisle. It depicts the kneeling figure of a layman †1520. Looking down on him is an old carved face, plump and smiling (at least I hope it is smiling and not grimacing) that acts as the western respond for the north arcade and therefore can be no more recent than the 13th century. No doubt there are other treasures and antiquities that I have missed but not too many — piscinas and a remodelled sedilia, yes, I do acknowledge.

The churchyard earns praise from Pevsner who found it 'exceptionally well planted'. It is extensive and certainly well planted with headstones, ancient and modern, dispersed amongst the usual crop of yews, conifers, deciduous trees and miscellaneous bushes. A mature magnolia beside the tower, which one could hardly miss, and a sweet gum from North America (thoughtfully labelled to enlighten us ignoramuses) are perhaps what Pevsner had in mind. It is all very rural and secluded, with the pleasant houses which make up Ewhurst on two sides, fields and woods on the other two with the embanked river not far away.

After I left the church, I had my sandwich lunch looking across the flood plain of the Rother towards Bodiam Castle. As I munched away, I watched a flight of small birds wheeling and diving as one, as if driven by one single controlling impulse. Coming from the church, these disciplined acrobatics could hardly fail to suggest to me that something similar may, just as likely, direct everything else, including us. Who would have thought that a visit to Ewhurst church and flight of birds could revive doubts about the concept of individual freewill — which we like to think we all possess.

St Peter's, Chailey, should not be confused with St Mary's, north Chailey, or St Martin's chapel of the Heritage Craft School for crippled children, admirable though both the latter are. Here we are concerned with the original parish church which acts as the focus of the long irregular parish of Chailey that runs south from Sheffield Park almost to the uplift of the Downs.

This focus consists of a triangular green beside the A275 around which are grouped old houses of more than one period as well as the church. I saw no village shops but nearby there is the Five Bells Inn of considerable antiquity, part genuine and part reproduction. Unless one lives here, Chailey seems the sort of place through which one passes without stopping on the way from A to B.

The church, though, deserves a visit, as does the Five Bells and both, on the damp February day when I was there, engaged my attention. The church stands in a fine wide-spread churchyard that descends southwards towards one of those modest streams that combines with others to water the upper reaches of the Ouse. As a churchyard, it is notable, I found, for an unusual number of dark, moss-covered, old chest tombs in varying stages of decay. There are also three enormous old yews, entirely compatible with what lies all around. To-day, the countryside and village look sparsely populated; not in the past if the churchyard is a reliable witness.

The church itself is a bit of a mixture. A 13th century west tower occupies the eye as one approaches from the lych-gate. It is a top-heavy feature now; solid and square basically with buttresses of a darker stone and pierced by later windows (in my enthusiasm for the past I think I detected a small blocked square that once was a window in the south face) but what I am sure is an anachronism is the silvery, shingled cap. This seems too large and leads one to infer that competition with the strapping yews may have been its genesis. Crowning it is a weather vane in the shape of a cockerel, dated 1772, and I daresay the spire may be of a similar age.

The chancel is about thirty years older than the tower — rough old sandstone walling with lancet windows, north and south. As elsewhere in the church, there has been reconstruction here but it is not obvious externally. A picture from the Burrell Collection, dated 1780, shows a priest's doorway and a low-side window; these had gone by 1845 as had the nave. Restoration in 1846, followed by enlargement in 1878 has left the church as we now find it — Early English chancel, Victorian nave and north aisle with a lean-to extension and a south aisle which partly escaped Mr Scott. He was the architect son of Sir George Gilbert Scott and built the other church in the parish. Sir George's sons were 'competent and careful like their father' says Pevsner in his Dictionary and the work here confirms that compliment. If only Victorian architects could have carried a 'distressing' tool in their kitbags.

A Victorian nave and aisles has inevitably affected the interior and its memorials from the past. These, in the shape of wall tablets, now concentrate in the chancel except for that of Richard Bourchier, †1770, one-time Governor of Bombay, who now rules in solitary state at the base of the tower. Who would care to shift a colonial governor in all his earthly (or should it be heavenly?) pomp.

I cannot claim any acquaintance with the Heritage Craft School on North Common, just over a mile away from St Peter's, but the former must, one feels, be what the area is noted for now. Whether this is to the disadvantage of the old church I don't know but I rather doubt it. If I lived here I would be grateful for its present less conspicuous role, important though it still will be for some that live around. One's attitude to any church must depend, I suppose, on which is held to be of more consequence, the here and now or the hereafter, and that is liable to change with age.

If anything can dispel the magic of the Downs, 1930s seaside housing can and does. There is a lot of it about east of Brighton; doubtless it is pleasant to live within sight and sound of the sea but how much better it would be if the coastal downs were left to the sheep and seabirds and the occasional isolated hamlet. Such a place, clearly, once was Ovingdean. No longer — houses in which to retire and grow old have seen to that. By a miracle, though, this church and a few period flint and cobblestone houses have managed to conceal themselves at the bottom of a fold in the downs. In this brief, withdrawn spot, one can step into the comely past (in architectural terms, at any rate) and forget picture windows, TV aerials and ribbon development.

I was lucky to come here on the scheduled day in the week when a very senior trio attended to their churchyard duties. They had the all-important key and one, an ex-churchwarden (who still managed to cut the grass amongst the closely-cluttered graves and curbstones depsite a game leg) very amiably remained to instruct me in all there was to know.

This is a dear little church, crouching low to the ground which rises fairly sharply towards a bare, empty shoulder of the Downs to windward. Sheltered by the lie of the land and by a ring of tall sycamores, St Wulfran's has lasted here from 1066. No wonder the ex-churchwarden and his cronies take pleasure and pride in preserving church and churchyard for the benefit of past and future generations and for the occasional amateur sketcher. There are plenty of the former and room on the slope of the Downs for more of the latter.

Externally the church, like the churchyard wall, is all flint. And mostly Norman, too. The square, low tower, topped and shaded by the trees in summer, is 13th century; it has one bell, said to be 500 years old, and tiny apertures to emit its sound. On the south wall of the nave, still visible, are the scorched stones that once formed an arcade for an aisle; the aisle has gone, popularly said to have been destroyed by the retreating French on their way back to the sea after an attack on Lewes in 1377. Not so, said my informative friend — the French are far too readily blamed for wanton destruction along the south coast. Presumably we are accused similarly by the French for our transgressions, genuine or imaginary. Genuine, I hope.

Past the dense protective yew that overhangs the little Victorian porch, one finds oneself in a cosy, intimate interior, lit by a mixture of Norman and lancet windows. The predominant architectural feature is the chancel arch, wide and Norman. It is impressive, made more so by two smaller flanking arches, added as a Victorian afterthought making the whole not unlike a screen in stone. The chancel contains a font that is unique in my experience. Reputed to be old but judged modern by my informant, it is embedded in a window sill so that only the lip of the bowl projects visibly. It is rather as if an old piscina had been pressed into use. To the south of the chancel is a minute chapel, more like an anchorite's cell, it seemed to me. A blocked arch suggests that it might have been an extension to the south aisle which the French, in their hurry to escape to sea, omitted to burn down. Pevsner is silent and Ovingdean too modest to attract much in the way of erudite hypotehises.

It is a fact that some churches become more or less exclusively identified with past members of prominent local families. Ovingdean and the Kempes are a case in point, more especially with Charles Kempe, †1907. He is famous for his stained-glass windows all over Sussex (scoring 55 mentions from Pevsner). Most of the windows here, tall, narrow and glowing with colour, are his and bear his wheatsheaf signature. He painted the chancel ceiling and bought and brought from Oberammergau carved rood figures which he installed above the central chancel arch. He also designed the family vault near the porch, but if I interpret Mee correctly, he is buried and memorialised in Chichester cathedral. I daresay he might be more at home in homely Ovingdean.

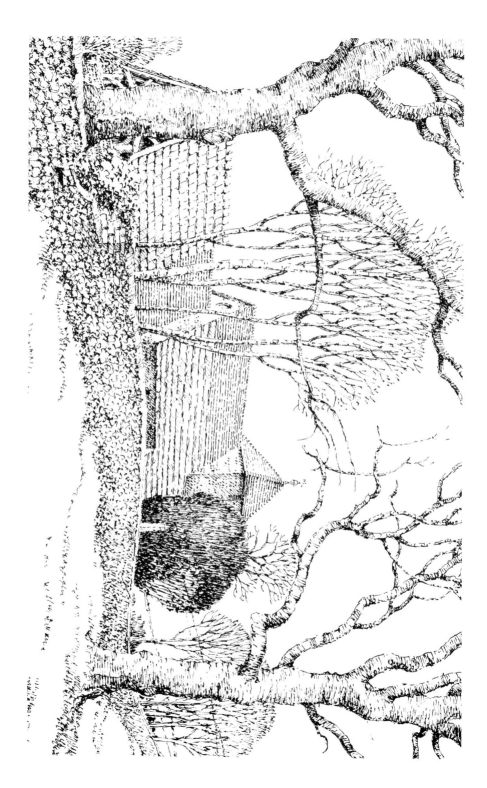

STREAT
Dedication not known (by me)

Roman road

Streat chuch is a modest little building nicely placed on a ridge looking south across the plain towards the Downs a couple of miles away, which here are conspicuous for the famous V-shaped plantation commemorating Queen Victoria's Jubilee. So the church, a Victorian-looking building in flint, confronts at a respectful distance a Victorian celebration in beech, fir and lime. Immediately adjacent to the north stands the impressive Jacobean facade of Streat Place — a mansion into which mounted Royalists sought hurried refuge from pursuing Roundheads, if Arthur Mee is to be believed. Peace reigns now and the echoes of war are confined to anecdote and the ubiquitous war memorials.

Despite its appearance, the church or rather its underlying framework is Early English with rectors dating from 1255 in the reign of Henry III. To-day the 'Benefice is held in sequestration' and the church is in the care of a priest-in-charge. Nevertheless, when I sketched, it was open and the lighting worked; it is not neglected and the money safe is emptied daily so visitors are expected and my mite will not languish.

What gives the church its Victorian appearance is the wall cladding. The church was restored in 1852, says my 'Notes on Sussex Churches', which also defined it as Early English but it must have been at this restoration that the flints, which compose the external surface of the walls virtually throughout, were arranged in a sort of strident crazy-paving pattern with prominent ribbon pointing. The effect is not attractive (compare the short length of nave wall not so treated) and rather spoils a church which has so much going for it scenically. No doubt the restored flint, set firmly in place by its proud pointing, will have the lasting qualities hoped for and give a fresh lease of life. It is attendance that really could do with a fresh lease of life.

In plan the church is noticeably asymmetrical with a north chapel balancing in an offset way a short south aisle. The north chapel is described as a 'dormitory' in my 'Notes' — a term I have not seen used before in respect of part of a church. Now this 'dormitory' is used as a vestry where the bulky organ allows room but I have no doubt that torpid parishioners have snoozed comfortably in this chamber in the days of long-winded sermons. One couldn't sleep there now nor would long-winded sermons be tolerated.

The interior of the church is small and compact. It may all look Victorian superficially and restored here too but it does rejoice in some memorials that any church would be happy to display. Two large alabaster wall tablets, complete with cherubs, armorial bearings, broken pediments and urns, occupy most of the north wall of the nave. On the gangway below are two 18th century cast-iron slabs, one sufficiently large to accommodate several deaths occurring in one family between 1714 and 1754. There are also two older stone slabs by the chancel steps, dated 1636, roughly contemporary with those exciting events at Streat Place and long before Victorian rescue cast its all-embracing gloss over this medieval structure.

Well looked after as this little church is, and has been, one suspects that its operational days are nearing their end. It is sad; although still standing and apparently unchanged, a redundant church is somehow petrified and not the same thing as a living church. Sad too for those whose memorials can no longer attract our attention or remembrance for that is why they were put there on the walls and on the floors in the first place. Set apart in its pleasant churchyard on a ridge in the quiet Sussex countryside, all Streat church lacks to-day is a sufficient demand for its religious services. I may be doing those who live in the scattered houses that make up Streat an injustice but I rather doubt it. I am sure they are fond of their church but possibly more in the way that I look upon churches and less in the way for which they were originally designed and built. The fault lies with us and not with the churches. It is we that have changed and not the churches.

WIVELSFIELD
St Peter and St John the Baptist

Wifel's open land

This little church continues to nestle within its compact rural hamlet as it has for centuries while latterly most of the population has elected to drift away to Wivelsfield Cross, a much more scattered community. That dispersal may be to the advantage of St Peter and St John; it has retained the church in its compatible surroundings and it has allowed the churchyard to develop southwards for an uninterrupted prospect of the long level line of the Downs. Sadly, though, this churchyard extension commemorates two members of one family who gave their lives in the successive great wars of this century. It is a gracious gift and honours their memory. When the church was sketched in 1787 there were no yews to obstruct the view. Now they are all around. On the south side they are comparatively immature, for yews; less than two hundred years old. To the north where the churchyard is restricted by houses and the village road, they are more close set. One specimen by the north doorway is said to be at least a thousand years old and indeed older than the present church. But maybe not older than the original church for churches must always have preceded their familiars, the sepulchral yews.

Anyway, Wivelsfield's ancient tree is only just older than the present church for, removed and re-installed in the Victorian north aisle, is an arched doorway that dates from circa 1070. Seen from outside, Norman one would say, and indeed that is what the chuch guide does say, but seen from inside, where the floor level is lower as is normal inside a church, the doorway looks tall and narrow and one would say Saxon — as do my 'Notes'. To-day, after its removal from the Norman nave to the Victorian aisle and in view of its origin at the collision of two cultures, it is probably safest to assess it as Saxo-Norman-Victorian.

The church as it stands to-day is distinctly composite although all composed of the same agreeable sandstone. The nave was Norman, whence the doorway but, of course, with the addition of the aisles, north and south, the stonework that once defined the nave has gone; nevertheless it was Norman in situation at least. Next, the south chantry is Early English; the south aisle Perpendicular; the chancel also Early English but now after extension, modern; the tower 15th century and the north aisle Victorian. I hope I have got all that right. When I built a small brick wall in my garden years ago, I embedded on its surface, with justified pride, a few coins of the year in question. What a pity the medieval masons didn't date their work permanently. All we have to go on for the most part is the style they adopted. For somewhere like Wivelsfield which began life as a chapel-of-ease to Ditchling, the masons may not have been of the first rank and possibly old fashioned which could make dating by style unreliable. That would be my excuse if I have got Wivelsfield all wrong.

When it comes to the interior, the body of the church is rather unremarkable. There are two recesses; that on the east wall of the chantry was once decorated with a black and white lozenge pattern (so the Revd Henry Rush found it in 1870 when he reported in Volume XXII of the Sussex Archaeological Collections), now it is hidden by a curtain and a reproduction of da Vinci's Last Supper — not an improvement, I would say. The other recess, in the north wall of the chancel, may have enclosed a tomb, says the guide. Now it is obscured by the reredos which previously stood behind an earlier altar. It seems an odd re-arrangement — a reredos should be behind, not before, as its name implies.

The memorials seem to have migrated to the base of the tower. Here there is a very fine alabaster wall tablet above what looks like 17th century ledger stones. One of these has the distinction of a supplementary inscription in upside down lettering. Flat on the floor, as it probably was originally, it could be read easily enough; vertically it is virtually impossible to decipher.

Prior to the memorials, upside downery also existed on the label stops of the Tudor doorway inside the porch where two grotesques dare one to enter. They are not welcoming, threatening more like. Evidently the prudent Victorian did not care to trifle with such menacing finials and left well alone when they did up the church. Very wise, too.

166

SLAUGHAM
St Mary

Sloe water meadow

Slaugham, a tiny picturesque hamlet, lies about six miles south of Crawley, off the beaten track and just off the fringes of what might be described as rhododendron-infested Sussex where the great houses and gardens like Nymans and Wakehurst Place hold sway. Slaugham, indeed, did have its great house, now no more than a ruin, where the Covert family held sway from the time of Henry II to Charles II. It is said that their 'manors extended from the banks of the Thames to the English Channel'. Now their sway is confined, it seems, to the sanctuary and their chapel in Slaugham church. How do such families manage to cease to exist, one wonders. Presumably their connections survive; the Covert females and their dowries surely were eminently desirable and marriageable. Some, at least, survive metallically and monumentally here in the recesses of the church.

Externally, the church is best seen from a distance — say from the Cheques Inn across the green. Close-to, the appearance of much of its old sandstone walling is rather spoilt by black ribbon pointing — something Alec Clifton-Taylor would certainly have criticised. Nor does the later stonework, severe grey ashlar blocks, make too warm an impresion. It seems a pity for a church that can boast a blocked Saxon or early Norman doorway of strength and simplicity. The Normans left us the nave, the Plantagenets the chancel, south aisle and lower half of the tower to which the Victorians economically added the upper half as well as providing a southwards extension to the aisle. The Coverts gave us their south chapel in the 17th century while the 20th century bestowed the transeptal vestry-cum-organ chamber. And Mr Kempe gave the stained glass that does so much to enrich the interior. Would that Grimm had been here to show us how the tower was finished before the Victorians got to work on it. My guess; much the same but without the shingled cap.

Which brings me to the more interesting interior. First, this church is, or was, famous for its wall paintings, discovered under several coats of whitewash'. They now only exist in barely discernible reproductions at the base of the tower. Fortunately the same hand seems to have reproduced them in Volume XIII of the Sussex Archaeological Collections of 1861. They represent the Scourging, the Crucifixion, a fish caught in a net (very symbolic), a fragment of the Last Supper and a soul borne heavenwards. The Revd Campion, who wrote the article, suggested that paintings like these covered all the interior walls — the nave anyway, I suppose.

Thence to the chancel and the chapel and to the Coverts. Chronologically, one finds Richard, †1452, and his three wives kneeling in brass at the back of the Easter recess in the sanctuary; next John, †1494, in full armour under a canopy, in brass vertically against the chapel wall (he came from the chancel, it is thought); then Richard, †1579, kneeling with his two wives and 14 children in a serried rank in stone in a magnificent wall monument — fluted columns Corinthian capitals and Tudor roses, all under a classical cornice; finally in brass, in another recess in the sanctuary, Dame Jane, †1586. Thereafter the Coverts seem to vanish from monumental history. What happened to the 14 children? I cannot leave the chapel without remarking on Captain Ellison RN who suvived the heat of battle at sea against the Napoleonic French only to succumb in 1817 'after a long and painful attack of gout'. I felt a twinge when I read that.*

Although this church looks best from the green, I could not resist the gable ends of chancel and chapel. Here, in considerable state, is the sepulchre of the Matchams. The family pedigree, detailed at length in stone, reveals that George Matcham's wife, Catherine, was the daughter of the Revd Edmund Nelson of Burnham Thorpe in Norfolk and thus the sister of the great Horatio. It gives me no small satisfaction to claim to have sketched three of the churches associated with the 'immortal memory'; these two and that at Tenterden where his daughter, Horatia, was the wife of the vicar.

---

* Gout is agonising; poor Captain Ellison.

Coming, as I do, from Kent where the Culpepers lie in state in many a country church, it is a pleasure to encounter them in strength here at Ardingly. Fore-warned by Pevsner, I had expected to find them but, at first sight of the interior, I feared I should be thwarted by the comprehensive tartan carpeting. Fortunately a framed plan of the church (there was no guide) saved the day and hinted where they could be found — under a moveable runner in the centre of the chancel. Beneath this protective fabric, framed by their inset Gothic canopies, supported by illuminated armorial shields and reproduced in stylised brass effigy, lie Richard and Nicholas Culpeper with their respective wives. In the case of Nicholas and his wife, they are accompanied by their 18 children. No wonder the Culpepers are so ubiquitous. There are two further Culpeper brasses, both female, which I missed but not so the reliable Mee who includes them in his 'Brass Portrait Gallery of Sussex'. One of the male Culpepers married a Wakehurst, presumably a daughter of Wakehurst Place, which explains the Culpeper presence in such unKentish territory as Sussex. What Tudor could forgo Wakehurst Place when retainers to keep it up were still feudal, abundant and economical. To-day, or rather when I was there, the Place was eclipsed by an ostentatious Antiques Fair at the County Agricultural Show Ground which separates Place from church. Actually, of course, church and Place each qualify as very senior antiques. Happily commerce and collectors avoided the church that day.

The Culpepers are not alone in their glory. In the chancel they are anticipated by an alabaster effigy of a priest, prostrate and rather mutilated, in a crocketted recess, and by a grand tomb chest, also in a recess, bearing on a black marble slab the brasses of Richard Wakehurst, †1455, and his wife. 1455, incidentally, was the year of the onset of the War of the Roses but I don't imagine the effects of that dynastic struggle were felt by those living in the depths of the Weald. Macaulay advanced such a view in his History — 'In a week the peasant was driving his team and the esquire flying his hawks over the field of Towton or of Bosworth as if no extraordinary event had interrupted the regular course of human life'. If peace returned so swiftly to Bosworth field, the Wakehurst and their retainers at Ardingly can hardly have known of its disturbance. But later, sad to say, the dangerous, merciless rule under Mary did reach down here to send Thomas Avyngton to the stake at Lewes.

The glamour of the Culpepers and their predecessors apart, this compact little church presents a fairly conventional medieval aspect, especially from the south (my view, more or less); warm, honey-coloured sandstone, squat low tower and ancient walls amidst a plethora of mossy, lichen-speckled tombs. It all looks just right externally (and would internally but for that tartan carpet) with the crowded stalls of the antique dealers, like Bosworth, worlds away. The nave and chancel date from 1330, the south aisle not quite so old, the tower and screen Perpendicular and the north aisle and vestry Victorian. Such is this pretty church which has rested so comfortably down a lane on the outskirts of its village for six hundred years.

When I arrived, I was lucky enough to find someone cutting the grass and the air was heavy with the summery scent which that activity brings. There is much to cut, round about the headstones, but that didn't prevent the grass-cutter taking time off to show me parallel grooves in the soft sandstone of one of the buttresses. They came, he said, from medieval bowmen sharpening the heads of their arrows against the stone; it seemed improbable to me. It is a nice thought but why are such scratchings not prevalent wherever the stone is suitable? Later, a policeman appeared. Apparently, the grass-cutter explained, two suspicious people had been reported lurking in the churchyard. One was him, the other me! One can't be too careful when fairs are in progress.

CROWHURST
St George

Wooded hill frequented by crows

Crowhurst is better known, I imagine, for its massive old yew and for the remnant of the 13th century manor house than it is for its church. The yew, said to be the oldest in Sussex, is vigorous still (1993) with plenty of new foliage at the extremities of its contorted branches. Hollow, but held together by iron bands and propped by timber crutches, protected by a circular iron railing and with a life that spans most of the recorded history of these islands and certainly that of the manor of Crowhurst, it is a must for any sketch of Crowhurst church.

Standing as it does in the shadow of this celebrated yew, the church strikes a more modest note, although no church within the Pelham domains or bearing their famous buckle can really be described as modest. It is just that it is outranked in age by its venerable companion — by a considerable margin, too. The four-square Perpendicular ironstone tower is what remains from the Pelham ownership; well buttressed against instability, it was never a likely candidate for Mr Teulon's rescue of the rest in 1856. To be fair it should be the then rector's rescue for he alone bore the £1,500 cost of demolishing and replacing a dilapidated nave and chancel to which was added a north aisle to accommodate the increased population of the village. A very respectable job was done, clearly, since apart from a disparity in weathering, the church now looks all of a piece and 14th century into the bargain.

With the demolition of the old church went the memorials, if any there were. Pevsner mentions none and the excellent guide only those I take to be post-reconstruction. Surely there might have been a brass of a Pelham or a Papillon or even a monk or two from the priory at Hastings. The light and airy, antiseptic almost, interior loses some character thereby but I think Pevsner's comment 'a run-of-the-mill interior' is unfair. How else can a relatively recent interior look unless the local grandee uses the interior decoration to express his convictions rather as did Beresford Hope with his richly decorated creation at Kilndown in Kent. Without such indulgence here, the simple stone pulpit becomes prominent; it must be the post-Victorian being entirely free of the fussy extravagances the Victorians were unable to resist.

Ideally, one would like to sketch the church from the south, in the garden of Court Lodge, so that the ruins of the original manor house could be included in the picture but in spring and summer the foliage of the intervening trees effects a total prohibition. The fragments of walling, particularly the shell of the east window, ecclesiastical in appearance though they may be, were I was assured by the present-day owner all that remains of the manor house. To-day, these old stones contribute greatly to the ambience of the church and no depiction can be complete without them or the historic yew. At least I managed to include the latter — as did Mr Lambert when he drew Crowhurst church in 1770, long before it received Mr Teulon's attention. Superficially there doesn't seem to have been a great deal of change.

A glance at the map suggests that William the Conqueror's army, or part of it, might have passed this way as it began to assemble before attacking the Saxon fyrd which Harold had drawn up on the ridge south of where Battle now is. It can't have been an easy time for either side; anticipation of engagement never is. Crowhurst was one of Harold's manors and, like all Saxon property, was promptly appropriated for the benefit of William's companions in his hazardous enterprise. Very likely the unknown Saxon who lived here died with Harold on that fateful day. Tranquil though it all now seems and secure as the church may look above the winding road, it could well have been the scene of yet another crisis in our history if Hitler had chanced his arm in 1940 as William did in 1066.

WEST HOATHLY
St Margaret

St Margaret's, West Hoathly, is fairly typical of the churches that one finds on the northern perimeter of the Ashdown Forest. Solidly made of sandstone, parts of it have been here since the 11th century. What gives it its distinctive wealden character, I think, is the uncomplicated west tower* with its overlapping, broached needle spire. Unlike many towers in Kent, they seem to manage in Sussex, as here, without the addition of any external stair turret to provide access to the bells and upper stages. I rather miss the stair turrets. Local sandstone must also have been used for the front of the manor house** which faces and complements the tower. Together with the Priest's House and various other period houses on three sides, this church perches very snugly in its crowded churchyard. 'Perches' is the right word for, on the fourth, east side, the churchyard descends very rapidly to the wooded valley below.

Apart from the tower, the church consists of nave, chancel, south aisle and south chapel involving construction in the 13th and 14th centuries. This is ironfounder territory and, appropriately, one enters through a door heavily studded with nail heads, dated 1626. Probably those nails came from the foundry of the Infields, two of whom are commemorated in the south chapel by rough, heavy, cast-irong grave slabs dated 1619 and 1624. The Infields lived at Gravetye, one of the great houses hereabouts; as later did William Robinson who presented the compatible sandstone lych-gate. Mr Robinson was a gardener of repute, not an iron master, and I expect some of the handsome trees in the churchyard came from him.

Once inside, I was particularly impressed by the floor; flagged throughout, its austere medieval effect could not entirely be dispelled by the serried ranks of yellow chairs, bolted together, instead of pews. In fact one might say the stone flags rescue the interior. Although the Norman origin is confirmed by two windows, visible externally, there is no sign of them internally. Piecemeal medieval reconstruction is evident though from the design of the arcade pillars and responds. Reading from west to east, there is a semi-circular respond followed by a circular pillar; then part of the original wall with octagonal responds; next, between chancel and chapel, an octagonal pillar and finally, at the east end, an octagonal respond. In a collection of china, all this might be described as a harlequin set. It makes up in interest what it may lack in coherence.

West Hoathly church and its surroundings may be the picture of a serene county village now but a small brass in the aisle says that it has not always been so. It was from here that the unfortunate Ann Tree was taken in 1556 to be burnt at the stake in the high street in East Grinstead. This church, any church, offers the way to salvation, or claims to; in the time of Mary, disagreements with its pronouncements could and did lead to an agonising death. These old stones now offer nothing but welcome and almost any beliefs are accepted. How times have changed and how lucky we are to have the churches without the bigotry or the benefit of the Holy Office.

The churchyard is bounded by a well-built standstone wall. In the 18th century, the major landowners were responsible for its maintenance. One can see why; maintenance is still essential to prevent the churchyard spilling down the precipitous eastern slope. Within its perimeter are packed the many flaking headstones and disintegrating table tombs of those who did not offend. The most elegant, to my mind, I found by the churchyard rubbish heap. One can imagine the family pride which attended the commissioning and installation of this distinguished sarcophagus. Now, eroded and anonymous and distorted by the penetrating ivy, it keeps company with the bonfire and an upturned wheelbarrow. 'Death is the great leveller' they say — ivy and frost, too.

---

* My 'Notes' say there are Norman traces in the tower. I failed to see them.
** Arthur Mee says Anne of Cleeves lived in this house after she was separated from Henry VIII.

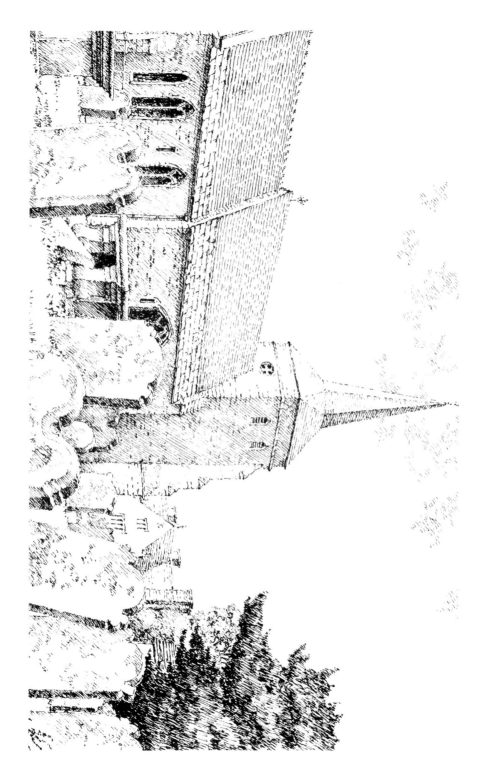

Ditchling village, a cross-roads at the heart of Sussex, seems to me to be the rural epitome of the county. As such, facing south towards the escarpment of the Downs, it is not surprising that it attracts the day-tourist, one of whom I must reluctantly include myself. It is difficult to say which is the magnet, the 13th century flint church or the ancient house opposite which was given to Anne of Cleeves but which Pevsner dismisses as 'nothing to do with her'.

The church has also attracted the thief and, when I arrived, was firmly locked with no guarantee that the vicar would be at home to surrender the key. Fortunately for me a solitary flower arranger was in the churchyard and, after a slight hesitation, she admitted me to the interior via the 'back way'. The church is cruciform in shape and it is under the north transept that one finds the 'back way'. Access is gained down a glass-covered tunnel to an underground vault, now converted to a modern sort of 'come-in-handy' meeting room, and from thence up into the body of the church through the transept. The latter is completely modernised and what memorials there were in this reconstructed chamber are now elsewhere.

Once out from behind the organ which blocks off the transept, the modern world evaporates and one is confronted initially by the tall, shafted pillars that support the central tower and constitute the crossing. They are an impressive quartet and are said to be the work of men brought over from Normandy whence also came the Caen stone. To the west lies the nave, unmarkble and two bays in length; to the east is the chancel of similar size but more evident of the past with its splayed and shafted windows, crowned with hood moulds terminating in carved heads. Alongside the chancel, of comparable dimensions, is the south chapel variously known as the Abergavenny or Neville chapel. Like the chancel, its windows are shafted inside with embracing hood moulds. My 'Notes', which are dated 1920, say that 'behind the organ in the north transept is an elaborate mural tablet to Henry Poole, †1580.' To-day this tablet, which displays three emblazoned shields and one blank (still awaiting another armigerous connection?), decorates the wall of the south chapel and, by virtue of Henry Poole's marriage to a Neville, thus entitles the chapel, I would suppose. Henry Poole is better here than hidden in the obscurity of the brutally refurbished north transept. The chapel, ex vestry, is now fenced about by elegant wooden screens which, although dated 1947, are eminently appropriate as protection for a 14th century sanctum.

Three other memorials, if that is the right word, deserve a mention even if all are totally anonymous. They are stone coffin lids, now preserved vertically in the south porch. One still retains its foliate cross, the other two so eroded as to be featureless but all three are of sufficient antiquity and redolent of mystery to give pause to all who enter the church conventionally through the porch — as one would were the inner door not locked.

To revert to the thieves who ultimately are responsible for the locked door, the church was the proud possessor of a pitch pipe (a sort of flute which gave the note to the choir in the days before the organ was installed). Now all that remains is its small glass case, empty on a shelf in the chancel. Who would possibly want to steal such an object, but go it did in 1992. There are two chests, one extremely pitted with a pitched lid. It was dusty and empty; such an honourable old chest deserves continued use, I think — stowage for hymn books perhaps. Previously there were three chests but one went with the thieves I was told by the flower lady. One sympathises with locked churches; a policy which, while it may preserve what remains inside, must also eliminate uncovenanted contributions from casual visitors. It is all so unfair here because Ditchling is the sort of place that really looks as if butter wouldn't melt in its mouth.

Church thieves do have a lot to answer for and one only hopes that answer they will be made to make here or in the hereafter.

As well as the famous abbey, commissioned by William on the spot and on the aftermath of the battle, there is also a parish church in this small town. The latter was founded by Abbot Ralph in 1115 in order that the abbey church could remain the exclusive province of the monks — for men only. In the event, the ladies have triumphed: the monks and their church are no more, the abbey became a girls' school and the parish has a really splendid church to which all are admitted. On my day, I was shown round by the admirable lady steward who is currently in charge of all the stewards, male and female, who invigilate here for the benefit of visitors. How times change.

St Mary's appears to have had five lives or five more or less complete buildings over the years 1115, 1150, 1250, 1350 and 1450, getting large and grander on each occasion so that now one finds a virtually complete Perpendicular church close under the north wall of the abbey grounds. Near enough one might say to show that the parish had not taken umbrage over their exclusion from William's abbey and retired in dudgeon to the other end of the town. Of the first church, all that remains is the trace of the Norman arch between the chancel and what is now the south chapel but was the base of the first tower. There is also from Norman times that long-lived article, the font.

It was at the final building campaign, which also saw the construction of the west tower, that the present nave was installed. Looking back from the chancel one can see how the line of the nave deviates. There are two theories here to account for this displacement — one, the chancel cants to the south in symbolic representation of Christ on the Cross; the other, the land here falls away to the north and so the new nave was given a nudge to the south to find a sounder footing. The substantial tower does call for something solid underneath and has evidently found it.

The nave is notable for its five-bay arcades, north and south. They are supported by alternate round and octagonal pillars which also alternate north and south. Even if this arrangement looks contrived (and why shouldn't it be?) they do look distinguished, topped by their capitals of large pointed leaves, in one case where the mason, all too humanly, muffed his calculations. Above the north arcade, between the clerestory windows, still remain faint frescoes recording the life of St Margaret of Antioch (why her, 'of whom nothing certain is known', in a church dedicated to Mary?). The frescoes continued above the chancel arch until Butterfield in his wisdom in the 1840s raised the chancel arch — to attract the eyes of the congregation towards heaven, I was told. In the process the frescoes, more likely to attract the eyes heavenwards, went. As in politics, a parochial example of an unintended consequence.

The most splendid memorial here, brasses not excepted, is the alabaster chest tomb of Sir Antony Browne, KG, †1548, and his wife, Dame Alis. They lie, side by side, on their gilded, semi-shafted, armorial chest; he in armour, she enrobed, both with their hands clasped in prayer — or so they would be had not Cromwell's soldiers, when stabled in the aisles, lopped their hands off. What was the symbolism of that spiteful act, I wonder. Sir Antony came into the abbey at the dissolution of the monasteries; he was an executor of Henry's will, tutor to the future Elizabeth I, 'Master of the King's Majesties Horcys and one of the Honourable Privy Council of our most dread Sovereign Lord'. Dread seems the right word for this particular sovereign.

A modern (1984) memorial, entirely appropriate to this parish church, is the stained-glass 'Senlac' window in the south aisle. Here are shown King Harold and Duke William contemplating each other against a background of scenes repeated from the Bayeux tapestry. One could spend a lot of time looking at this window, reliving that turning point in our history. One could also spend time deciphering the open page of the Geneva Bible in its glass case — a translation into English made in Geneva in the 1560s by exiles from the Marian persecution. It reeks of our contentious history as, of course, does this golden church, the whole town and abbey of Battle.

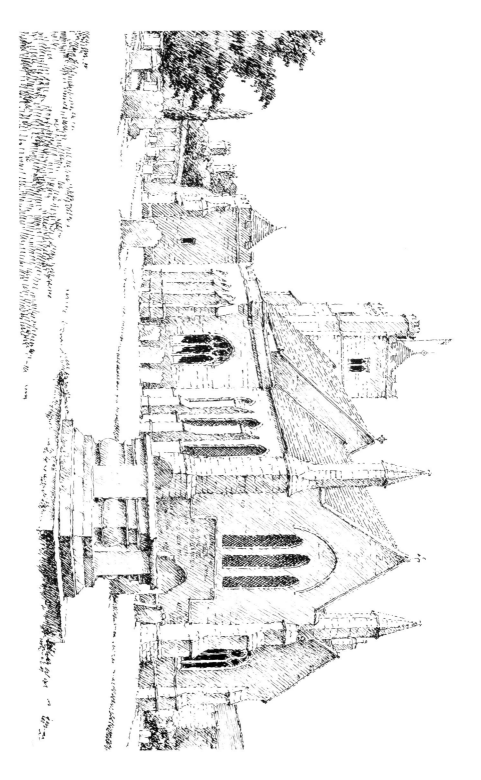

Waldron lies enmeshed in a confusing network of minor roads which can easily lead the newcomer astray.* When Waldron is eventually run to earth, one finds the epitome of a country village, hamlet more like, grouped around its mellow church. Here development might seem to have stopped over a century ago. Nevertheless, enterprise is not entirely absent; almost opposite the lych-gate is a thriving vineyard which must be modern, if it isn't Roman which I doubt.

The church, mostly constructed of tawny sandstone blocks, is Early English in origin, that is it dates from the 12th century. It is unlikely to have been the first church here, vide the Saxon font which now reposes outside on the grass facing the north porch. Fonts need a church, I think one may safely assume. This font, rediscovered in a neighbouring farm, is huge — any bowl, roughly four feet in diameter and rough in texture and, although described as 'one of the church's treasures', must be safe from theft, casual lifting theft, at any rate.**

Moving on two hundred years, the Early Englishness is continued by the chancel lancets, one with much-admired stained glass. Two others, now blocked, are separated by the east chancel window which, Pevsner suggests, replaced three other lancets that once combined to form an ordered group of five. There are two aisles to the four-bay nave; the north is 13th century, the south Victorian. A Perpendicular west tower, embattled with an inset cap and north east stair turret which might have come from Kent, provides the finial. Such is the basic structure of this typical and completely satisfying village church.

The interior is notable for the fine lofty arch at the base of the tower and for the absence of any chancel arch. Was there one once? Generally speaking, chancel arches far outrank any other arches in the church — Waldron may be an exception to prove the rule. Along the central gangway of the nave are six large, handsome armorial ledger stones and two with small brass plaques. One's eyes, though, are soon diverted from the nave floor, good though it is, to the north aisle where a huge flat obelisk (of slate, I think) rests above a marble sarcophagus to commemorate Major Jack Fuller, †1722. He must have been related to 'Mad Jack Fuller' of Brightling who was blessed (if that is the right word) with an even more conspicuous memorial, a pyramid-shaped mausoleum in the churchyard there. The Fullers were not inclined to do things by halves evidently. But then, what is so extravagant about a spectacular memorial? I expect Mad Jack is more remembered for his mausoleum than for his lifetime achievements or eccentricities.

Waldron church excites a hobby horse of mine. Mee, Pevsner and the guide each mention, as one of the church treasures, a pair of bronze, 16th century Italian candlesticks, nearly five feet high, the gift of the family who lived at Possingworth. A few years ago these candlesticks were sold. Should a third party, or inheritor, sell other people's gifts? I think not. Others will argue otherwise, I am sure, as does the guide. If the Huths had known their candlesticks were to be sold, I think they would have done better to keep the candlesticks in their manor or their money in their pockets.

After my solitary exploration here, I had my sandwich lunch by the stile at the untended, overgrown edge of the churchyard, shaded on one side by an oak and by a giant ash on the other. At this extremity, where the mower and scythe do not trespass, the nettles and saplings are waist high and jostle the jumbled headstones for light and air. The only movement came from a herd of black and white cows as they sluggishly circled the field below me. It was all sublimely peaceful and I felt as if I had been translated from the Sussex of rhododendrons to the untamed Andredeswald, or what remains of it.

* Could those confusing lanes be the descendants of Saxon trackways through the forest?
** Rereading this sentence, I now realise that this font must have been stolen once to fetch up in a 'neighbouring farm'.

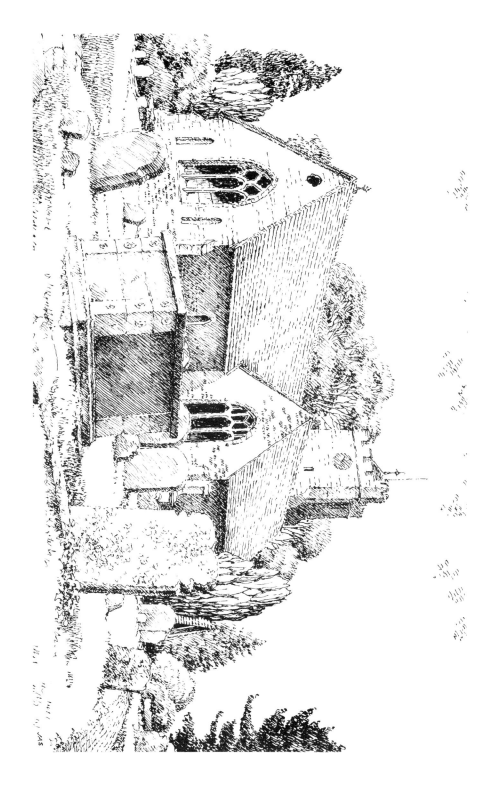

So far as I can remember, there are only two churches in eastern Sussex to have been built entirely of brick. East Guldeford, on the edge of the Romney Marsh, is one; Twineham is the other. East Guldeford dates from 1505, Twineham from the early years of Henry VIII's reign when England was finally emerging from its medieval past. There must have been some reason to provoke the change here from conventional stone or flint to brick and the guide suggests that it might have been due, in Twineham's case, to a local influx of Flemish brickmakers. Flemish they may have been, it was English bond (alternate courses of headers and stretchers) which they tactfully used to bind the walls of the church. In Tudor times, bricks were smaller than those we use to-day — an 18th century example of tax avoidance. Those here are of that distinctive size that one always associates with Tudor buildings. It appears as if they were at some time covered with rendering so that the overall effect now is of walls of mellow rosy brick splashed here and there with patches of a transparent silvery bloom. Will modern red-brick churches ever age half so well?

Twineham can never have been more than a scattered rural parish lying between two minor arms of the river Adur so it was not to be expected that those early Tudors could, or would, manage anything elaborate here in the heart of the forest. And nor did they. What they left us, still virtually unchanged, is a small nave joined to a smaller chancel by a crude depressed arch. There are no buttresses or hood moulds above the restrained, round-headed windows, nothing to cast a shadow or disturb the smooth run of the brickwork. Added to this economy is the tower for two bells, five now, equally austere if buttressed, and a south porch.

This porch is said by the guide to be contemporary with the rest but a notably well-informed contributor to the Sussex Archaeological Collections of 1918, Dr Grayling, says it is earlier. Certainly, for so modest a structure, the timbers that frame it seem unduly massive and their fastenings primitive. It has a look of antiquity that puts me in mind of the 14th century porch at Westmeston. Perhaps there was a wooden church here to which this porch belonged before the Flemings arrived to bring Twineham into the post-medieval age with their new-fangled clay bricks. The list of rectors, dating from 1287, would confirm an earlier church here.

Inside, the past is pleasantly evoked by the unrestored flooring and by the ledger stones below which lie the members of a prominent local family. And the simplicity of the aisleless nave is accentuated by the plain, whitewashed walls which, to judge by the depth of the window splays, are at least two feet thick — as they would need to be to bear the considerable weight of the Horsham slabs on the roof. Of the original furnishings, the one Elizabethan box pew, comprehensively carved, remains to be supported by the Jacobean pulpit. Above them, somewhat disproportionate to its surroundings, hangs a large reproduction of an Italian painting of the Holy Family. To redress this Continental display, three nice watercolours of the church represent indigenous talent. The font, as fonts invariably are, is old — 13th century says the guide. It bears 'the indent of a cross fylfot on the bowl' says the learned Dr Grayling. Not certain what I was looking for, I could find no cross. Later at home, my dictionary informed me that the cross fylfot is the swastika!*

If it wasn't for the chest tombs and headstones dotted about the churchyard, one might imagine the church was standing in the middle of a field. There are fields on all sides, no yews to convey the authentic churchyard atmosphere, but instead, scythed grass and several majestic oaks to remind one of the forest. In a corner by the rustic gate a plot was set aside in 1694 for use as a Quaker burial ground. It seemed odd; in all that churchyard the only place where the grass had been suffered to grow tall and feathery was the plot reserved for the Society of Friends. Can they still be friendless here 300 years after the Act of Toleration?

* In non-Christian terms, the swastika is said amongst other things, to be a symbol of fertility.

Poynings church presents a considerable challenge to the would-be sketcher. It stands on a restricted mound, so embowered with trees that one can only get a decent stand-off view by perching vulnerably in the middle of the road, fortunately not a very busy one. Which, presumably, is why the Sussex artist, F L Griggs, made his drawing look down on the roof tops from the Devil's Dyke, that great prehistoric fort on the Downs behind the church. In effect, Griggs' drawing consists almost entirely of trees stretching north into the distance across the blue Weald. His is more accomplished than mine (he was an ARA) but I have more church to show for my labours.

The church is equi-cruciform; chancel, nave and transepts all being equal in size, a Greek cross in plan. Separating these is the great square tower which looks Norman but isn't. The whole church was built, in one go about 1370, of knapped flints with particular care taken to square the flints that face the porch — ashlared flints, one might say. Elsewhere, here and there, occasional limestone blocks interrupt the dark, flint facade. I wondered if there could be some design to account for the position of these random stones; 'erratic', the word geographers use to describe the boulders left behind by retreating glaciers, would seem to apply equally to Poynings' intermittent blocks. Could it be that from time to time, the flint-knappers failed to keep pace with the flint-layers?

Externally and internally, what seems prodigious in this downland church is the excess of height to length; outside the effect is towering, inside cavernous, and yet remarkably economical with the number of buttresses needed to keep the structure upright. When Michael and Joan de Ponyngges subscribed 400 marks towards its building in 1369, they must have had something very grand in mind — imposing enough to dominate the plain to the north and substantial enough to stand comparison with the ramparts of the Devil's Dyke immediately behind to the south. I am sure they would be more than satisfied to see how well and unchanged their church has survived the passage of time.

Inside, the great arches that support the central tower dominate. They reach almost to the ridges of the roofs. They are pointed, as also are all the windows which makes the church Early Perpendicular, as the pundits have it. 'Perpendicular' couldn't be a more apt description in the case of Holy Trinity.

The north transept, the Montague Chapel, is now given over to the organ, the vestry and the house-keeping impedimenta that every church inevitably accumulates. The chapel has not benefited thereby and is now nondescript internally. Opposite, the Poynings Chapel is protected by a Perpendicular screen. It is rather empty with no sign of the de Ponyngges. On the floor is a large, damaged coffin slab that looks as if it came from elsewhere. Under a strip of carpet lies an indented grave slab bordered by Lombardic inscriptions; Lombardic lettering always defeats me but this memorial has a clerical look to it, I thought.

The chancel, large as it is, is spaciously uncluttered. A few wall tablets, a triple sedilia, and a pair of silvery oak pews is all. Pevsner identifies these as family pews; the families must have felt rather exposed when in occupation and I would imagine these pews are now the province of the choir, if any. The high walls of the nave, bare of memorials, speak eloquently of medieval austerity to which nothing of structural significance has been added or subtracted since. Apart from one window in the south transept, this absence of change applies to the whole church. The founders, the de Ponyngges, may have no sepulchral memorial here so their inviolate church must serve as their remembrance. Which it does and what could be better?

One cannot leave Poynings church without remarking the benches in the porch. They are long and strikingly rough and ready. They hardly look as if they began life as seats, rafters rescued from elsewhere more likely, but now enjoying an honourable retirement. Somehow, they seem to epitomise a great church whose great days are over.

WHATLINGTON
St Mary Magdalene

Farmstead of Hwaetel's people

Whatlington may not be one of the great or famous churches of Sussex, far from it, but I am very glad to have included it in my catalogue, all the same. Plaudits from the pundits are few and comments insufficient to attract any but the persistent. If one wants to see a great church and ancient, historic ruins, Battle is only two miles away. So one can be fairly confident of peace and solitude at Whatlington. Maybe that is why Malcolm Muggeridge chose it. As I absent-mindedly munched my sandwiches under the belt of lime trees, I was surprised to find myself confronting his grey headstone — 'Malcolm Muggeridge, 1903-1990, writer'. In his later years he was affectionately known, I believe, as the 'Sage of Robertsbridge' and Salehurst churchyard was where I had assumed he would be. To stand beside the grave of someone to whom, not so long ago, one had listened with pleasure and seen on the television seemed vaguely disturbing; most of those we encounter in stone are invariably too distant in time to provoke a similar reaction.

The church stands well back from and well above the road; the only sound of traffic comes from the occasional passing Hastings train. The churchyard is convex, bounded by indeterminate hedges and well away from where the centre of gravity of the village may be. The grass had recently been close cut; I had rather hoped to find myself waist-deep in long grass and cow parsley and it would not have been inappropriate. I had expected the church to be locked, it was, and half expected to find it redundant. But, if the notices in the porch are anything to go by, it is far from redundant and regularly in use. The annual finances are posted; from an amateur interpretation of these, it did seem that the diocesan demands of Chirchester had become something of a problem for this minor parish church struggling in the shadow of Battle. Doubtless the diocese has problems, too.

It is an odd-looking little building. The responsibility for this rests with Mr S W Tracey who, in 1862, substituted his Victorian-style tower, on the north side, for an earlier west tower. There is no sign of the latter now, where and how it joined the nave and no recollection of what it looked like. Although Mr Tracey's tower cum porch is relatively innocuous here, I think it might do would-be architects good to come to Whatlington to compare the elaboration of Victoriana with the medieval simplicity of the church's lancet windows. Some elaboration, string courses for instance, is desirable to cast a shadow and to relieve the deadening monotony here of the stucco which embalms the walls (it looks as if the east end of the chancel has been stripped of its stucco, to its obvious benefit aesthetically) but, even allowing for the incompetence of my draughtsmanship, most people would, I suspect, consider the tower's east window unfortunate and similarly the patterned tiling on the spire. For all that, Mr Tracey has made an intriguing addition to what essentially was a very simple nave and chancel housed under a single roof line. The apsidal vestry is his too but no-one could object to that. He does, though, seem to have been torn between reproducing the past, the vestry, and following the latest fashion, the tower. Does that sound pompous and patronising from an unqualified observer; probably it is and I daresay a modern architect would take me to task for disparaging the new and clinging to the old. The trouble is the old seems so much better.

Of the interior I have no personal experience apart from the tower porch. Here three bellropes hang down so there must be three bells, doubtless saved from the previous tower. Presumably the bellringers have learnt how to cope with a passing congregation without losing their concentration. Inside, it is said there is some early Norman walling still extant, a 1627 brass and a carved wooden pulpit of sufficient distinction to have been exhibited at the Great Exhibition in Hyde Park in 1851. It must be something of a change for anything to exchange the glare of public exposure at the Crystal Palace for the rural seclusion of the nave of Whatlington church. Surprising it may be but not necessarily a change for the worse could be maintained.

SELMESTON
St Mary?

Sigehelm's farmstead

Grouped pastorally under the lee of the Downs with its older neighbours, Alciston and Berwick, Selmeston church gives the impression of a little, flint Victorian church pretending to be a medieval country church. Which, in fact, is what it is or was; Early English say my 'Notes' but partly rebuilt in 1867, by Ewart Christian, no less. Externally, the unknapped flints, neo-Decorated windows, pristine buttresses and catslide roof over the new south aisle all belie the medieval origin implied by modest size and a long list of vicars stretching back over the years. It all looks so unweathered to-day.

The south aisle is Mr Christian's although he would hardly have introduced timber arcade pillars unless an earlier aisle had been here before. They appear to mimic columns of stone, I would say; octagonal to the carved capitals, thence arching braces, rather like king posts, to the roof above. The only other church that I can remember to have timber pillars is Wingham in Kent; Wingham used chestnut, here they are oak. Wingham's are huge and 400 years old, Selmeston's are shortish Victorian replacements, one is already split and I can't see them lasting as long as Wingham's.

Four other aspects of the interior call for comment. First, the unusually attractive floor of unpatterned rosy tiles set diagonally. Down the centre of the gangways are set brass commemorative plates of a similar size; two rectangular plates with elegant brass crosses on black grounds and a square ledger of 1741 with an inscribed coat of arms bordered by brass add variety. Although spanning a hundred years or more, the whole set looks to be one coherent design and is remarkably effective. There are not many church floors, particularly those that have been largely rebuilt, as attractive as this one — could it be down to Mr Christian?

Of the windows, the oldest in appearance is that on the north side of the chancel; it also appears at first glance to contain the oldest stained glass, soft blues and greys — medieval grisaille, one might say, until the tiny golden wheatsheaf, low down on the left hand side reveals the hand of Charles Kempe. Very much in demand towards the end of the 19th century, Kempe's work can be found all over the county and it gives one a sort of Sherlock Holmes satisfaction to locate his tell-tale logo.

The bell turret is a bit of a conundrum, to me at least. After several careful circuits, I could find no aperture through which the sound of the bell or bells might carry. Bell or bells there must be, why else the turret? Inside, under it and fastened to the west wall, there is a curious wooden, lever-shaped contraption connected heavenwards by wire. I longed to give it a tug to see, or hear, what would happen but my courage failed me.

A watercolour by one of the vicar's daughters at the west end of the church is joined by four faded reproductions of the interior. They were discovered in a London art shop by Lord Keynes. John Maynard Keynes we know as a man of great distinction, compared in his day to such economic heavyweights as Adam Smith and David Ricardo; it would have needed a very observant Keynesian eye to identify these watercolours as representing Selmeston. Only the timber aisle pillars and arching braces say Selmeston. The rest looks pre-Christian and might be anywhere — a flattened chancel arch and an east window of level lancets whereas in Keynes' day the arch was and is pointed and the window neo-Deocrated. These pictures, rescued from a distant exile, seem to suggest mammon (in the guise of a benevolent economist and bohemian) bestowing favours on a spiritual haven. Evidently Keynes was not all materialistic and hedonist and he did take his title from hereabouts.

After I had finished my sketch, I enjoyed an undisturbed lunch contemplating the flint walls of the church across the long grass and partly hidden headstones with only the occasional gatekeeper butterfly to distract the eye. It was entirely idyllic and I have to thank the memory of Mrs Woodhams for the use of her commemorative seat. Pevsner says there were neolithic pits south east of the chancel. That corner of the churchyard is now a tangle of briars and nettles and impenetrable. Rightly or wrongly, I have always understood that nettles thrive where humans have been. Perhaps the bank of nettles at the edge of Selmeston churchyard is a legacy from our stone-age predecessors. I would like to think so.

BOLNEY
St Mary Magdalene

Bolla's island

When I came to Bolney my head was full of the Revd Joseph Dale's disapproving comments as he took up his incumbency here in 1849. However, before reaching the source of his discontent, the visitor must first negotiate a 20th century lych-gate. This is a splendid entrance to Bolney churchyard, twice the usual size, roofed with Horsham slabs and furnished with an emblazoned, coffin-shaped plinth on which to rest the bier. Mee says it is 'the most massive we have seen'; I can't remember a better one at any of those churches illustrated in this little book.

Beyond and up the path to the stone porch, built in 1718, I was ready to endorse Mr Dale's strictures only to find they had been acted upon. His complaint, and discovery, was that a Saxon doorway lay behind and was largely obscured by one of the beams in the porch. No longer: the beam has gone and the tall, narrow doorway with its semi-circular arch of six receeding rolls is revealed in all its primitive authority. The doorway is 9 feet high and 3 feet wide and is reached up 4 steps. To touch its ancient stones with the tips of one's fingers is almost to establish contact with our pre-Conquest forbears by handling stones they handled.

Mr Dale, one might think, had his heart in the right place when it comes to ancient architecture. But, as one learns that the north aisle was added four years after his induction, doubts begin to emerge. The south walls of the nave and chancel (Saxon presumably because there is a Saxon window and I cannot believe that such an inconspicuous opening would not have been swept away if the wall had been renewed in the 12th century, say) are a warm, rough and ready construction of ironstone. By contrast, the walling of the Victorian aisle and later vestry is too terrible to contemplate — a sort of ashlared crazy-paving. Avoid the northern half of the churchyard is my recommendation and remain in the sunlit south.

In comparison, the 16th century tower, straightforward and solid and dignified and crowned with conical pinnacles, each flaunting its own weather vane, does not offend at all, quite the reverse. The Tudors did their own thing but their coursed, dressed blocks harmonise perfectly with the rougher old Saxon work. The Tudors would also be offended by the crazy-paving, I am sure.

After the Saxon doorway, the interior seems rather commonplace and devoid of interest, at least to this visitor. The floor is paved with stone but so uniform as to suggest its recent installation. Ground-level memorials do grace a floor; their prohibition to-day is to be regretted, I think, although I can understand the reluctance to permit internal burial. Could we not have one without the other, as it is with wall tablets? There are 17th century brasses to 3 families, the ubiquitous Culpepers amongst them, old chests and stained glass to brighten the Saxon windows in the chancel. And if I didn't hear the silvery chimes of the eight bells in the tower, I did have an agreeable drink in the Eight bells pub opposite the famous lych-gate.

Two unusual memorials attracted my attention. In the porch there is a cast-iron plaque recording the grant of £116 for the enlargement of the church subject to the reservation of 510 seats for the poorer members of the parish. Can one imagine the necessity of such a provision to-day?

The other is a set of curious grave markers which proliferate here but nowhere else that I can remember. They consist of an horizontal stone member terminated at each end by a sort of collared boss. There is an example in the foreground of my sketch. Bolney probably was very isolated when these memorials were popular here and contact with the funerary fashions of the day may have been restricted. Their originality put me in mind of Easter Island and its mysterious stone figures but I hardly think Bolney can have been quite as remote as the Pacific island. Now, with the crowded and dangerous highways by-passing the village, peace here is assured and those interred under their idiosyncratic markers can rest at ease with only the persistent roar of the displaced traffic to remind us of what they have escaped.

LITTLE HORSTED   *Horse place*
St Michael and All Angels

Little Horsted, or Horsted Parva as the antiquarian Mark Antony Lower had it when he investigated this church in 1869. It stands about 3 miles south of Uckfield, just off the road to Lewes. Admirably situated on high ground, it looks south, clear across fields and woods to the distant Downs. All it lacks is any sign of a village. The Black Death reached England in 1348 and the church was standing then. Did the plague take the population? Possibly; it only numbered 296 when Mr Lower wrote and I doubt if it is as much to-day. Then why the strong Perpendicular tower and a restoration of 1863, both coming after a clearance with no apparent recovery. This is a fine looking church but the question remains — why is it and its by no means empty churchyard here in the empty countryside? All rather confusing to the stranger.

It consists very simply of the tower, the reconstructed nave and chancel with only the north wall of the chancel to speak of its origins. And this the latter does, eloquently, through its four blind arcades. This piece of wall is rough and uncoursed, gingery in colour whereas the stonework of the rest of the church is coursed, dressed and greyish. The blind arcade, say my 'Notes', is reminiscent of the Saxon chapel at Bradford-on-Avon near Bath. Old it certainly looks as do the two early Norman windows within two of the arches. Inside the church is a watercolour of the building as it stood before Mr Scott's restoration. If the watercolour is accurate in the essentials, and I hardly think it would be inaccurate, there were no windows in the arcade then, no pointed windows in the nave, no porch and no octagonal pinnacle crowning the stair turret — altogether a simpler church as one might expect. But those Norman windows in the chancel arcade must either have been uncovered in the restoration or be bogus. I can't believe the latter. The restoration did uncover things as will also be seen inside.

Apart from the arcading of the exterior of the north wall, the inside surface of this wall is the next most interesting thing about Horsted Parva. Here at the time of the restoration, was uncovered in the chancel at ground level a flattened arched recess in which lay, or now lies anyway, a foliated sepulchral slab. This, Mr Lower suggests, marks the entombment of the founder of the church or that of an early prior of St Pancras, Lewes (the priory now lies under the railway line — what a downfall). To-day unless you had been fore-warned, you would be unlikely to notice this ancient tomb; it is almost entirely hidden by the back of the everyday choir stalls — what a cavalier way to treat a reputed father of this church.

Not so antique but interesting all the same is the tower's western doorcase; square headed but perhaps an afterthought if the arched voussoir stones above are anything to go by. In the southern spandrel one is confronted by a Green Man chewing a bough. He is a bit of a surprise and hardly welcoming. On either side, as label stops, he is joined by two mutilated medieval heads. In their present condition they look distinctly sinister, not spirits to be trifled with.

At a more reassuring level is the rood beam across the chancel arch with its rood and the figures of St Mary the Virgin and St John the Evangelist on either side. It commemorates a young man who died in Flanders in 1915 — one of so many lives brutally ended in that desolating war but at least he has his memorial.

So here is a well-built little church, carefully restored at considerable expense I expect, standing alone on its eminence, open and welcoming, a satellite of Uckfield and a sort of staging post en route to Lewes and the Downs. It is a delight to come and sketch and to explore but where do its parishioners live and how many of them are there? And how is the money to be found to keep it going? A problem that is likely to loom larger now that we learn (summer 1993) that the Church Commissioners have lost so much of the Church's capital in misguided investment in the property market. St Michael and All Angels is a property that deserves to be preserved.

Sedlescombe village runs north and south, along the A229 Hastings road. It seems to have the subsidiary title on my map of Sedlescombe Street and that describes it better. It is noticeable that where the houses are, on the whole, the church is not. The church guide claims the church stands at the geographical centre of the parish; that may be so in geometrical terms but not in terms of the centre of gravity of the village. The guide also suggests that the church might have been preceded by a wooden Saxon church followed, on more definite but now lost evidence, by a Norman successor. Of either of these there is no trace to-day and it could be that, while the church, however changed, has maintained its inherited site, the village has shifted southwards. I think that a more credible explanation than the need for geographical centralism in a sparsely populated countryside where what population there is has concentrated elsewhere. Not that the church suffers thereby although the present-day congregation may, but perhaps not unduly.

The first glimpse of the church from the road, gained through the glossy, dark-green leaves of a screen of Spanish chestnuts, is impressive. Here, above the bank, stands the 15th century west tower — solid ironstone blocks, eroded maybe but more than usually substantial — towering up amongst the shielding trees. This looks to be the oldest part of the church although the weathered wall of the north aisle may support the guide's claim of some 13th century work still standing. The rest, I think results from the restoration of 1866 which has now given us a mostly unweathered-looking church of nave, north and south aisles and chancel, all of uniform honey-coloured ironstone blocks, and of course the handsome Perpendicular tower of genuine antiquity. It is set in an extensive wooded churchyard, criss-crossed with neat brick-paved paths, and bearing a wide range of monumental masonry, the whole pleasantly redolent of the heady scent of recently cut grass when I was there.

Inside, it is what you might expect after a fairly major Victorian restoration which apprently took 8 years to complete. There are a few wall tablets to members of the prominent local families, a Sackville funeral helm and one hatchment. The guide's enthusiasm for the latter sent me to Lawrence Jones for the conventions governing the design of these memorials. It is surprising how precise these conventions are. For instance, by the arrangement of the coats of arms and the application of white or black backgrounds, the person commemorated can be defined, but not named, as widow or widower, bachelor or spinster. The colours also determine, of married couples, who died first although I should have thought the description of widow or widower made this clear enough. Hatchments seem to have been fashionable only briefly at the turn of the 18th century; by no means as informative as the invariably eulogistic stone memorials, they are nevertheless decorative and bring colour and light to many a gloomy aisle. We have 8 in Hadlow church, if I may be forgiven the boast, and they do much to relieve the monotony of the bare white-washed walls of our nave.

In the north aisle lies the cast-iron slab of an ironmaster, †1664, his wife and granddaughter. Unless they all died more or less simultaneously, their commemoration here called for two amending slabs after the first. That is the trouble with cast-iron memorials; inscriptions can't be added and the slab must be renewed. I presume that is what happened here.

In the course of exploring the churchyard, one of its enticing paths led me to the burial plot of the Weston family where they lie together beneath 5 sarcophagi and one headstone. I could not resist them and they form the foreground of my somewhat eccentric view of the church. Now-a-days, families are so dispersed that a concentration like that of the Westons must be rather a rarity but to my mind an achievement if it can be managed. When I try to concentrate my wife's mind on this proposition for the Syms family, she seems strangely unresponsive.

CATSFIELD
St Lawrence

Wild cats open land
(or St Chadd's(field) as the church guide hints)

I had not expected too much from Catsfield (ignored by Betjeman and rather disdained by Pevsner) and when I arrived at the map reference my spirits fell more. Here in the village stands a neo-Gothic pile of monstrous disproportions; fortunately it turned out to be the one-time Methodist church, now in course of conversion to secular use. The real church, St Lawrence, is half a mile outside the village on the Crowhurst road. One finds it perched perilously above this road in imminent danger, one might think, of being pushed over the edge of the bank by Catsfield manor, the garden wall of which barely leaves one room to squeeze past the end of the chancel. As the church must antedate the manor, the latter must at some time have enclosed part of the consecrated ground; do ghosts linger there, I wonder. Spirits apart, or included, it's all a great relief after the first encounter.

The church consists of a 10th century nave, vide the lofty arch of the inner doorway, a 12th century tower, a 13th century chancel and a Victorian north aisle, chapel and vestry and about the last three less said the better. Terrible is Pevsner's verdict. The south wall of the nave is remarkable for much erratic herring-bone work which the egregious Mr Carpenter, who is responsible for the north aisle, stabilised by a prominent application of ribbon pointing. Without it, the wall might have crumbled but, with it, much of the aura of ancient survival is dispelled. To be practical I suppose one should accept the pointing, as one has to now it is there, but under protest so to speak. From the presence of three grey quoin stones in the face of the tower, one can deduce that the tower was intruded into the western few feet of the nave. Quite understandable in view of the proximity of the abyss but why leave the quoin stones to disclose the encroachment — a 12th century protest against the expropriation of prior space, perhaps.

I was lucky enough to meet a flower arranger in the porch, one who had once attended a lecture by Pevsner, no less, so I listened to what she had to say about the church and its luminaries with profit and pleasure. We admired the black ledger stones in the chancel, one to the 'virtuous and pious Lady Pelham', †1686, another to the sister of a sort of Sussex Gilbert White; we viewed from a distance the Nollekens wall tablet, too high to discern properly, which commemorates an uncle of Mad Jack Fuller, he with the Pharaonic pretensions in Brightling churchyard. And we spent time in considering the life and achievements of Thomas Brassey, †1870, commemorated here by the west window of the aisle. His activities included the construction of railways as far apart as Canada, Australia, India and the Crimea. Travel was made easier (now it is too easy) by the time he came to retire to Catsfield. So he deserves his granite sarcophagus but surely not the forlorn strip of churchyard that runs along the north side of the church where he lies. He would be better beside the churchyard path. To Brassey must also be credited, I was informed, the memorial to the four men of the village who lost their lives in the Crimean War — the only such memorial I have ever seen.

At the manor lived the Burrell Hayleys. In the mid 1800s they provided a rector and one assumes that they provided the two framed sketches of the church from the Burrell Collection — one by the splendidly-named Swiss, Hieronymous Grimm, the other by James Lambert of Lewes. Both pictures are interesting. They show the dormer window, now gone but recalled by the shading of the tiles and both, possibly out of respect for their patron, Sir William Burrell, are careful to omit the encroachment of the manor upon the churchyard. Tactful and sensible but, of course to be fair, the garden wall that rubs shoulders with the chancel may be after their time.

Unlike the secularisation which has overtaken the other church in the village, St Lawrence is obviously still going strong — services held, flowers arranged and the churchyard (most of it) cared for. It seems to me that the most serious threat is subsidence under the tower; no-one here would be unwise or sacriligious enough, I imagine, to attribute that eventuality to an Act of God.

ALBOURNE
St Bartholomew

Alder stream

A small, compact church at the end of a lane that leads to nowhere. I imagine though, that those who live in the 17th century tile-hung, old rectory beside the church would dispute the 'nowhere'. It must be somewhere to them and I am sure they like living next to this lonely church as much as anyone would. If one draws a triangle with Albourne village, Albourne Place and the Bishop's Palace as the apexes, the church occupies the middle ground. That could be why it is where it is — in splendid isolation but more or less equidistant from what matters in this unfrequented tract of the Sussex countryside.

Externally, the church presents rather plain facades of pebbly, unknapped flints, bonded at the corners by undefaced sandstone blocks none of which, blocks or flints, yet reflect the mellowing of weather over time. This is because it is all new, or at least Victorian, having been rebuilt in 1853. There is a nave, north aisle and chancel. The chancel may have retained some of its earlier features vide the small Norman window and the lancets. The rest is Mr Scott's handiwork but which Scott architect, Pevsner doesn't say; there were at least five of them. If the bellcote is squat and diminutive, it is nevertheless distinctive and houses a single bell, c1300, which makes it a very old bell indeed. Assuming the bell has always been here, its age corroborates the evidence of the Norman window which says that a church has long stood on this spot.

The unadorned nave is three bays in length to which was added, long before Scott, a north aisle. Although the nave is probably ample for its congregation to-day, no doubt more room was required in the days of religious furore. For instance, in 1593 an 'Act against Seditious Sectaries' threatened dire punishment, even death, to those who refused to go to church. Few seemed to escape its net. At Catsfield, near Battle, in that same year, so influential a Sussex lady as a Pelham was brought to tiral by compurgators (whoever they may have been but they don't sound too charming) 'for not frequenting the church'. I hope she escaped unscathed. So it seems much more likely that the Elizabethan locals of Albourne attended their church in the requisite numbers than that Mr Scott should have found it necessary to add an aisle in 1859. Therefore what we see to-day could well stand on what was here before.

The oldest part of the interior, genuine in appearance if not in fact, is the cell-like chancel with its low, round archway and Norman moulding. Pevsner says the zigzag orders of this arch are a replacement by Mr Scott; my 'Notes' makes no such debunking assertion. In the face of expert disagreement, us lay church enthusiasts do best, I feel, to seek refuge in that hackneyed modern cliche 'an open mind'. The chancel is so restricted that the altar is perforce lodged within a pointed-arched recess which Pevsner says is what remains of an eastern apse. Certainly the brief extension to the chancel looks to be a late, economical addition so I think we should accept the great man's ruling. If there are two opinions about the chancel arch, there can be little doubt, I think, about the fragment of an arch which is inconspicuously embedded at the foot of the churchyard wall. Its moulding is worn but I could identify to my satisfaction the Norman beakhead motif that betrays a Viking ancestry. Could this half buried relic be part of the original chancel arch which Mr Scott took care to preserve in the churchyard? If so, 5 out of 10, for why not reinstate it. Should all this sound presumptuous speculation in an amateur, it is, for an amateur, a stimulating way of looking at an old church in the absence of much in the way of factual information.

Albourne Place was the home of the Juxon family*. One of their number, a bishop, supported Charles I on the scaffold on that raw January day in 1649. Albourne, miles from anywhere, must then have seemed infinitely preferable to the Whitehall scene. To my mind, it still does.

---

* There are no Juxon memorials in the rebuilt church. Mr Scott again? No, it can't be.

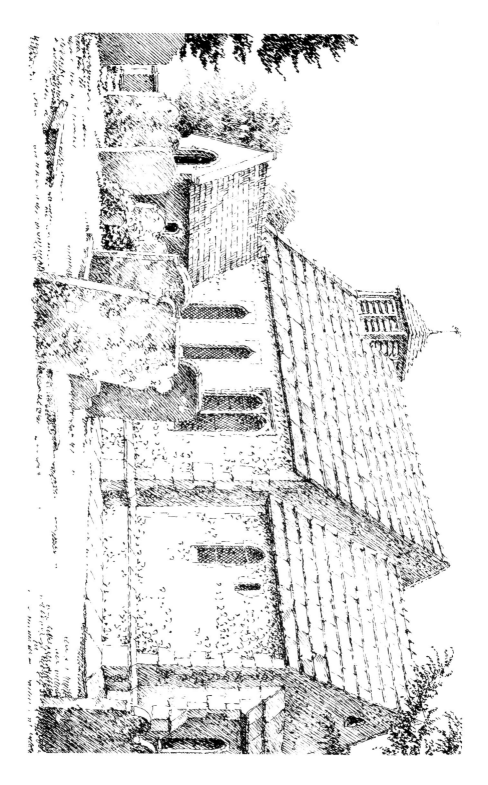

OLD HEATHFIELD
All Saints

Open land covered with heather

Old Heathfield should not be confused with the commercial town of Heathfield. One finds this unspoilt rural village of period houses, and, of course, the church, safe beyond the walls and acres of Heathfield Place. The approach to the church puts one in mind of Framfield — a brief street flanked by cosy, tiled and boarded houses, a sturdy lych-gate at the end and, beyond, the olivine walls of All Saints. It is a different world from the railway town of Heathfield, with its natural gas, only a mile away.

The church consists of a nave with north and south aisles plus north and south porches, all resulting from the rebuildings of 1861 and 1869, an Early English west tower of mottled sandstone and ironstone, lit by long slit apertures in its upper levels and topped by a dominanting shingled spire, a chancel that looks partly original and partly renewed and, finally, a south chapel, now vestry and organ chamber, that looks wholly Victorian. Despite the renewals, it all looks harmonious and stands well on the crown of a sweeping churchyard from which most of the headstones have been cleared to allow the mower its right of way. The displaced headstones now reinforce the walls and line the base of the church to act as run-offs for the rain water from the eaves. If headstones are not permitted to mark their proper graves, their role as a sort of monumental soakaway seems an eminently practical and satisfactory alternative.

Inside, an impression of height and light is conveyed by the clerestory windows, north and south, below which four splendid hatchments find their place. By some dispensation, the nave was allowed to retain its homely floor of plum-coloured bricks, its row of ledger stones and its complete set of box pews; but of the reputed squint, there is no sign. Happily, the Victorian renovation seems therefore to have been largely confined to the exterior where no doubt it was necessary.

Historically, Heathfield says George Augustus Elliot, Lord Heathfield and, of course, Gibraltar. When I looked for signs of the valiant defender of the Rock, all I could find was his ghost in the shape of a wall tablet which replaced the original, removed when his remains were taken from the crypt here for reburial in his wife's family vault at Buckland Monachorum. She was a Drake so one can hardly blame him, or her. But as we know, the great sailor and scourge of the Dons is, in fact, 'slung atween the round-shot in Nombre de Dios Bay'. They had the same enemy if not the same mausoleum.

Old Heathfield is also justly proud of its vicar of 1602, Robert Hunt. Bravely forsaking his comfortable parish, he sailed in the spring of 1607 in the Susan Constant as chaplain to the expedition which established the 'first permanent (just) English settlement of Jamestown, Virginia', America*. There were 105 settlers — no women, strangely, which implies a lack of confidence in the future, I think — mostly described in the church's list as gentlemen, a few as carpenters and even less as labourers. The Indians were hostile (who can blame them) and life in the wilderness was harsh and brutal; sad to say, our vicar did not survive the winter of 1607-8. If all the above seems an unnecessary digression when considering the present church, I can plead that it is remarkable and worth recording how often one encounters a country church and village which has had an historical effect in the great world out of all proportion to its status in its own little world through the exploits of those who once lived there. Frant is another case in point.

* I cannot resist remarking (after all, this is a strictly personal account) that, when living in Virginia years ago, we visited the restored stockade at Jamestown which the State of Virginia has made into one of the local sights of the Chesapeake Bay area. Remembering our picnic there gives me a distinct feeling of affinity with Robert Hunt and indeed with the parish of Old Heathfield in its Jacobean days.

EDBURTON
St Andrews

Eadburga's farmstead

If you stand in the porch here and look through its lofty arch, the Downs loom disconcertingly close above. If you climb these downs and look down on the church, hiding amongst its trees, the slope seems to verge on the vertical; from the side, the angle looks to be 45° which is steep enough for anybody. Why then did the Princess Eadburga, granddaughter of Alfred, choose this spot on which to build her church? Maybe the narrow road that runs past was then a crucial highway squeezed between the upland downs and the impenetrable weald. It must have been something like that. To-day there is less than a dozen houses and an enterprise that smokes salmon; barely enough to keep the church even moderately full on Sundays. Perhaps, at Fulking, where there is no church, they divide on geographical lines between Poynings and Edburton.

One hopes that Eadburga's church has survived, unobtrusively in material terms, in some of the exterior walling and as the crowns of the two low-side windows which are hewn from single blocks of stone. The rector of the 1930s thought the four vestigial scratch dials were also Saxon but his scholarly notes on the subject are now prefaced by a disclaimer in a later reprint. The Saxons had sundials, why not scratch dials? There is also a portable relic known as the 'chained stone'. This small circular stone dish, now secured to a chain, is said to be the 'ground priscina of a stone altar in the ancient Saxon church'. It looks old enough and rugged enough but a piscina on the ground?

The church offers an explanation for low-side windows that I have not heard before. These small windows, obviously not designed for illumination, were introduced, it is alleged, to circumvent an edict by one of the popes forbidding Franciscan friars from hearing confessions within a church. Obeying the letter of the law but hardly the spirit, the friar sat inside beside the low window while the penitent remained outside. And the friars were not only in trouble with the pope; they also antagonised the Lancastrians in the early 1400s by questioning the legitimacy of Henry IV as king. Several were imprisoned and some executed. Fortunately, the hostility to the Franciscans does not seem to have extended to the low-side windows of which there is no shortage in Sussex churches.

To come at length to the essentials of the church, the longish nave and chancel are Early English, built of rubbly flint and covered here and there by patches of faded rendering — exhibiting an appropriately weathered texture. The north chapel is somewhat later; it should more properly be described as the north transept, I would say, as its roof line runs at right angles to the rest of the church. The tower and porch are Perpendicular, the former faced with rows of exactly squared and sized knapped flints. It clearly is the 'chef d'oeuvre' of the church and justifies all the labour it must have incurred.

Inside one should not fail to remark the lead font, one of only three in Sussex, nor the altar rails and pulpit, said to have been given by Archbishop Laud himself. The Archbishop of Canterbury has 'always been the patron here' and indeed the guide claims that Laud actually preached here. I am sure the church was full that day.

After Eadburga, the next notability here was the Revd George Keith. He was a Scotsman, born in 1638, who came south to England to preach Quaker unorthodoxy and experience the inside of our prisons. In 1684 he emigrated to New Jersey as Surveyor General where nevertheless he continued to preach. Back in England in 1694, he found himself rejected by the Quakers but adopted by the Society for the Propogation of the Gospel. Another spell of preaching along the eastern seaboard of America followed before he finally came to rest as rector of Edburton. He is remembered here by a medallion in a lancet and by a monumental sarcophagus in the churchyard, subscribed to by the ten States in which he preached in America, and inscribed:

'His work is remembered, his memory honoured'

No mean life and no mean tribute.

NINFIELD
St Mary the Virgin

Like its village, which runs along the crest of a ridge four miles south west of Battle, the church of St Mary is unassuming. The village, mostly modern, nonetheless remembers its historic past for here, on Standard Hill, Duke William is said to have raised his standard (a sort of medieval summons to battle, I take it). The recent development of Standard Close would seem to mark this pregnant spot. The church, however, lies some way distant on the southern edge of the village and looks south through its tangle of trees towards the sea, across the Pevensey marshes where William landed, and on to the grey bulk of the Sussex Downs.

It is difficult now to put a date to the church because so much was rebuilt in 1885 but its origin is Early English, hence the lancets in the chancel. It is modest in size; nave, north aisle and chancel is all, plus a pretty little brick porch, dated 1735, and a white wooden turret to house the single bell. When I arrived I was very taken with the blocked priest's doorway with its long and short Saxon stonework for the jambs so I was rather put out to see the inscription 'IB 1671' on its angled arch. If not Saxon, it is certainly a very good imitation. The walls of the church suffer from a flush surface of much crazy-paving, particularly fortissimo on the north side. What can have possessed Mr George Gilbert Scott (or was it Sir Arthur Blomfield?) but at least the culprit did include three large Saxon stones, saved from the earlier church, in his execrable walling. Perhaps like IB of 1671, he hankered after Saxon memorabilia. Fortunately also, he left alone the faded rendering on the south side of the nave and the rough rubble stonework at the western end of the nave. The latter's Early English purity, however, was violated by the insertion of a window suitably inscribed to record Queen Victoria's Diamond Jubilee. All the same, the outside of this church is an attractive hotch potch but would be more so without the crazy-paving.

Inside, all looks new but sympathetically restored; one could not take exception to anything, not even the 'Norman' chancel arch. There is much to admire; the sumptuous, dark polished, poppy-head choir stalls, the iron-work altar rails (they must, I assume, have come from Ashburnham forge in the century when the Earls of Ashburnham were patrons of the living), the minstrells gallery, high at the end of the nave and now inaccesible, the carved arms of James I beneath it and the tiny rectangular font with a Jacobean cover (from the same stable as the choir stalls?). Riches indeed from an unassuming little church that welcomes one with an open door.

But most of all, it was the insistent ticking of a clock in an empty church that will be remembered by me. The clock is located under the bell turret in a glass-fronted cabinet. Here one finds a large assembly of cogs and wheels turning imperceptibly under the influence of the measured swing of a long pendulum. As I watched, fascinated, a sudden convulsion of movement and whirring resulted in the bell above striking one o'clock. In these days of miniaturisation, it is a relief for once to see the opposite working so well. The church has reason to be proud of its clock and grateful to those who made it so well and to those who subscribed to its installation in 1898.

Remembering those Saxon stones in the north aisle wall, I stopped in Powdermill Lane, south of Battle, on my way home to gaze across the peaceful park-like fields that lead up to the ridge on which Harold had drawn up his fyrd on that fateful day in October 1066. To my nautical mind, Harold's position looked daunting, as it must have to the Normans who had to assault it. But assault it they did, successfully too, although I cannot avoid the opinion that Harold might be criticised for failing to hold it and, equally, William for attacking it so impetuously. Fortune favours the bold — they were all brave that day; they had to be, they were fighting for their lives. Ours, too, in the long run.

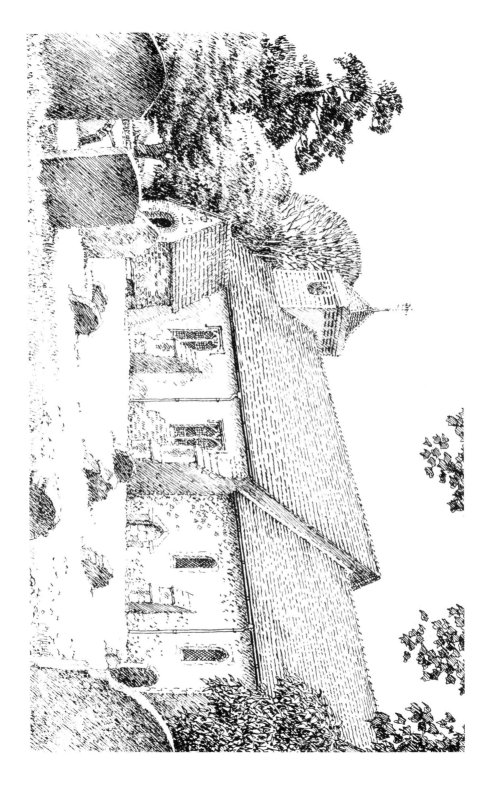

WORTH
St Nicholas

Enclosure

St Nicholas's church, Worth, must surely be one of the most famous parish churches in Sussex and few gazeteers overlook it. Few church enthusiasts can be unaware of it; I hope, though, that those who know all about this church will be tolerant of my observations, based as they are on just one visit in February.

A notice board by the lych-gate says the church was built between 871 and 901 AD. Most commentaries are more cautious and attribute a less precise date of early 11th century. All seem agreed, nevertheless, that it has 'the unique distinction of being the only Saxon cruciform edifice in the country that is complete and untouched in plan'. Think of that; what those masons set out a thousand years ago still holds good to-day, the only one!

They planted this church, of cathedral proportions in terms of Anglo-Saxon England, in the middle of a forest. If the lych-gate dates are accurate, Alfred the Great was king of Wessex when they did so and the forest of Andredesweald covered most of Sussex. Worth may have been a royal manor but why such grandeur here, one may ask. If the manor was largely used for hunting, what else, who were the people who would worship here in numbers? The heathen Danes were rampant then and, indeed, it was only a hundred years later that Canute became king of England so I wonder if this church was designed and intended as some sort of hidden refuge for the native Saxon nobility. It seems a possibility. To-day the church is menaced by equally intrusive threats — the spread of housing from Crawley in the west and the thunderous roar of the M23 in the east. The church and churchyard have become a refuge from the 20th century as they once were a sanctuary from the marauding Danes amongst the trees and thickets of Andredesweald.

The plan which the Saxons left us consists of a nave, north and south transepts and an apsidal chancel. Their enclosing walls still rise from their foundation plinth essentially as first built, witness the thin pilasters which are placed at intervals below the string course that runs around the building. Pilaster strips look more ornamental than functional, I think, suggesting a well-found confidence in foundations on which to base the towering structures so typical of Saxon architecture. Another Saxon practice which evidently answers satisfactorily, despite avoidance by others, is their method of binding corners by 'long and short work' (see over). It does not inspire confidence in appearance.

The church is tall for its proportions but yet to-day there is only one buttress to keep it upright. Doubtless transepts and an apsidal chancel can provide as much, or more, stability than a row of buttresses; such may have been the opinion of Mr Salvin when he came to restore the church in 1871. A picture of the church, from the north east, prior to the restoration, shows two buttresses supporting the chancel apse with a small Perpendicular window centrally above the string course. All gone — to be replaced by a circlet of five equally-spaced lancets. At the same time, the architect replaced the wooden structure that used to suppoort a shingled spire above the north transept with a dark stone tower that now nestles in the corner formed by chancel and transept. Elsewhere, Decorated and Perpendicular windows had previously been introduced to provide more light inside but fortunately three of those characteristic, divided Saxon windows (see over) still remain. So the Saxon walls, however many liberties have been taken with them over the years, still stand tall above the surrounding churchyard as their Saxon builders always intended they should.

The roofing is mostly new; it gave me an uneasy twinge of 'mea culpa' to read that the previous nave roof was destroyed by fire in 1986 on my birthday!

Inside, through the 14th century west door and not through the blocked Saxon doorways, north and south, which were tall enough to permit entry on horseback, one finds oneself standing on a modern floor of French limestone amongst new golden, habitat-style, pews. The initial impression is of a spacious uncluttered interior, both nave and especially chancel, which might be the work of some modernistic interior designer — probably was for much money was spent on improvement in 1988. Such an illusion of new creation is soon dispelled. The transepts contain the memorials; six really sumptuous armorial ledger stones pave the floor in one and

206

many wall tablets, of the languishing angels and urn category, cover the walls of both. Interesting and elegiac as these may be, they can't hold one's attention.

For here we are confronted by the Saxon arches that more than anything else in this church confirm its reputation. There are three, one to each transept and the greatest of all, the chancel arch, standing 22 feet high. Rough-hewn as they were with primitive mallets and chisels, one can still feel the abrasions made a thousand years ago and wonder what they were like who made them — not incompetent at all, I am sure. Many of the stones are too bulky to be handled by men unaided; they must have had ropes and tackles and sheer-legs. Even with lifts and slings, there is always the problem of how to disengage the sling when the stone is lowered flush on to its bed. In medieval times, they had, one gathers, a clever, collapsible gadget called a 'three-legged Lewis' to do the trick. Did the Saxon builders of Worth have something similar? They must have. And what about Stonehenge? Surely they didn't have a Lewis. How did they manage their trilithons?

To sum up this splendid church — it is a glorious tribute to Anglo-Saxon civilization before the Conquest and, it must be acknowledged, to the Victorian architect who restored the ancient virility to its structure. Nor should one forget the guardians who care for it so well to-day. If only it could escape the clutches of Crawley and settle down in some remote tract of the Sussex countryside, what an adornment it would be. But churches are for people and isolation defeats its purpose. What a conundrum.

Since 'long and short work' may be a somewhat cryptic term, I have reproduced opposite a sketch of the stonework forming the north east corner of the north transpt. It does seem an odd, but no doubt effective, way of reinforcing corners. Round-headed windows, that Saxon hallmark, are something of a rarity so I have similarly reproduced on the facing page one of the windows lighting the north side of the nave. One could hardly do justice to Worth church without emphasising both constructs.

I can't resist adding a few words about Worth Abbey church in the school of its name. Dedicated by the Apostolic Delegate to the United Kingdom in 1968, it is a massive rotunda in corn-coloured brick, lit by a great central lantern directly above a stark and simple altar. Whoever it was commissioned and designed this non-traditional church, they clearly intended to do justice to the school, the abbey and the Cardinale Archbishop. And so they have. Had it been made of stone and perhaps less cluttered externally by subsidiary buildings, it would look stunning and a splendid modern response to its Saxon namesake a couple of miles away.

And now I must bid a reluctant farewell to this collection of Sussex churches. Never fear, surely they will.